I0528743

www.ingramcontent.com/pod-product-compliance
Lightning Source LLC
Chambersburg PA
CBHW041113120626
46547CB00019B/2694

ספר שופטים

# THE
# ISRAEL
# BIBLE

*From Chaos to Redemption:*
*Contemporary Teachings from*
*the Book of Judges*

**By Rabbi Elie Mischel**

*From Chaos to Redemption: Contemporary Teachings from the Book of Judges*
First Edition 2023
The Israel Bible was produced by Israel365 in cooperation with Teach for Israel and
is used with permission from Teach for Israel. All rights reserved.
All rights reserved.
Cover design: Chani Gordon & Inbal Rose. Typesetting: Chani Gordon
**ISBN 978-1-957109-50-3, softcover**
*From Chaos to Redemption: Contemporary Teachings from the Book of Judges is a holy book
that contains the name of God and should be treated with respect.*

# Table of Contents

| ז | ו | ה | ד |
|---|---|---|---|
| Zayin<br>'Z' | Vav<br>'V' | Hay<br>'H' | Dalet<br>'D' |
| מ | ל | ך | כ |
| Mem<br>'M' | Lamed<br>'L' | Final Khaf<br>'KH' | Khaf<br>'KH' |
| ף | פ | פ | ע |
| Final Pey<br>'F' | Fay<br>'F' | Pay<br>'P' | Ayin<br>Silent[1] |
| ת | ת | שׂ | שׁ |
| Sav<br>'T' | Tav<br>'T' | Sin<br>'S' | Shin<br>'SH' |

**Notes:**

If there is a vowel underneath the letter, the sound of the vowel is pronounced. If there is no vowel underneath, the letter remains silent.

[1] In Hebrew there are 2 types of Sh'vas. A Sh'va na is considered a vowel and is pronounced. This is represented in our transliteration by the apostrophe (') and pronouced like the 'e' in father. The other sh'va, the sh'va nakh, indicates the end of a syllable. It does not have its own sound, and therefore no phonetic representation.

[3] A kamatz katan looks like a regular kamatz but is pronounced like a kholam.

[4] The Hebrew alphabet has a unique feature known as gematriya , in which every letter is assigned a numerical value.

Above each letter is its numeric value[4]

| אֻ/אוּ | אֶ |
|---|---|
| Shuruk/Kubutz<br>'u' junior | Segol<br>'e' in Edward |
| אְ | אֵ |
| Sh'va[2]<br>' (apostrophe) | Tzayray<br>'ay' in day |

# ABET CHART

| | | | |
|---|---|---|---|
| ג<br>Gimel<br>'G' | ב<br>Vet<br>'V' | בּ<br>Bet<br>'B' | א<br>Aleph<br>Silent[1] |
| כ<br>Kaf<br>'K' | י<br>Yud<br>'Y' | ט<br>Tet<br>'Tet' | ח<br>Chet<br>'KH' |
| ס<br>Samekh<br>'S' | ן<br>Final Nun<br>'N' | נ<br>Nun<br>'N' | ם<br>Final Mem<br>'M' |
| ר<br>Raysh<br>'R' | ק<br>Kuf<br>'K' | ץ<br>Final Tzadi<br>'TZ' | צ<br>Tzadi<br>'TZ' |

Vowels: The Aleph is silent[1] so we will use it in the example for each sound

| | | | |
|---|---|---|---|
| אִ<br>Kheerik Khasayr<br>'i' in igloo | אָ<br>Kamatz Katan[3]<br>'o' in host | אַ<br>Patakh<br>'a' in hurrah | אָ<br>Kamatz<br>'a' in hurrah |
| אִי<br>Kheerik Malay<br>'ee' in street | אֹ/אוֹ<br>Kholam<br>'o' in host | אַי<br>Patakh + Yud<br>'ai' in aisle | אָי<br>Kamatz + Yud<br>'ai' in aisle |

# Chart of the Judges of Israel

The following is a chart of the Judges of Israel, the tribes they were from, and the amount of time they served.

| English Name | Hebrew Name | Tribe | Approximate Years | Relevant Verses |
|---|---|---|---|---|
| **Othniel son of Kenaz** | *Otniel ben Kenaz* | Judah | 40 | Judges 3:8-11 |
| **Ehud son of Gera** | *Ehud ben Gera* | Benjamin | 80 | Judges 3:15-30 |
| **Shamgar son of Anath** | *Shamgar ben Anat* | Not recorded | 1 | Judges 3:31 |
| **Deborah wife of Lapidoth** | *Devora eishet Lapidot* | Ephraim | 40 | Judges 4-5 |
| **Gideon son of Joash** | *Gidon ben Yoash* | Manasseh | 40 | Judges 6-6 |
| **Abimelech son of Gideon** | *Avimelech ben Gidon* | Manasseh | 3 | Judges 9:1-56 |
| **Tola son of Puah** | *Tola ben Puah* | Issachar | 23 | Judges 10:1-2 |
| **Jair the Gila-dite** | *Yair haGiladi* | Manasseh | 22 | Judges 10:3-5 |
| **Jephthah the Giladite** | *Yiftach haGiladi* | Manasseh | 6 | Judges 11:1-12:7 |
| **Ibtzan of Beth-lehem** | *Ivtzan of Beit Lechem* | Judah | 7 | Judges 12:8-10 |

| Elon the Zebulunite | *Eilon haZevuloni* | Zebulun | 10 | Judges 12:11-12 |
|---|---|---|---|---|
| **Abdon son of Hillel** | *Avdon ben Hillel* | Ephraim | 8 | Judges 12:13-15 |
| **Samson son of Manoah** | *Shimshon ben Manoach* | Dan | 20 | Judges 13-16 |
| **Eli the Priest** | *Eli haKohen* | Levi | 40 | I Samuel 1-4 |
| **Samuel the Prophet** | *Shmuel haNavi* | Levi | 11 | I Samuel 1-17 |

# Preface

*Rabbi Tuly Weisz*

Israel today stands at a crossroads, grappling with internal divisions that echo the challenges faced by the ancient twelve tribes. In the Book of Judges, the twelve tribes struggled mightily to remain united, their unique strengths and weaknesses both a source of pride and a seed for discord. Even when facing powerful enemies, the tribes often failed to find common ground, mirroring the contemporary struggles of modern Israel. Is Civil War on the Horizon? This question, and others, resonate in this study of the Book of Judges.

The struggle of the twelve tribes to remain united at the time of the judges is reflected in the modern state of Israel, where tribes have given way to varied groups - religious Jews, secular Jews, and Jews from diverse locations such as Russia, the United States, Ethiopia, and the Middle East. Like the twelve tribes of the Bible, these modern tribes struggle to work together, even as Israel faces continuous external threats.

One contemporary example is the recent upheaval over proposed judicial reforms in modern Israel, a disagreement that has stirred fierce debate and threatens to splinter the nation. The ancient narratives of the Book of Judges are not just stories of the past, but urgent parables for the present. They are tales of pride and independence, of unity and discord, of leadership and failure, of faith and resilience.

At the same time, the United States is experiencing a period of extreme polarization, as woke activists relentlessly work to overturn traditional values. Like the twelve tribes and the modern state of Israel, Americans are finding it increasingly difficult to forge a common vision for the future. These internal struggles offer a poignant parallel to the disunity faced by the tribes in the Book of Judges, serving as a cautionary tale for the pressing need for unity and common purpose.

"From Chaos to Redemption: Contemporary Teachings from the Book of Judges," aims to explore the eternal themes present in the biblical Book of Judges, and show how they are very relevant even today. It is a call to reflect, understand, and, hopefully, to act. As we delve into these ancient stories, may we find wisdom and guidance for our times, learning from the successes and mistakes of the past and finding hope for a united future.

May this commentary be a bridge between the ancient and the modern, between the lessons of the past and the challenges of today. Let it serve as a reminder that, even in our deepest struggles, there is a path forward, guided by faith, wisdom, and the unending pursuit of unity.

*Rabbi Tuly Weisz*
*Founder of Israel365 and Publisher of The Israel Bible*
*Ramat Beit Shemesh, Israel*
*Elul 5783 / September 2023*

**INTRODUCTION:**

# Why Study Judges in the 21st Century?

What is the point of studying the Book of Judges in modern times?

Yes, I know this sounds heretical. But it's a fair question. We live in a modern world that appears, at first glance, to have very little in common with the stories of the Book of Judges.

During the people of Israel's two-thousand-year exile following the destruction of the Second Temple, the books of the Bible, and particularly historical books like the Book of Judges, were often neglected in the standard Jewish curriculum. In yeshivas (Jewish religious schools), students were almost exclusively taught Talmud, the masterwork of Jewish law, and philosophy written between the 4th and 6th centuries. Though everyone studied the five books of the Torah and became familiar with Psalms, most students rarely studied the other books of the Bible.

This seems shocking. How could Jewish schools largely ignore the Bible itself, the most important book given to the world by the Jewish people?

Throughout the millennia, the Jewish people have sought practical guidance from its sacred texts. The five books of the Torah contain the commandments and laws that guide our day-to-day life, and so these books were studied very closely even after the Jewish people were exiled from Israel. But what could Jews living in exile learn from studying the historical books of Joshua and Judges, Samuel and Kings? What practical guidance could they possibly derive from the monarchs, wars and politics of ancient Israel? These books described a society that was distant from the world they lived in and dealt with challenges that were alien to them.

## Eternal Prophecies

The sages explain that every book included in the Hebrew Bible is critically important – for all generations:

"Many prophets arose for Israel, double the number of [the Israelites] who came out of Egypt. But only the prophecies which contained a lesson for future generations were written down, and that which did not contain such a lesson was not written down." (Talmud Megillah 14a)

Over the course of millennia, hundreds of thousands of prophets prophesied to the people of Israel. Though their prophecies were authentic, the vast majority of their teachings were not written down and included in the Hebrew Bible, for their teachings were only relevant to their own generation. By contrast, any book of prophecy that was included in the Hebrew Bible is, by definition, relevant for all generations – forever.

Why write a commentary on Judges? What relevance does this ancient Book of Judges have to our world today?

The Book of Judges is not merely relevant for our generation; it is essential. For the people of Israel in our own time are, in many ways, reliving the Book of Judges as we speak!

Rabbi Moshe Zvi Neria (1913-1995), one of modern Israel's leading rabbis, once wrote that "One must come to the land of Israel with a Hebrew Bible in hand – not simply as an ancient book, but as the book of books that is alive and well, whose words are words of fire, warming and illuminating with a constant and eternal flame." The Book of Judges is not merely a story about ancient Israel. It is an eternal guidebook that offers essential guidance for the modern Israelites of our own generation.

## Reliving the Books of the Bible

First, some context. The Book of Joshua, which immediately precedes the Book of Judges, tells the story of the people of Israel's first 15 years in the Holy Land, beginning with the miraculous crossing of the Jordan River and culminating with Joshua's death. The Book of Judges picks up the story after the death of Joshua, covering the next 400 years of Israel's history in a mere 21 chapters. Sadly, many of the stories in the Book of Judges follow the same pattern: the people of Israel stray from God, God sends an enemy nation to oppress them, the people cry out to God, and God sends a savior to redeem His people.

What do the stories of Joshua and Judges have to do with our generation? A lot more than you might think.

When the Jewish people first returned to the Land and established the modern State of Israel in 1948, they relived and reenacted the Book of Joshua. Just as Joshua led the nation in battle against powerful enemies and conquered the Land for the first time, the modern Jewish people overcame great odds in 1948 to conquer the Land. Just as Joshua defeated seven ancient nations that were occupying the Land, the young State of Israel defeated the five Arab nations that sought to destroy the newly created country.

In the 75 years since the founding of Israel in 1948, the Jewish people – now rulers of the Land – have sacrificed greatly to defend the Jewish State from enemy Arab states and terrorists. This stage of Israeli history, in which the Jewish people must fight every day to hold onto the Land that God gave them, closely parallels the story of the Book of Judges. In many ways, the story of the State of Israel in our time is a repetition of the story of the Book of Judges.

In the Book of Judges, the people of Israel struggled to remain true to God and avoid the dangerous influences of the surrounding pagan cultures. "And the children of Israel dwelt among the Canaanites, the Hittites, and the Amorites, and the Perizzites, and the Hivites, and the Jebusites; and they took their daughters to be their wives, and gave their own daughters to their sons, and served their gods (Judges 3:5-6). Just as the Roman Empire first conquered Greece but then adopted Greek culture, the ancient Israelites defeated the local pagan tribes in war but ultimately adopted much of the pagan culture of these vanquished tribes. Throughout the books of Judges, Samuel and Kings, the Israelites were engaged in a perpetual culture war – between the defenders of tradition and the Bible on the one hand, and dangerous pagan influences on the other.

The very same struggle, between Israelis who have adopted Western culture and those who have remained true to the Bible, is playing out in modern Israel today. The tension between the religious and secular Jews of Israel is a repetition, in many ways, of the internal struggles first described in the Book of Judges.

In the Book of Judges, the twelve tribes of Israel struggled to remain united, even when facing dangerous enemies. Each tribe was proud and independent, with unique strengths and weaknesses. This, of course, is also the story of modern Israel; a nation of many "tribes" who struggle to work together, all while Israel constantly faces external threats. The many tribes of modern Israel – religious Jews and secular Jews, Jews from Middle Eastern countries, Russia, Ethiopia and the United States – directly parallel the ancient tribes of Israel. Their struggles are the same struggles we face today.

And just as the Israelites in the Book of Judges faced a wide array of enemy states and internal terrorists, modern Israelis are threatened by dangerous nations like Iran and the Arab terrorists who threaten to destroy Israel from within.

Though the Book of Judges may have seemed irrelevant to powerless Jews living in exile in European ghettos in the Middle Ages, it has now, with the return of the Jewish people to Israel, come back to life!

## *Hope in Turbulent Times: Judges and the Book of Ruth*

The Book of Judges is clearly relevant for our time – but on its surface, it is a book filled with failure and disappointment. After the death of Joshua, the tribes pulled apart from one another, the people frequently turned away from God and worshiped the pagan gods of surrounding nations, and God repeatedly sent enemies to punish the Israelites and awaken them from their stupor. Yes, the Book of Judges is eerily similar to our time. But why study such a depressing book?

Though other nations rise and fall, Israel follows a different trajectory. Even during the darkest times, God has promised that He will never abandon the people of Israel. "With everlasting love have I loved you; therefore have I drawn you to Me with loving-kindness" (Jeremiah 31:2). Though Israel will stumble, Israel is also destined to rise up, again and again.

Incredibly, as the nation sunk to spiritual lows during the era of the Judges, the seeds of Israel's salvation were being sown in the most unlikely of ways.

Ibzan from Bethlehem was one of the lesser-known judges of Israel; the Book of Judges dedicates only three verses to his life:

"And after him Ibzan of Bethlehem judged Israel. And he had thirty sons, and thirty daughters he sent abroad, and thirty daughters he brought in from abroad for his sons. And he judged Israel for seven years. and Ibzan died, and was buried at Bethlehem." (Judges 12:8-10)

Though the Bible shares very little about Ibzan other than his remarkably large number of children, the sages provide a fascinating backstory to Ibzan's life. Tragically, Ibzan's wife and all of his sons and daughters died during his lifetime. Bereft and alone, Ibzan needed to start his life anew, and so he chose to take on a new name: Boaz, meaning "in strength." In other words, the sages explain that Ibzan is actually Boaz of Bethlehem from the story of Ruth!

The Book of Ruth tells one of the most powerful personal stories of the Bible – a story with national implications. After selflessly following her mother-in-law to Judea, Ruth is rewarded with a life of poverty and no marriage prospects. When she and her mother-in-law return to Naomi's hometown of Bethlehem, the people stare at Naomi, widowed and aged, and say "Is this broken woman really Naomi?" Living on the edge of town with no means of support, Naomi calls herself "Mara," "the bitter one" – and who can blame her?

Ruth amazingly stumbles onto Boaz's farm, and he is kind to her; you can almost hear the wedding bells! But once again, Ruth is disappointed. The harvest season ends and nothing happens. Boaz fails to act. In a bold move, Naomi instructs Ruth to sneak into the threshing floor where Boaz is asleep. And yet, instead of a romantic scene, Boaz essentially tells Ruth: "There may be another redeemer instead of me. Wait, and let's see what happens." This other relative is given the opportunity to marry Ruth, but he turns it down – yet another moment of rejection and disappointment. It is only then, at the very end of the book, that we finally reach the moment we've been waiting for. Boaz steps up to the plate and says "I will redeem her!" And from this union the Messiah is born.

The Book of Judges is defined by disappointment and failure. And yet, in the midst of that dark time, the love and kindness of Ruth, Boaz and Naomi brought a powerful light to the world and planted the seeds of Israel's future redemption. The prophet Samuel, author of both the Book of Judges and the Book of Ruth, alludes to this light within the darkness in the very first verse of the Book of Ruth: "And it came to pass in the days when the judges judged…" (Ruth 1:1). Ruth and Boaz will plant the seeds of redemption during the dark times of the judges!

This, it seems, is God's playbook for redemption. As we see throughout the story of Ruth and the entire era of the Book of Judges, the path to redemption is neither straightforward nor easy. There will be generations of darkness and years of sin and oppression before the people of Israel find their way to God. But that day will certainly come, as Samuel would later declare: "The Eternal One of Israel will not lie nor change His mind; for He is not a man, that He should change His mind" (I Samuel 15:29).

"It was the best of times, it was the worst of times, it was the age of wisdom, it was the age of foolishness, it was the epoch of belief, it was the epoch of incredulity, it was the season of light, it was the season of darkness, it was the spring of hope, it was the winter of despair" (Charles Dickens, A Tale of Two Cities).

We are living through complicated times. It is a time of miracles and prophecies fulfilled, when three-thousand-year-old prophecies are coming to life as the people of Israel return to their homeland from all over the world. But it is also a painful time, when terrorism has become a daily phenomenon, when the people of Israel are at risk of once again tearing themselves apart through internal divisions. From this perspective, we are living through an era of great pain and national disappointment.

But the Books of Judges and Ruth teach us that it is precisely during times like these that the seeds of redemption are sown. Perhaps, at this very moment of civil strife and external threats, the story of the final redeemer is being set in motion – right under our noses!

During the dark era of the judges, a small family brought great light to the world and transformed it. Instead of sinking into justifiable depression over all that he had lost, Boaz found the strength and hope he needed, as his new name implied, to begin his life anew with Ruth. And the extraordinary kindness that Ruth, Boaz and Naomi – the three bereaved protagonists of the story – show to one another led to the union of Ruth and Boaz and, ultimately, to the birth of their great-grandson: King David.

The Books of Judges and Ruth remind us that the people of Israel and its faithful friends must never give up hope, for God will never forsake His people. Like Boaz, Ruth and Naomi, we must find strength, place our hope in God, and show kindness to one another. Together, we can illuminate the darkness and bring redemption!

# 1

א

| After the death of Joshua, the Israelites inquired of GOD, "Which of us shall be the first to go up against the Canaanites and attack them?" | *vai-HEE, a-kha-ray mot y'-ho-SHU-a, va-yish-a-LU b'-NAY yis-ra-AYL ba-do-NAI lay-MOR: mee ya-a-leh LA-nu el ha-k'-na-a-NEE ba-t'-khi-LAH, l'-hi-LA-khem BO* | וַיְהִי אַחֲרֵי מוֹת יְהוֹשֻׁעַ וַיִּשְׁאֲלוּ בְּנֵי יִשְׂרָאֵל בַּיהוָה לֵאמֹר מִי יַעֲלֶה־לָּנוּ אֶל־הַכְּנַעֲנִי בַּתְּחִלָּה לְהִלָּחֶם בּוֹ׃ |

א

| GOD replied, "Let [the tribe of] Judah go up. I now deliver the land into their hands." | *va-YO-mer a-do-NAI, y'-hu-DAH ya-a-LEH hi-NAY na-TA-tee et ha-A-retz b'-ya-do.* | וַיֹּאמֶר יְהוָה יְהוּדָה יַעֲלֶה הִנֵּה נָתַתִּי אֶת־הָאָרֶץ בְּיָדוֹ׃ |

ב

| Judah then said to their brother-tribe Simeon, "Come up with us to our allotted territory and let us attack the Canaanites, and then we will go with you to your allotted territory." So Simeon joined them. | *va-YO-mer y'-hu-DAH l'-shim-ON a-KHEEV a-LAY i-TEE b'-go-ra-LEE v'-ni-la-cha-MAH ba-k'-na-a-NEE, v'-ha-lakh-TEE gam a-NEE i-t'-KHA b'-go-ra-LE-kha va-YAY-lekh i-TO shim-ON.* | וַיֹּאמֶר יְהוּדָה לְשִׁמְעוֹן אָחִיו עֲלֵה אִתִּי בְגֹרָלִי וְנִלָּחֲמָה בַּכְּנַעֲנִי וְהָלַכְתִּי גַם־אֲנִי אִתְּךָ בְּגוֹרָלֶךָ וַיֵּלֶךְ אִתּוֹ שִׁמְעוֹן׃ |

ג

| When Judah advanced, GOD delivered the Canaanites and the Perizzites into their hands, and they defeated ten thousand of them at Bezek. | *va-YA-al y'-hu-DAH va-yi-TAYN a-do-NAI et ha-k'-na-a-NEE v'-ha-p'-ree-ZEE b'-ya-DAM va-yak-KUM b'-VE-zek a-SE-ret a-la-FEEM EESH.* | וַיַּעַל יְהוּדָה וַיִּתֵּן יְהוָה אֶת־הַכְּנַעֲנִי וְהַפְּרִזִּי בְּיָדָם וַיַּכּוּם בְּבֶזֶק עֲשֶׂרֶת אֲלָפִים אִישׁ׃ |

ד

5

At Bezek, they
encountered Adoni-
bezek, engaged
him in battle,
and defeated the
Canaanites and the
Perizzites.

*va-yim-tz'-U et a-do-NEE
VE-zek b'-VE-zek va-yi-
la-cha-MU BO va-ya-KU
et ha-k'-na-a-NEE v'-et
ha-p'-ri-ZEE.*

וַיִּמְצְאוּ אֶת־אֲדֹנִי
בֶזֶק בְּבֶזֶק וַיִּלָּחֲמוּ בּוֹ
וַיַּכּוּ אֶת־הַכְּנַעֲנִי וְאֶת־
הַפְּרִזִּי:

ה

6

Adoni-bezek fled, but
they pursued him
and captured him;
and they cut off his
thumbs and his big
toes.

*va-YA-nas a-DO-nee
VE-zek, va-yir-d'-FU
a-kha-RAV va-yo-kha-ZU
o-TO vai-ka-tz'-TZU et
b'-ho-NOT ya-DAV v'-
rag-LAV.*

וַיָּנָס אֲדֹנִי בֶזֶק וַיִּרְדְּפוּ
אַחֲרָיו וַיֹּאחֲזוּ אֹתוֹ
וַיְקַצְּצוּ אֶת־בְּהֹנוֹת
יָדָיו וְרַגְלָיו:

ו

7

And Adoni-bezek
said, "Seventy kings,
with thumbs and big
toes cut off, used
to pick up scraps
under my table; as I
have done, so God
has requited me."
They brought him
to Jerusalem and he
died there.

*va-YO-mer a-do-ni
VE-zek, shiv-eem m'-la-
KHEEM, b'-ho-NOT
y'-day-HEM v'-rag-lay-
HEM m'-ku-tza-TZEEM
ha-YU m'-la-k'-TEEM
TA-khat shul-kha-NEE
ka-a-SHER a-SEE-tee,
kayn shi-lam LEE e-lo-
HEEM; vai-vee-U-hu
y'-ru-sha-LA-yim, va-YA-
mot sham.*

וַיֹּאמֶר אֲדֹנִי־בֶזֶק
שִׁבְעִים מְלָכִים בְּהֹנוֹת
יְדֵיהֶם וְרַגְלֵיהֶם
מְקֻצָּצִים הָיוּ מְלַקְּטִים
תַּחַת שֻׁלְחָנִי כַּאֲשֶׁר
עָשִׂיתִי כֵּן שִׁלַּם־לִי
אֱלֹהִים וַיְבִיאֻהוּ
יְרוּשָׁלַם וַיָּמָת שָׁם:

ז

8

The Judahites
attacked Jerusalem
and captured it; they
put it to the sword
and set the city on
fire.

*va-yi-la-kha-MU v'-NAY
y'-hu-DAH bee-ru-sha-
LA-yim, va-yil-k'-DU
o-TAH, va-ya-KU-ha
l'-FEE KHA-rev; v'-et
ha-EER shi-l'-KHU va-
AYSH.*

וַיִּלָּחֲמוּ בְנֵי־יְהוּדָה
בִּירוּשָׁלַם וַיִּלְכְּדוּ
אוֹתָהּ וַיַּכּוּהָ לְפִי־חָרֶב
וְאֶת־הָעִיר שִׁלְּחוּ
בָאֵשׁ:

ח

| | | |
|---|---|---|
| 9 | After that the Judahites went down to attack the Canaanites who inhabited the hill country, the Negeb, and the Shephelah. | *v'-a-KHAR ya-r'-DU b'-NAY y'-hu-DAH l'-hi-la-KHAYM ba-k'-na-a-NEE yo-SHAYV ha-HAR v'-ha-NE-gev v'-ha-sh'-fay-LAH* | וְאַחַר יָרְדוּ בְּנֵי יְהוּדָה לְהִלָּחֵם בַּכְּנַעֲנִי יוֹשֵׁב הָהָר וְהַנֶּגֶב וְהַשְּׁפֵלָה: ט |
| 10 | The Judahites marched against the Canaanites who dwelt in Hebron, and they defeated Sheshai, Ahiman, and Talmai. (The name of Hebron was formerly Kiriath-arba.) | *va-YAY-lekh y'-hu-DAH el ha-k'-na-a-NEE ha-yo-SHAYV b'-khev-RON v'-shaym khev-RON l'-fa-NEEM kir-YAT ar-BA; va-ya-KU et shay-SHAI v'-et a-khee-MAN, v'-et tal-MAI.* | וַיֵּלֶךְ יְהוּדָה אֶל־הַכְּנַעֲנִי הַיּוֹשֵׁב בְּחֶבְרוֹן וְשֵׁם־חֶבְרוֹן לְפָנִים קִרְיַת אַרְבַּע וַיַּכּוּ אֶת־שֵׁשַׁי וְאֶת־אֲחִימַן וְאֶת־תַּלְמָי: י |
| 11 | From there they marched against the inhabitants of Debir (the name of Debir was formerly Kiriath-sepher). | *va-YAY-lekh mi-SHAM, el yo-sh'-VAY d'-VEER; v'-shaym d'-VEER l'-fa-NEEM, kir-yat SAY-fer.* | וַיֵּלֶךְ מִשָּׁם אֶל־יוֹשְׁבֵי דְּבִיר וְשֵׁם־דְּבִיר לְפָנִים קִרְיַת־סֵפֶר: יא |
| 12 | And Caleb announced, "I will give my daughter Achsah in marriage to the man who attacks and captures Kiriath-sepher." | *va-YO-mer ka-LAYV a-sher ya-KEH et kir-YAT SAY-fer ul-kha-DAH, v'-na-ta-TEE lo et akh-SAH vi-TEE l'-i-SHAH* | וַיֹּאמֶר כָּלֵב אֲשֶׁר־יַכֶּה אֶת־קִרְיַת־סֵפֶר וּלְכָדָהּ וְנָתַתִּי לוֹ אֶת־עַכְסָה בִתִּי לְאִשָּׁה: יב |
| 13 | His younger kinsman, Othniel the Kenizzite, captured it; and Caleb gave him his daughter Achsah in marriage. | *va-yil-k'-DAH ot-nee-AYL ben k'-NAZ a-KHEE ka-LAYV ha-ka-TON mi-ME-nu, va-yi-ten LO et akh-SAH vi-TO l'-i-SHAH* | וַיִּלְכְּדָהּ עָתְנִיאֵל בֶּן קְנַז אֲחִי כָלֵב הַקָּטֹן מִמֶּנּוּ וַיִּתֶּן־לוֹ אֶת־עַכְסָה בִתּוֹ לְאִשָּׁה: יג |

**14** When she came [to him], she induced him to ask her father for some property. She dismounted from her donkey, and Caleb asked her, "What is the matter?"

*vai-HEE b'-vo-AH, va-t'-see-TAY-hu lish-OL may-ayt a-VEE-ha ha-sa-DEH, va-titz-NAKH may-AL ha-kha-MOR, va-yo-mer LAH ka-LAYV, mah LA-kh.*

וַיְהִי בְּבוֹאָהּ וַתְּסִיתֵהוּ לִשְׁאוֹל מֵאֵת־אָבִיהָ הַשָּׂדֶה וַתִּצְנַח מֵעַל הַחֲמוֹר וַיֹּאמֶר־לָהּ כָּלֵב מַה־לָּךְ: יד

**15** She replied, "Give me a present, for you have given me away as Negeb-land; give me springs of water." And Caleb gave her Upper and Lower Gulloth.

*va-TO-mer LO ha-vah LEE v'-ra-KHAH, KEE E-retz ha-NE-gev n'-ta-TA-nee, v'-na-ta-TAH LEE gu-LOT MA-yim, va-yi-ten LAH ka-LAYV AYT gu-LOT i-LIT, v'-AYT gu-LOT takh-TEET.*

וַתֹּאמֶר לוֹ הָבָה־לִּי בְרָכָה כִּי אֶרֶץ הַנֶּגֶב נְתַתָּנִי וְנָתַתָּה לִי גֻּלֹּת מָיִם וַיִּתֶּן־לָהּ כָּלֵב אֵת גֻּלֹּת עִלִּית וְאֵת גֻּלֹּת תַּחְתִּית: טו

**16** The descendants of the Kenite, the father-in-law of Moses, went up with the Judahites from the City of Palms to the wilderness of Judah; and they went and settled among the people in the Negeb of Arad.

*uv-NAY kay-NEE cho-TAYN mo-SHEH a-LU may-EER ha-t'-ma-REEM, et b'-NAY y'-hu-DAH mid-BAR y'-hu-DAH a-SHER b'-NE-gev a-RAD; va-YAY-lekh, va-YAY-shev et ha-AM.*

וּבְנֵי קֵינִי חֹתֵן מֹשֶׁה עָלוּ מֵעִיר הַתְּמָרִים אֶת־בְּנֵי יְהוּדָה מִדְבַּר יְהוּדָה אֲשֶׁר בְּנֶגֶב עֲרָד וַיֵּלֶךְ וַיֵּשֶׁב אֶת־הָעָם: טז

**17** And Judah with its brother-tribe Simeon went on and defeated the Canaanites who dwelt in Zephath. They proscribed it, and so the town was named Hormah.

*va-YAY-lekh y'-hu-DAH, et shim'-ON a-KHEEV, va-ya-KU et ha-k'-na-a-NEE yo-SHAYV tz'-FAT; va-ya-kha-REE-mu o-TAH, va-yik-RA et shaym ha-EER khor-MAH.*

וַיֵּלֶךְ יְהוּדָה אֶת־שִׁמְעוֹן אָחִיו וַיַּכּוּ אֶת־הַכְּנַעֲנִי יוֹשֵׁב צְפַת וַיַּחֲרִימוּ אוֹתָהּ וַיִּקְרָא אֶת־שֵׁם־הָעִיר חָרְמָה: יז

18 | And Judah captured Gaza and its territory, Ashkelon and its territory, and Ekron and its territory. | *va-yil-KOD y'-hu-DAH et a-ZAH v'-ET g'-vu-LAH, v'-et ash-k'-LON v'-et g'-vu-LAH, v'-et ek-RON, v'-et g'-vu-LAH.* | וַיִּלְכֹּד יְהוּדָה אֶת־עַזָּה וְאֶת־גְּבוּלָהּ וְאֶת־אַשְׁקְלוֹן וְאֶת־גְּבוּלָהּ וְאֶת־עֶקְרוֹן וְאֶת־גְּבוּלָהּ: יח

19 | GOD was with Judah, so that they took possession of the hill country; but they were not able to dispossess the inhabitants of the plain, for they had iron chariots. | *vai-HEE a-do-NAI et y'-hu-DAH, va-YO-resh et ha-HAR: KEE LO l'-ho-REESH et yo-sh'-VAY ha-AY-mek, kee RE-khev bar-ZEL la-HEM.* | וַיְהִי יְהֹוָה אֶת־יְהוּדָה וַיֹּרֶשׁ אֶת־הָהָר כִּי לֹא לְהוֹרִישׁ אֶת־יֹשְׁבֵי הָעֵמֶק כִּי־רֶכֶב בַּרְזֶל לָהֶם: יט

20 | They gave Hebron to Caleb, as Moses had promised; and he drove the three Anakites out of there. | *va-yi-t'-NU l'-kha-LAYV et khev-RON, ka-a-SHER di-BER mo-SHEH; va-YO-resh mi-SHAM, et sh'-lo-SHAH b'-NAY ha-a-NAK.* | וַיִּתְּנוּ לְכָלֵב אֶת־חֶבְרוֹן כַּאֲשֶׁר דִּבֶּר מֹשֶׁה וַיּוֹרֶשׁ מִשָּׁם אֶת־שְׁלֹשָׁה בְּנֵי הָעֲנָק: כ

21 | The Benjaminites did not dispossess the Jebusite inhabitants of Jerusalem; so the Jebusites have dwelt with the Benjaminites in Jerusalem to this day. | *v'-ET ha-y'-vu-SEE yo-SHAYV y'-ru-sha-LA-yim, lo ho-REE-shu b'-NAY vin-ya-MIN; va-YAY-shev hai-vu-SEE et b'-NAY vin-ya-MIN bee-ru-sha-LA-yim, AD ha-YOM ha-ZEH.* | וְאֶת־הַיְבוּסִי יֹשֵׁב יְרוּשָׁלַם לֹא הוֹרִישׁוּ בְּנֵי בִנְיָמִן וַיֵּשֶׁב הַיְבוּסִי אֶת־בְּנֵי בִנְיָמִן בִּירוּשָׁלַם עַד הַיּוֹם הַזֶּה: כא

22 | The House of Joseph, for their part, advanced against Bethel, and GOD was with them. | *va-ya-a-LU vayt yo-SAYF gam HAYM, beit AYL; va-do-NAI, i-MAM.* | וַיַּעֲלוּ בֵית־יוֹסֵף גַּם־הֵם בֵּית־אֵל וַיהֹוָה עִמָּם: כב

| | | | |
|---|---|---|---|
| 23 | While the House of Joseph were scouting at Bethel (the name of the town was formerly Luz), | *va-ya-TEE-ru vayt yo-SAYF, b'-vayt AYL; v'-SHAYM ha-EER l'-fa-NEEM, LUZ.* | וַיָּתִירוּ בֵית־יוֹסֵף בְּבֵית־אֵל וְשֵׁם־הָעִיר לְפָנִים לוּז: כג |
| 24 | their patrols saw someone leaving the town. They said to him, "Just show us how to get into the town, and we will treat you kindly." | *va-yir-U ha-sho-m'-REEM, EESH yo-TZAY min ha-EER; va-yo-m'-ru LO, har-AY-nu NA et m'-VO ha-EER, v'-a-SEE-nu i-m'-kha KHA-sed.* | וַיִּרְאוּ הַשֹּׁמְרִים אִישׁ יוֹצֵא מִן־הָעִיר וַיֹּאמְרוּ לוֹ הַרְאֵנוּ נָא אֶת־מְבוֹא הָעִיר וְעָשִׂינוּ עִמְּךָ חָסֶד: כד |
| 25 | He showed them how to get into the town; they put the town to the sword, but they let the man and all his relatives go free. | *va-yar-AYM et m'-VO ha-EER, va-ya-KU et ha-EER l'-FEE KHA-rev; v'-ET ha-EESH v'-et kol mish-pakh-TO, shi-LAY-khu.* | וַיַּרְאֵם אֶת־מְבוֹא הָעִיר וַיַּכּוּ אֶת־הָעִיר לְפִי־חָרֶב וְאֶת־הָאִישׁ וְאֶת־כָּל־מִשְׁפַּחְתּוֹ שִׁלֵּחוּ: כה |
| 26 | The man went to the Hittite country. He founded a city and named it Luz, and that has been its name to this day. | *va-YAY-lekh ha-EESH, E-retz ha-khi-TEEM; va-YI-ven EER, va-yik-RA sh'-MAH LUZ hu sh'-MAH, ad ha-YOM ha-ZEH.* | וַיֵּלֶךְ הָאִישׁ אֶרֶץ הַחִתִּים וַיִּבֶן עִיר וַיִּקְרָא שְׁמָהּ לוּז הוּא שְׁמָהּ עַד הַיּוֹם הַזֶּה: כו |

27

Manasseh did not dispossess [the inhabitants of] Beth-shean and its dependencies, or [of] Taanach and its dependencies, or the inhabitants of Dor and its dependencies, or the inhabitants of Ibleam and its dependencies, or the inhabitants of Megiddo and its dependencies. The Canaanites persisted in dwelling in this region.

*v'-LO ho-REESH m'-na-SHEH et bayt sh'-AN v'-et b'-no-TE-ha v'-ET ta-NAKH v'-ET b'-no-TE-ha v'-et yo-sh'-VAY dor v'-et b'-no-TE-ha v'-ET yo-sh'-VAY yiv-l'-AM v'-et b'-no-TE-ha v'-et yo-sh'-VAY mi-gi-DO ve-et b'-no-TE-ha va-YO-el ha-k'-na-a-NEE la-SHE-vet ba-A-retz ha-ZOT*

וְלֹא־הוֹרִישׁ מְנַשֶּׁה אֶת־
בֵּית־שְׁאָן וְאֶת־בְּנוֹתֶיהָ
וְאֶת־תַּעְנַךְ וְאֶת־בְּנֹתֶיהָ
וְאֶת־[יוֹשְׁבֵי] (יושב)
דוֹר וְאֶת־בְּנוֹתֶיהָ וְאֶת־
יוֹשְׁבֵי יִבְלְעָם וְאֶת־
בְּנֹתֶיהָ וְאֶת־יוֹשְׁבֵי
מְגִדּוֹ וְאֶת־בְּנוֹתֶיהָ
וַיּוֹאֶל הַכְּנַעֲנִי לָשֶׁבֶת
בָּאָרֶץ הַזֹּאת:

כז

28

And when Israel gained the upper hand, they subjected the Canaanites to forced labor; but they did not dispossess them.

*vai-HEE kee kha-ZAK yis-ra-AYL va-YA-sem et ha-k'-na-a-NEE l'-MAS; v'-ho-RAYSH, LO ho-ree-SHO.*

וַיְהִי כִּי־חָזַק יִשְׂרָאֵל
וַיָּשֶׂם אֶת־הַכְּנַעֲנִי לָמַס
וְהוֹרֵישׁ לֹא הוֹרִישׁוֹ:

כח

29

Nor did Ephraim dispossess the Canaanites who inhabited Gezer; so the Canaanites dwelt in their midst at Gezer.

*v'-ef-RA-yim LO ho-REESH et ha-k'-na-a-NEE ha-yo-SHAYV b'-GA-zer; va-YAY-shev ha-k'-na-a-NEE b'-kir-BO b'-GA-zer.*

וְאֶפְרַיִם לֹא הוֹרִישׁ
אֶת־הַכְּנַעֲנִי הַיּוֹשֵׁב
בְּגָזֶר וַיֵּשֶׁב הַכְּנַעֲנִי
בְּקִרְבּוֹ בְּגָזֶר:

כט

30 Zebulun did not dispossess the inhabitants of Kitron or the inhabitants of Nahalol; so the Canaanites dwelt in their midst, but they were subjected to forced labor.

*z'-vu-LUN LO ho-REESH et yo-sh'-VAY kit-RON v'-et yo-sh'-VAY na-ha-LOL va-YAY-shev ha-k'-na-a-NEE b'-kir-BO va-yih-YU la-MAS*

זְבוּלֻן לֹא הוֹרִישׁ אֶת־יוֹשְׁבֵי קִטְרוֹן וְאֶת־יוֹשְׁבֵי נַהֲלֹל וַיֵּשֶׁב הַכְּנַעֲנִי בְּקִרְבּוֹ וַיִּהְיוּ לָמַס: ל

31 Asher did not dispossess the inhabitants of Acco or the inhabitants of Sidon, Ahlab, Achzib, Helbah, Aphik, and Rehob.

*a-SHAYR LO ho-REESH et yo-sh'-VAY a-KO v'-ET yo-sh'-VAY tzee-DON; v'-et akh-LAV v'-et akh-ZEEV v'-et khel-BAH v'-et a-FEEK v'-et r'-KHOV.*

אָשֵׁר לֹא הוֹרִישׁ אֶת־יֹשְׁבֵי עַכּוֹ וְאֶת־יוֹשְׁבֵי צִידוֹן וְאֶת־אַחְלָב וְאֶת־אַכְזִיב וְאֶת־חֶלְבָּה וְאֶת־אֲפִיק וְאֶת־רְחֹב: לא

32 So the Asherites dwelt in the midst of the Canaanites, the inhabitants of the land, for they did not dispossess them.

*va-YAY-shev ha-A-shay-REE b'-KE-rev ha-k'-na-a-NEE yo-sh'-VAY ha-A-retz: KEE LO ho-ree-SHO.*

וַיֵּשֶׁב הָאָשֵׁרִי בְּקֶרֶב הַכְּנַעֲנִי יֹשְׁבֵי הָאָרֶץ כִּי לֹא הוֹרִישׁוֹ: לב

33 Naphtali did not dispossess the inhabitants of Beth-shemesh or the inhabitants of Beth-anath. But they settled in the midst of the Canaanite inhabitants of the land, and the inhabitants of Beth-shemesh and Beth-anath had to perform forced labor for them.

*naf-ta-LEE, lo ho-REESH et yo-sh'-VAY vayt SHE-mesh v'-et yo-sh'-VAY vayt a-NAT; va-YAY-shev b'-KE-rev ha-k'-na-a-NEE yo-sh'-VAY ha-A-retz; v'-yo-sh'-VAY vayt SHE-mesh u-VAYT a-NAT ha-YU la-HEM la-MAS.*

נַפְתָּלִי לֹא־הוֹרִישׁ אֶת־יֹשְׁבֵי בֵית־שֶׁמֶשׁ וְאֶת־יֹשְׁבֵי בֵית־עֲנָת וַיֵּשֶׁב בְּקֶרֶב הַכְּנַעֲנִי יֹשְׁבֵי הָאָרֶץ וְיֹשְׁבֵי בֵית־שֶׁמֶשׁ וּבֵית עֲנָת הָיוּ לָהֶם לָמַס: לג

| | | |
|---|---|---|
| 34 | The Amorites pressed the Danites into the hill country; they would not let them come down to the plain. | *va-yil-kha-TZU ha-e-mo-REE et b'-nay DAN ha-HA-rah kee LO n'-ta-NO la-RE-det la-AY-mek* |

וַיִּלְחֲצוּ הָאֱמֹרִי אֶת־בְּנֵי־דָן הָהָרָה כִּי־לֹא נְתָנוֹ לָרֶדֶת לָעֵמֶק: לד

| | | |
|---|---|---|
| 35 | The Amorites also persisted in dwelling in Har-heres, in Aijalon, and in Shaalbim. But the hand of the House of Joseph bore heavily on them and they had to perform forced labor. | *va-YO-el ha-e-mo-REE la-SHE-vet b'-har KHE-res b'-a-ya-LON uv-sha-al-VEEM va-tikh-BAD YAD bayt yo-SAYF va-yih-YU la-MAS* |

וַיּוֹאֶל הָאֱמֹרִי לָשֶׁבֶת בְּהַר־חֶרֶס בְּאַיָּלוֹן וּבְשַׁעַלְבִים וַתִּכְבַּד יַד בֵּית־יוֹסֵף וַיִּהְיוּ לָמַס: לה

| | | |
|---|---|---|
| 36 | The territory of the Amorites extended from the Ascent of Akrabbim—from Sela—onward. | *ug-VUL ha-e-mo-REE mi-ma-a-LAY ak-ra-BEEM may-ha-SE-la va-MA-lah* |

וּגְבוּל הָאֱמֹרִי מִמַּעֲלֵה עַקְרַבִּים מֵהַסֶּלַע וָמָעְלָה: לו

# The Quiet Heroes of Our Time

Othniel, the first judge of Israel described in the book of Judges, was a courageous warrior and military leader. When Caleb, the aging leader of the tribe of Judah, sought a younger man to lead the men of Judah in battle, Othniel volunteered:

"And Caleb announced, 'I will give my daughter Achsah in marriage to the man who attacks and captures Kiriath-sepher.' His younger kinsman, Othniel the Kenizzite, captured it; and Caleb gave him his daughter Achsah in marriage." (Judges 1:12-13)

This, it would seem, is the conclusion of the story. Othniel leads the men of Judah to victory, and is rewarded by being given the hand of Achsah, daughter of the legendary Caleb, in marriage.

But then the Book of Judges then shares a short, strange story about Achsah, Othniel's new wife:

"When she came [to him], she induced him to ask her father for some property. She dismounted from her donkey, and Caleb asked her, 'What is the matter?' She replied, 'Give me a present, for you have given me only Negeb-land [in the desert]; give me springs of water.' And Caleb gave her Upper and Lower Gulloth." (Judges 1:14-15)

After marrying Othniel, it seems that Caleb gave his daughter and son-in-law a portion of land in the tribe of Judah's territory in the Negev desert, in southern Israel. Achsah, however, wasn't satisfied with her father's gift, for her father had given her and Othniel desert lands without water - and what, really, can you do with land if you don't have water? At Achsah's urging, Caleb gave the young couple an additional portion of land, the Upper and Lower Gulloth, that contained springs of water.

When I first read these verses, I was confused. Why is this short personal story about Achsah and her request for water for her farm recorded in the Bible? What relevance does this story have to the great national and religious themes of the Book of Judges?

Every verse in the Bible is essential, and every story is there to teach us something important and eternal. This short story about Achsah and her request for water is no exception.

In the first chapter of Judges, Othniel is the brave hero who leads his people and succeeds in conquering the Land from its idolatrous inhabitants. But the Book of Judges wants us to understand that victory in battle is only the beginning. To fully acquire the land of Israel, the Jewish people must not only *conquer* but also *settle* the Holy Land.

This is why we are told the story of Achsah and her tenacious determination to acquire water for her new farm. Achsah understood that military victories are critical - but that the land must also be settled and made to bloom and prosper. Had Achsah not acquired water for her land, her husband's military exploits would have been for naught!

In our generation, when the people of Israel have returned to the Land of Israel and are struggling to conquer and settle it, the story of Achsah and Othniel is particularly relevant. Beginning in the late 1960s, after the Six-Day War, Rabbi Moshe and Miriam Levinger, of blessed memory, led the struggle to rebuild the Jewish community of Hebron, despite great opposition from local Arabs and the Israeli government. Hebron, of course, is part of the ancient tribal portion of Judah and the second holiest city in Israel, which Caleb and Othniel first captured thousands of years ago!

Though Rabbi Levinger was better known to the broader Israeli public, it was his wife, Miriam, who was a "modern-day Achsah." Miriam often joked that she "brought the first Jewish refrigerator to Hebron." While her husband gave public speeches and helped lead the settlement movement, Miriam ensured that the small and endangered Jewish community of Hebron continued to function and grow. Because of her sacrifice, the Jewish community of Hebron and adjacent Kiryat Arba is now over 10,000 strong.

When Miriam passed away in 2020, a friend eulogized her: "She dreamed of a renewed Hebron which would be visited each year by hundreds of thousands, where children could play freely in the streets and in the ancient field by the Cave of the Patriarchs, and she was blessed, through her efforts, and through the efforts of all those whom she inspired, to see her dream come true."

Miriam, like so many other extraordinary women in modern Israel, worked quietly behind the scenes to ensure that the Jewish people not only conquer the land of Israel, but also settle it and make it their own. May their holy sacrifice never be forgotten.

**2**　　　　　　　　　　　　　　　　　　　　**ב**

| | | |
|---|---|---|
| 1 | An angel of GOD came up from Gilgal to Bochim and said, "I brought you up from Egypt and I took you into the land that I had promised on oath to your fathers. And I said, 'I will never break My covenant with you. | *va-YA-aL mal-ach a-do-NAI min ha-gil-GAL el ha-bo-KHEEM va-YO-mer a-a-LEH et-KHEM mi-mitz-RA-yim, va-a-VEE et-KHEM el ha-A-retz a-SHER nish-BA-tee la-a-vo-tay-KHEM, va-o-MAR, lo a-FAYR b'-ree-TEE i-t'-KHEM l'-o-LAM.* |

וַיַּעַל מַלְאַךְ־יְהוָה מִן־הַגִּלְגָּל אֶל־הַבֹּכִים וַיֹּאמֶר אַעֲלֶה אֶתְכֶם מִמִּצְרַיִם וָאָבִיא אֶתְכֶם אֶל־הָאָרֶץ אֲשֶׁר נִשְׁבַּעְתִּי לַאֲבֹתֵיכֶם וָאֹמַר לֹא־אָפֵר בְּרִיתִי אִתְּכֶם לְעוֹלָם: א

| | | |
|---|---|---|
| 2 | And you, for your part, must make no covenant with the inhabitants of this land; you must tear down their altars.' But you have not obeyed Me—look what you have done! | *v'-a-TEM lo tikh-r'-TU v'-REET l'-yo-sh'-VAY ha-A-retz ha-ZOT miz-b'-kho-tay-HEM ti-to-TZUN v'-lo sh'-ma-TEM b'-ko-LEE mah ZOT a-see-TEM.* |

וְאַתֶּם לֹא־תִכְרְתוּ בְרִית לְיוֹשְׁבֵי הָאָרֶץ הַזֹּאת מִזְבְּחוֹתֵיהֶם תִּתֹּצוּן וְלֹא־שְׁמַעְתֶּם בְּקוֹלִי מַה־זֹּאת עֲשִׂיתֶם: ב

| | | |
|---|---|---|
| 3 | Therefore, I have resolved not to drive them out before you; they shall become your oppressors, and their gods shall be a snare to you." | *v'-GAM a-MAR-tee lo a-ga-RAYSH o-TAM mi-p'-nay-KHEM v'-ha-YU la-KHEM l'-tzi-DEEM, vay-lo-hay-HEM, yih-YU la-KHEM l'-mo-KAYSH.* |

וְגַם אָמַרְתִּי לֹא־אֲגָרֵשׁ אוֹתָם מִפְּנֵיכֶם וְהָיוּ לָכֶם לְצִדִּים וֵאלֹהֵיהֶם יִהְיוּ לָכֶם לְמוֹקֵשׁ: ג

| | | | |
|---|---|---|---|
| 4 | As the angel of GOD spoke these words to all the Israelites, the people broke into weeping. | *vai-HEE k'-da-BAYR mal-AKH a-do-NAI et ha-d'-va-REEM ha-AY-leh, el kol b'-NAY yis-ra-AYL va-yis-U ha-AM et ko-LAM, va-yiv-KU.* | וַיְהִי כְּדַבֵּר מַלְאַךְ יְהֹוָה אֶת־הַדְּבָרִים הָאֵלֶּה אֶל־כָּל־בְּנֵי יִשְׂרָאֵל וַיִּשְׂאוּ הָעָם אֶת־קוֹלָם וַיִּבְכּוּ: ד |
| 5 | So they named that place Bochim, and they offered sacrifices there to GOD. | *va-yik-r'-U shaym ha-ma-KOM ha-HU bo-KHEEM; va-yiz-b'-khu SHAM la-do-NAI.* | וַיִּקְרְאוּ שֵׁם־הַמָּקוֹם הַהוּא בֹּכִים וַיִּזְבְּחוּ־ שָׁם לַיהֹוָה: ה |
| 6 | When Joshua dismissed the people, the Israelites went to their allotted territories and took possession of the land. | *vai-sha-LAKH y'-ho-SHU-a et-ha-AM va-yay-l'-KHU v'-NAY yis-ra-AYL EESH l'-na-kha-la-TO la-RE-shet et-ha-A-retz.* | וַיְשַׁלַּח יְהוֹשֻׁעַ אֶת־ הָעָם וַיֵּלְכוּ בְנֵי־יִשְׂרָאֵל אִישׁ לְנַחֲלָתוֹ לָרֶשֶׁת אֶת־הָאָרֶץ: ו |
| 7 | The people served GOD during the lifetime of Joshua and the lifetime of the older people who lived on after Joshua and who had witnessed all the marvelous deeds that GOD had wrought for Israel. | *va-ya-av-DU ha-AM et a-do-NAI KOL y'-MAY y'-ho-SHU-a v'-KHOL y'-MAY ha-z'-kay-NEEM, a-SHER he-e-REE-khu ya-MEE a-kha-RAY y'-ho-SHU-a a-SHER ra-U AYT kol ma-a-SAY a-do-NAI ha-ga-DOL, a-SHER a-SAH l'-yis-ra-AYL.* | וַיַּעַבְדוּ הָעָם אֶת־יְהֹוָה כֹּל יְמֵי יְהוֹשֻׁעַ וְכֹל יְמֵי הַזְּקֵנִים אֲשֶׁר הֶאֱרִיכוּ יָמִים אַחֲרֵי יְהוֹשֻׁעַ אֲשֶׁר רָאוּ אֵת כָּל־מַעֲשֵׂה יְהֹוָה הַגָּדוֹל אֲשֶׁר עָשָׂה לְיִשְׂרָאֵל: ז |
| 8 | Joshua son of Nun, the servant of GOD, died at the age of one hundred and ten years, | *va-YA-mot y'-ho-SHU-a bin NUN E-ved a-do-NAI, ben may-AH va-E-ser sha-NEEM.* | וַיָּמָת יְהוֹשֻׁעַ בִּן־נוּן עֶבֶד יְהֹוָה בֶּן־מֵאָה וָעֶשֶׂר שָׁנִים: ח |

| | | | |
|---|---|---|---|
| 9 | and was buried on his own property, at Timnath-heres in the hill country of Ephraim, north of Mount Gaash. | *va-yik-b'-RU o-TO big-VUL na-kha-la-TO, b'-tim-nat KHE-res b'-HAR ef-RA-yim, mi-tz'-FON, l'-har GA-ash.* | וַיִּקְבְּרוּ אוֹתוֹ בִּגְבוּל נַחֲלָתוֹ בְּתִמְנַת־חֶרֶס בְּהַר אֶפְרָיִם מִצְּפוֹן לְהַר־גָּעַשׁ: ט |
| 10 | And all that generation were likewise gathered to their ancestors. Another generation arose after them, which had not experienced GOD's deliverance or the deeds that had been wrought for Israel. | *v'-GAM kol ha-DOR ha-HU ne-es-FU el a-vo-TAV va-YA-kom DOR a-KHAYR a-kha-ray-HEM a-SHER lo ya-d'-U et a-do-NAI, v'-GAM et ha-ma-a-SEH a-SHER a-SAH l'-yis-ra-AYL.* | וְגַם כָּל־הַדּוֹר הַהוּא נֶאֶסְפוּ אֶל־אֲבוֹתָיו וַיָּקָם דּוֹר אַחֵר אַחֲרֵיהֶם אֲשֶׁר לֹא־יָדְעוּ אֶת־יְהֹוָה וְגַם אֶת־הַמַּעֲשֶׂה אֲשֶׁר עָשָׂה לְיִשְׂרָאֵל: י |
| 11 | And the Israelites did what was offensive to GOD. They worshiped the Baalim | *va-ya-a-SU v'-NAY yis-ra-AYL et ha-RA b'-ay-NAY a-do-NAI; va-ya-av-DU et ha-b'-a-LEEM.* | וַיַּעֲשׂוּ בְנֵי־יִשְׂרָאֵל אֶת־הָרַע בְּעֵינֵי יְהֹוָה וַיַּעַבְדוּ אֶת־הַבְּעָלִים: יא |
| 12 | and forsook the ETERNAL, the God of their ancestors, who had brought them out of the land of Egypt. They followed other gods, from among the gods of the peoples around them, and bowed down to them; they provoked GOD. | *va-ya-az-VU et a-do-NAI e-lo-HAY a-vo-TAM ha-mo-TZEE o-TAM may-E-retz mitz-RA-yim va-yay-l'-KHU a-kha-RAY e-lo-HEEM a-khay-REEM may-e-lo-HAY ha-a-MEEM a-SHER s'-vee-vo-tay-HEM va-yish-ta-kha-VU la-HEM va-yakh-I-su et a-do-NAI.* | וַיַּעַזְבוּ אֶת־יְהֹוָה אֱלֹהֵי אֲבוֹתָם הַמּוֹצִיא אוֹתָם מֵאֶרֶץ מִצְרַיִם וַיֵּלְכוּ אַחֲרֵי אֱלֹהִים אֲחֵרִים מֵאֱלֹהֵי הָעַמִּים אֲשֶׁר סְבִיבוֹתֵיהֶם וַיִּשְׁתַּחֲווּ לָהֶם וַיַּכְעִסוּ אֶת־יְהֹוָה: יב |
| 13 | They forsook GOD and worshiped Baal and the Ashtaroth. | *va-ya-az-VU et a-do-NAI; va-ya-av-DU la-BA-al v'-la-ash-ta-ROT.* | וַיַּעַזְבוּ אֶת־יְהֹוָה וַיַּעַבְדוּ לַבַּעַל וְלָעַשְׁתָּרוֹת: יג |

14 Having become incensed at Israel, GOD then handed them over to foes who plundered them, surrendering them to their enemies on all sides; they could no longer hold their own against their enemies.

*va-yi-khar AF a-do-NAI b'-yis-ra-AYL va-yi-t'-NAYM b'-yad sho-SEEM va-ya-SHO-su o-TAM; va-yim-k'-RAYM b'-YAD o-y'-vay-HEM mi-sa-VEEV v'-lo ya-kh'-LU OD la-a-MOD lif-NAY o-y'-vay-HEM.*

וַיִּחַר־אַף יְהֹוָה
בְּיִשְׂרָאֵל וַיִּתְּנֵם בְּיַד־
שֹׁסִים וַיָּשֹׁסּוּ אוֹתָם
וַיִּמְכְּרֵם בְּיַד אוֹיְבֵיהֶם
מִסָּבִיב וְלֹא־יָכְלוּ עוֹד
לַעֲמֹד לִפְנֵי אוֹיְבֵיהֶם: יד

15 In all their campaigns, the hand of GOD was against them to their undoing—as GOD had declared and as GOD had sworn to them—and they were in great distress.

*b'-KHOL a-SHER ya-tz'-U yad a-do-NAI ha-y'-tah BAM l'-ra-AH ka-a-SHER di-BER a-do-NAI, v'-kha-a-SHER nish-BA a-do-NAI la-HEM; va-YAY-tzer la-HEM m'-OD.*

בְּכֹל אֲשֶׁר יָצְאוּ יַד־
יְהֹוָה הָיְתָה־בָּם לְרָעָה
כַּאֲשֶׁר דִּבֶּר יְהֹוָה
וְכַאֲשֶׁר נִשְׁבַּע יְהֹוָה
לָהֶם וַיֵּצֶר לָהֶם מְאֹד: טו

16 Then GOD raised up chieftains who delivered them from those who plundered them.

*va-YA-kem a-do-NAI sho-f'-TEEM va-yo-shee-UM mi-YAD sho-say-HEM.*

וַיָּקֶם יְהֹוָה שֹׁפְטִים
וַיּוֹשִׁיעוּם מִיַּד
שֹׁסֵיהֶם: טז

17 But they did not heed their chieftains either; they went astray after other gods and bowed down to them. They were quick to turn aside from the way their ancestors had followed in obedience to the commandments of GOD; they did not do right.

*v'-GAM el sho-f'-tay-HEM LO sha-MAY-u KEE za-NU a-kha-RAY e-lo-HEEM a-khay-REEM va-yish-ta-kha-VU la-HEM: SA-ru ma-HAYR min ha-DE-rekh a-SHER ha-l'-KHU a-vo-TAM lish-MO-a mitz-vot a-do-NAI lo A-su KHAYN.*

וְגַם אֶל־שֹׁפְטֵיהֶם
לֹא שָׁמֵעוּ כִּי זָנוּ
אַחֲרֵי אֱלֹהִים אֲחֵרִים
וַיִּשְׁתַּחֲווּ לָהֶם סָרוּ
מַהֵר מִן־הַדֶּרֶךְ אֲשֶׁר
הָלְכוּ אֲבוֹתָם לִשְׁמֹעַ
מִצְוֹת־יְהֹוָה לֹא־עָשׂוּ
כֵּן: יז

18 When GOD raised up chieftains for them, GOD would be with that chieftain— and would save them from their enemies during that chieftain's lifetime; for GOD would be moved to pity by their moanings because of those who oppressed and crushed them.

*v'-khee hay-KEEM a-do-NAI la-HEM sho-f'-TEEM, v'-ha-YAH a-do-NAI im ha-sho-FAYT v'-ho-shee-AM mi-YAD o-y'-vay-HEM, kol y'-MAY ha-sho-FAYT kee yi-na-KHAYM a-do-NAI mi-na-a-ka-TAM mi-p'-NAY lo-kha-tzay-HEM v'-do-kha-kay-HEM.*

וְכִי־הֵקִים יְהֹוָה לָהֶם שֹׁפְטִים וְהָיָה יְהֹוָה עִם־הַשֹּׁפֵט וְהוֹשִׁיעָם מִיַּד אֹיְבֵיהֶם כֹּל יְמֵי הַשּׁוֹפֵט כִּי־יִנָּחֵם יְהֹוָה מִנַּאֲקָתָם מִפְּנֵי לֹחֲצֵיהֶם וְדֹחֲקֵיהֶם:

יח

19 But when the chieftain died, they would again act basely, even more than the preceding generation — following other gods, worshiping them, and bowing down to them; they omitted none of their practices and stubborn ways.

*v'-ha-YAH b'-MOT ha-sho-FAYT ya-SHU-vu v'-hish-KHEE-tu may-a-vo-TAM la-LE-khet a-kha-RAY e-lo-HEEM a-khay-REEM, l'-ov-DAM ul'-hish-ta-kha-VOT la-HEM LO hi-PEE-lu mi-ma-a-l'-lay-HEM u-mi-dar-KAM ha-ka-SHAH.*

וְהָיָה בְּמוֹת הַשֹּׁפֵט יָשֻׁבוּ וְהִשְׁחִיתוּ מֵאֲבוֹתָם לָלֶכֶת אַחֲרֵי אֱלֹהִים אֲחֵרִים לְעָבְדָם וּלְהִשְׁתַּחֲוֹת לָהֶם לֹא הִפִּילוּ מִמַּעַלְלֵיהֶם וּמִדַּרְכָּם הַקָּשָׁה:

יט

20 Then GOD, having become incensed against Israel, said, "Since that nation has transgressed the covenant that I enjoined upon their ancestors and has not obeyed Me,

*va-yi-khar AF a-do-NAI b'-yis-ra-AYL va-YO-mer YA-an a-SHER a-v'-RU ha-GOY ha-ZEH et b'-ree-TEE a-SHER tzi-VEE-tee et a-vo-TAM v'-LO sha-m'-U l'-ko-LEE.*

וַיִּחַר־אַף יְהֹוָה בְּיִשְׂרָאֵל וַיֹּאמֶר יַעַן אֲשֶׁר עָבְרוּ הַגּוֹי הַזֶּה אֶת־בְּרִיתִי אֲשֶׁר צִוִּיתִי אֶת־אֲבוֹתָם וְלֹא שָׁמְעוּ לְקוֹלִי:

כ

| | | |
|---|---|---|
| 21 | I for My part will no longer drive out before them any of the nations that Joshua left when he died." | *gam a-NEE LO o-SEEF l'-ho-REESH EESH mi-p'-nay-HEM min ha-go-YIM a-sher a-ZAV y'-ho-SHU-a va-ya-MOT.* | גַּם־אֲנִי לֹא אוֹסִיף לְהוֹרִישׁ אִישׁ מִפְּנֵיהֶם מִן־הַגּוֹיִם אֲשֶׁר־עָזַב יְהוֹשֻׁעַ וַיָּמֹת: | כא |
| 22 | For it was in order to test Israel by them—[to see] whether they would faithfully walk in the ways of GOD, as their ancestors had done— | *l'-MA-an na-SOT BAM et yis-ra-AYL ha-sho-m'-REEM HAYM et DE-rekh a-do-NAI la-LE-khet BAM ka-a-SHER sha-m'-RU a-vo-TAM im LO.* | לְמַעַן נַסּוֹת בָּם אֶת־יִשְׂרָאֵל הֲשֹׁמְרִים הֵם אֶת־דֶּרֶךְ יְהוָה לָלֶכֶת בָּם כַּאֲשֶׁר שָׁמְרוּ אֲבוֹתָם אִם־לֹא: | כב |
| 23 | that GOD had left those nations, instead of driving them out at once, and had not delivered them into the hands of Joshua. | *va-ya-NAKH a-do-NAI e ha-go-YIM ha-AY-leh l'-vil-TEE ho-ree-SHAM ma-HAYR v'-LO n'-ta-NAM b'-yad y'-ho-SHU-a.* | וַיַּנַּח יְהוָה אֶת־הַגּוֹיִם הָאֵלֶּה לְבִלְתִּי הוֹרִישָׁם מַהֵר וְלֹא נְתָנָם בְּיַד־יְהוֹשֻׁעַ: | כג |

3

1 These are the nations that GOD left in order to test the Israelites who had not known any of the wars of Canaan,

*v'-AY-leh ha-go-YIM a-SHER hi-NEE-akh a-do-NAI, l'-na-SOT BAM et yis-ra-AYL, AYT kol a-SHER lo ya-d'-U AYT kol mil-kha-MOT k'-NA-an.*

וְאֵלֶּה הַגּוֹיִם אֲשֶׁר
הִנִּיחַ יְהֹוָה לְנַסּוֹת
בָּם אֶת־יִשְׂרָאֵל אֵת
כָּל־אֲשֶׁר לֹא־יָדְעוּ אֵת
כָּל־מִלְחֲמוֹת כְּנָעַן׃ א

2 so that succeeding generations of Israelites might be made to experience war—but only those who had not known the former wars:

*RAK l'-MA-an DA-at do-ROT b'-NAY yis-ra-AYL l'-la-m'-DAM mil-kha-MAH RAK a-sher l'-fa-NEEM lo y'-da-UM.*

רַק לְמַעַן דַּעַת דֹּרוֹת
בְּנֵי־יִשְׂרָאֵל לְלַמְּדָם
מִלְחָמָה רַק אֲשֶׁר־
לְפָנִים לֹא יְדָעוּם׃ ב

3 the five principalities of the Philistines and all the Canaanites, Sidonians, and Hivites who inhabited the hill country of the Lebanon from Mount Baal-hermon to Lebo-hamath.

*kha-MAY-shet sar-NAY f'-lish-TEEM, v'-khol ha-k'-na-a-NEE v'-ha-TZEE-do-nee, v'-ha-khi-VEE yo-SHAYV HAR ha-l'-va-NON may-HAR BA-al kher-MON, AD l'-VO kha-MAT.*

חֲמֵשֶׁת סַרְנֵי פְלִשְׁתִּים
וְכָל־הַכְּנַעֲנִי וְהַצִּידֹנִי
וְהַחִוִּי יֹשֵׁב הַר הַלְּבָנוֹן
מֵהַר בַּעַל חֶרְמוֹן עַד
לְבוֹא חֲמָת׃ ג

4 These served as a means of testing Israel, to learn whether they would obey the commandments that GOD had enjoined upon their ancestors through Moses.

*va-yih-YU l'-na-SOT BAM et yis-ra-AYL la-DA-at ha-yish-m'-U et mitz-VOT a-do-NAI a-sher tzi-VAH et a-vo-TAM b'-YAD mo-SHEH.*

וַיִּהְיוּ לְנַסּוֹת בָּם
אֶת־יִשְׂרָאֵל לָדַעַת
הֲיִשְׁמְעוּ אֶת־מִצְוֹת
יְהֹוָה אֲשֶׁר־צִוָּה אֶת־
אֲבוֹתָם בְּיַד־מֹשֶׁה׃ ד

5

The Israelites settled among the Canaanites, Hittites, Amorites, Perizzites, Hivites, and Jebusites;

*uv-NAY yis-ra-AYL ya-sh'-VU b'-KE-rev ha-k'-na-a-NEE, ha-khi-TEE v'-ha-e-mo-REE v'-ha-p'-ri-ZEE, v'-ha-khi-VEE v'-hai-vu-SEE.*

וּבְנֵי יִשְׂרָאֵל יָשְׁבוּ
בְּקֶרֶב הַכְּנַעֲנִי הַחִתִּי
וְהָאֱמֹרִי וְהַפְּרִזִּי וְהַחִוִּי
וְהַיְבוּסִי: ה

6

they took their daughters to wife and gave their own daughters to their sons, and they worshiped their gods.

*va-yik-KHU et b'-no-tay-HEM la-HEM l'-na-SHEEM, v'-et b'-no-tay-HEM na-t'-NU liv-nay-HEM; va-ya-av-DU et e-lo-hay-HEM.*

וַיִּקְחוּ אֶת־בְּנוֹתֵיהֶם
לָהֶם לְנָשִׁים וְאֶת־
בְּנוֹתֵיהֶם נָתְנוּ
לִבְנֵיהֶם וַיַּעַבְדוּ אֶת־
אֱלֹהֵיהֶם: ו

7

The Israelites did what was offensive to GOD; they ignored the ETERNAL their God and worshiped the Baalim and the Asheroth.

*va-ya-a-SU v'-nay yis-ra-AYL et ha-RA b'-ay-NAY a-do-NAI, va-yish-k'-KHU et a-do-NAI e-lo-hay-HEM; va-ya-av-DU et ha-b'-a-LEEM v'-et ha-a-shay-ROT.*

וַיַּעֲשׂוּ בְנֵי־יִשְׂרָאֵל
אֶת־הָרַע בְּעֵינֵי יְהוָה
וַיִּשְׁכְּחוּ אֶת־יְהוָה
אֱלֹהֵיהֶם וַיַּעַבְדוּ
אֶת־הַבְּעָלִים וְאֶת־
הָאֲשֵׁרוֹת: ז

8

GOD became incensed at Israel and surrendered them to King Cushan-rishathaim of Aram-naharaim; and the Israelites were subject to Cushan-rishathaim for eight years.

*va-yi-khar AF a-do-NAI b'-yis-ra-AYL va-yim-k'-RAYM b'-YAD ku-SHAN rish-a-TA-yim, ME-lekh a-RAM na-ha-RA-yim; va-ya-av-DU v'-NAY yis-ra-AYL et ku-SHAN rish-a-TA-yim, sh'-mo-NEH sha-NEEM.*

וַיִּחַר־אַף יְהוָה
בְּיִשְׂרָאֵל וַיִּמְכְּרֵם בְּיַד
כּוּשַׁן רִשְׁעָתַיִם מֶלֶךְ
אֲרַם נַהֲרָיִם וַיַּעַבְדוּ
בְנֵי־יִשְׂרָאֵל אֶת־כּוּשַׁן
רִשְׁעָתַיִם שְׁמֹנֶה
שָׁנִים: ח

9

The Israelites cried out to GOD, and GOD raised a champion for the Israelites to deliver them: Othniel the Kenizzite, a younger kinsman of Caleb.

*va-yiz-a-KU v'-NAY yis-ra-AYL el a-do-NAI, va-YA-kem a-do-NAI mo-SHEE-a liv-NAY yis-ra-AYL va-yo-shee-AYM AYT ot-nee-AYL ben k'-NAZ a-KHEE kha-LAYV ha-ka-TON mi-ME-nu.*

וַיִּזְעֲקוּ בְנֵי־יִשְׂרָאֵל
אֶל־יְהוָה וַיָּקֶם יְהוָה
מוֹשִׁיעַ לִבְנֵי יִשְׂרָאֵל
וַיּוֹשִׁיעֵם אֵת עָתְנִיאֵל
בֶּן־קְנַז אֲחִי כָלֵב הַקָּטֹן
מִמֶּנּוּ: ט

| | | | |
|---|---|---|---|
| 10 | The spirit of GOD descended upon him and he became Israel's chieftain. He went out to war, and GOD delivered King Cushan-rishathaim of Aram into his hands. He prevailed over Cushan-rishathaim, | *va-t'-HEE a-LAV RU-akh a-do-NAI va-yish-POT et yis-ra-AYL, va-yay-TZAY la-mil-kha-MAH, va-yi-TAYN a-do-NAI b'-ya-DO et ku-SHAN rish-a-TA-yim, ME-lekh a-ram; va-TA-oz ya-DO AL ku-SHAN rish-a-TA-yim.* | וַתְּהִי עָלָיו רוּחַ־יְהוָה וַיִּשְׁפֹּט אֶת־יִשְׂרָאֵל וַיֵּצֵא לַמִּלְחָמָה וַיִּתֵּן יְהוָה בְּיָדוֹ אֶת־כּוּשַׁן רִשְׁעָתַיִם מֶלֶךְ אֲרָם וַתָּעָז יָדוֹ עַל כּוּשַׁן רִשְׁעָתָיִם: י |
| 11 | and the land had peace for forty years. When Othniel the Kenizzite died, | *va-tish-KOT ha-A-retz ar-ba-EEM sha-NAH v'-YA-mot ot-nee-AYL ben k'-NAZ* | וַתִּשְׁקֹט הָאָרֶץ אַרְבָּעִים שָׁנָה וַיָּמָת עָתְנִיאֵל בֶּן־קְנַז: יא |
| 12 | the Israelites again did what was offensive to GOD. And because they did what was offensive to GOD, GOD let King Eglon of Moab prevail over Israel. | *va-yo-SI-fu b'-NAY yis-ra-AYL la-a-SOT ha-RA b'-ay-NAY a-do-NAI vai-kha-ZAYK a-do-NAI et eg-LON me-lekh MO-av al yis-ra-AYL AL kee a-SU et ha-RA b'-ay-NAY a-do-NAI* | וַיֹּסִפוּ בְּנֵי יִשְׂרָאֵל לַעֲשׂוֹת הָרַע בְּעֵינֵי יְהוָה וַיְחַזֵּק יְהוָה אֶת־עֶגְלוֹן מֶלֶךְ־מוֹאָב עַל־יִשְׂרָאֵל עַל כִּי־עָשׂוּ אֶת־הָרַע בְּעֵינֵי יְהוָה: יב |
| 13 | [Eglon] brought the Ammonites and the Amalekites together under his command, and went and defeated Israel and occupied the City of Palms. | *va-ye-e-SOF ay-LAV et b'-NAY a-MON va-a-ma-LAYK va-YAY-lekh va-YAKH et yis-ra-AYL va-yee-r'-SHU et EER ha-t'-ma-REEM* | וַיֶּאֱסֹף אֵלָיו אֶת־בְּנֵי עַמּוֹן וַעֲמָלֵק וַיֵּלֶךְ וַיַּךְ אֶת־יִשְׂרָאֵל וַיִּירְשׁוּ אֶת־עִיר הַתְּמָרִים: יג |
| 14 | The Israelites were subject to King Eglon of Moab for eighteen years. | *va-ya-av-DU v'-NAY yis-ra-AYL et eg-LON me-LEKH mo-AV sh'-mo-NEH es-RAY sha-NAH* | וַיַּעַבְדוּ בְנֵי־יִשְׂרָאֵל אֶת־עֶגְלוֹן מֶלֶךְ־מוֹאָב שְׁמוֹנֶה עֶשְׂרֵה שָׁנָה: יד |

15 | Then the Israelites cried out to GOD, and GOD raised up a champion for them: the Benjaminite Ehud son of Gera, a left-handed man. It happened that the Israelites sent tribute to King Eglon of Moab through him. | *va-yiz-a-KU v'-NAY yis-ra-AYL el a-do-NAI, va-YA-kem a-do-NAI la-HEM mo-SHEE-a et ay-HUD ben gay-RA ben hai-mee-NEE EESH i-TAYR yad y'-mee-NO va-yish-l'-KHU v'-NAY yis-ra-AYL b'-ya-DO min-KHAH l'-eg-LON ME-lekh mo-AV.* | וַיִּזְעֲקוּ בְנֵי־יִשְׂרָאֵל אֶל־יְהֹוָה וַיָּקֶם יְהֹוָה לָהֶם מוֹשִׁיעַ אֶת־אֵהוּד בֶּן־גֵּרָא בֶּן־הַיְמִינִי אִישׁ אִטֵּר יַד־יְמִינוֹ וַיִּשְׁלְחוּ בְנֵי־יִשְׂרָאֵל בְּיָדוֹ מִנְחָה לְעֶגְלוֹן מֶלֶךְ מוֹאָב: | טו

16 | So Ehud made for himself a two-edged dagger, a gomed in length, which he girded on his right side under his cloak. | *va-YA-as LO ay-HUD KHE-rev v'-LAH sh'-NAY fi-YOT GO-med or-KAH va-yakh-GOR o-TAH mi-TA-khat l'-ma-DAV AL YE-rekh y'-mee-NO* | וַיַּעַשׂ לוֹ אֵהוּד חֶרֶב וְלָהּ שְׁנֵי פֵיוֹת גֹּמֶד אָרְכָּהּ וַיַּחְגֹּר אוֹתָהּ מִתַּחַת לְמַדָּיו עַל יֶרֶךְ יְמִינוֹ: | טז

17 | He presented the tribute to King Eglon of Moab. Now Eglon was a very stout man. | *va-yak-RAYV et ha-min-KHAH l'-eg-LON ME-lekh mo-AV v'-eg-LON EESH ba-REE m'-OD* | וַיַּקְרֵב אֶת־הַמִּנְחָה לְעֶגְלוֹן מֶלֶךְ מוֹאָב וְעֶגְלוֹן אִישׁ בָּרִיא מְאֹד: | יז

18 | When [Ehud] had finished presenting the tribute, he dismissed the people who had conveyed the tribute. | *vai-HEE ka-a-SHER ki-LAH l'-hak-REEV et ha-min-KHAH vai-sha-LAKH et ha-AM no-s'-AY ha-min-KHAH* | וַיְהִי כַּאֲשֶׁר כִּלָּה לְהַקְרִיב אֶת־הַמִּנְחָה וַיְשַׁלַּח אֶת־הָעָם נֹשְׂאֵי הַמִּנְחָה: | יח

| | | | |
|---|---|---|---|
| 19 | But he himself returned from Pesilim, near Gilgal, and said, "Your Majesty, I have a secret message for you." [Eglon] thereupon commanded, "Silence!" So all those in attendance left his presence; | *v'-HU SHAV min ha-p'-see-LEEM a-SHER et ha-gil-GAL va-YO-mer d'-var SAY-ter LEE ay-LE-kha ha-ME-lekh va-YO-mer HAS va-yay-tz'-U may-a-LAV kol ha-o-m'-DEEM a-LAV* | וְהוּא שָׁב מִן־הַפְּסִילִים אֲשֶׁר אֶת־הַגִּלְגָּל וַיֹּאמֶר דְּבַר־סֵתֶר לִי אֵלֶיךָ הַמֶּלֶךְ וַיֹּאמֶר הָס וַיֵּצְאוּ מֵעָלָיו כָּל־הָעֹמְדִים עָלָיו: | יט |
| 20 | and when Ehud approached him, he was sitting alone in his cool upper chamber. Ehud said, "I have a message for you from God"; whereupon he rose from his seat. | *v'-ay-HUD BA ay-LAV v'-hu yo-SHAYV ba-a-li-YAT ha-m'-kay-RAH a-sher LO l'-va-DO va-YO-mer ay-HUD d'-VAR e-lo-HEEM LEE ay-LE-kha va-YA-kom may-AL ha-ki-SAY* | וְאֵהוּד בָּא אֵלָיו וְהוּא־יֹשֵׁב בַּעֲלִיַּת הַמְּקֵרָה אֲשֶׁר־לוֹ לְבַדּוֹ וַיֹּאמֶר אֵהוּד דְּבַר־אֱלֹהִים לִי אֵלֶיךָ וַיָּקָם מֵעַל הַכִּסֵּא: | כ |
| 21 | Reaching with his left hand, Ehud drew the dagger from his right side and drove it into Eglon's belly. | *va-yish-LAKH ay-HUD et YAD s'-mo-LO va-yi-KAKH et ha-KHE-rev may-AL YE-rekh y'-mee-NO va-yit-ka-E-ha b'-vit-NO* | וַיִּשְׁלַח אֵהוּד אֶת־יַד־שְׂמֹאלוֹ וַיִּקַּח אֶת־הַחֶרֶב מֵעַל יֶרֶךְ יְמִינוֹ וַיִּתְקָעֶהָ בְּבִטְנוֹ: | כא |
| 22 | The fat closed over the blade and the hilt went in after the blade—for he did not pull the dagger out of his belly—and the filth came out. | *va-ya-VO gam ha-ni-TZAV a-KHAR ha-LA-hav va-yis-GOR ha-KHAY-lev b'-AD ha-LA-hav KEE LO sha-LAF ha-KHE-rev mi-bit-NO va-yay-TZAY ha-par-sh'-DO-nah* | וַיָּבֹא גַם־הַנִּצָּב אַחַר הַלַּהַב וַיִּסְגֹּר הַחֵלֶב בְּעַד הַלַּהַב כִּי לֹא שָׁלַף הַחֶרֶב מִבִּטְנוֹ וַיֵּצֵא הַפַּרְשְׁדֹנָה: | כב |

| | | |
|---|---|---|
| 23 | Stepping out into the vestibule, Ehud shut the doors of the upper chamber on him and locked them. | *va-yay-TZAY ay-HUD ha-mis-d'-RO-nah va-yis-GOR dal-TOT ha-a-li-YAH ba-a-DO v'-na-AL* | וַיֵּצֵא אֵהוּד הַמִּסְדְּרוֹנָה וַיִּסְגֹּר דַּלְתוֹת הָעֲלִיָּה בַּעֲדוֹ וְנָעָל: כג |
| 24 | After he left, the courtiers returned. When they saw that the doors of the upper chamber were locked, they thought, "He must be relieving himself in the cool chamber." | *v'-HU ya-TZA va-a-va-DAV BA-u va-yir-U v'-hi-NAY dal-TOT ha-a-li-YAH n'-u-LOT va-yo-m'-RU AKH may-SEEKH HU et rag-LAV ba-kha-DAR ha-m'-kay-RAH* | וְהוּא יָצָא וַעֲבָדָיו בָּאוּ וַיִּרְאוּ וְהִנֵּה דַּלְתוֹת הָעֲלִיָּה נְעֻלוֹת וַיֹּאמְרוּ אַךְ מֵסִיךְ הוּא אֶת־רַגְלָיו בַּחֲדַר הַמְּקֵרָה: כד |
| 25 | They waited a long time; and when he did not open the doors of the chamber, they took the key and opened them—and there their master was lying dead on the floor! | *va-ya-KHEE-lu ad BOSH v'-hi-NAY ay-NE-nu fo-TAY-akh dal-TOT ha-a-li-YAH va-yik-KHU et ha-maf-TAY-akh va-yif-TA-khu v'-hi-NAY a-do-nay-HEM no-FAYL AR-tzah MAYT* | וַיָּחִילוּ עַד־בּוֹשׁ וְהִנֵּה אֵינֶנּוּ פֹתֵחַ דַּלְתוֹת הָעֲלִיָּה וַיִּקְחוּ אֶת־הַמַּפְתֵּחַ וַיִּפְתָּחוּ וְהִנֵּה אֲדֹנֵיהֶם נֹפֵל אַרְצָה מֵת: כה |
| 26 | But Ehud had made good his escape while they delayed; he had passed Pesilim and escaped to Seirah. | *v'-ay-HUD nim-LAT AD hit-mah-m'-HAM v'-HU a-VAR et ha-p'-see-LEEM va-yi-ma-LAYT ha-s'-ee-RA-tah* | וְאֵהוּד נִמְלַט עַד הִתְמַהְמְהָם וְהוּא עָבַר אֶת־הַפְּסִילִים וַיִּמָּלֵט הַשְּׂעִירָתָה: כו |
| 27 | When he got there, he had the ram's horn sounded through the hill country of Ephraim, and all the Israelites descended with him from the hill country; and he took the lead. | *vai-HEE b'-vo-O va-yit-KA ba-sho-FAR b'-HAR ef-RA-yim va-yay-r'-DU i-MO v'-NAY yis-ra-AYL min ha-HAR v'-hu lif-nay-HEM.* | וַיְהִי בְּבוֹאוֹ וַיִּתְקַע בַּשּׁוֹפָר בְּהַר אֶפְרָיִם וַיֵּרְדוּ עִמּוֹ בְנֵי־יִשְׂרָאֵל מִן־הָהָר וְהוּא לִפְנֵיהֶם: כז |

28 "Follow me closely," he said, "for GOD has delivered your enemies, the Moabites, into your hands." They followed him down and seized the fords of the Jordan against the Moabites; they let no one cross.

*va-YO-mer a-lay-HEM rid-FU a-kha-RAI kee na-TAN a-do-NAI et o-y'-vay-KHEM et mo-AV b'-yed-KHEM; va-yay-r'-DU a-kha-RAV, va-yil-k'-DU et ma-b'-ROT ha-yar-DAYN l'-mo-AV, v'-lo na-t'-NU eesh la-a-VOR.*

וַיֹּאמֶר אֲלֵהֶם רִדְפוּ אַחֲרַי כִּי־נָתַן יְהֹוָה אֶת־אֹיְבֵיכֶם אֶת־מוֹאָב בְּיֶדְכֶם וַיֵּרְדוּ אַחֲרָיו וַיִּלְכְּדוּ אֶת־מַעְבְּרוֹת הַיַּרְדֵּן לְמוֹאָב וְלֹא־נָתְנוּ אִישׁ לַעֲבֹר: כח

29 On that occasion they slew about 10,000 Moabites; they were all robust and brave men, yet not one of them escaped.

*va-ya-KU et mo-AV ba-AYT ha-HEE ka-a-SE-ret a-la-FEEM EESH kol sha-MAYN v'-khol EESH KHA-yil v'-LO nim-LAT EESH.*

וַיַּכּוּ אֶת־מוֹאָב בָּעֵת הַהִיא כַּעֲשֶׂרֶת אֲלָפִים אִישׁ כָּל־שָׁמֵן וְכָל־אִישׁ חָיִל וְלֹא נִמְלַט אִישׁ: כט

30 On that day, Moab submitted to Israel; and the land was tranquil for eighty years.

*va-ti-ka-NA mo-AV ba-YOM ha-HU, TA-khat YAD yis-ra-AYL; va-tish-KOT ha-A-retz sh'-mo-NEEM sha-NAH.*

וַתִּכָּנַע מוֹאָב בַּיּוֹם הַהוּא תַּחַת יַד יִשְׂרָאֵל וַתִּשְׁקֹט הָאָרֶץ שְׁמוֹנִים שָׁנָה: ל

31 After him came Shamgar son of Anath, who slew six hundred Philistines with an oxgoad. He too was a champion of Israel.

*v'-a-kha-RAV ha-YAH, sham-GAR ben a-NAT, va-YAKH et p'-lish-TEEM SHAYSH may-OT EESH, b'-mal-MAD ha-ba-KAR; va-YO-sha gam HU et yis-ra-AYL.*

וְאַחֲרָיו הָיָה שַׁמְגַּר בֶּן־עֲנָת וַיַּךְ אֶת־פְּלִשְׁתִּים שֵׁשׁ־מֵאוֹת אִישׁ בְּמַלְמַד הַבָּקָר וַיֹּשַׁע גַּם־הוּא אֶת־יִשְׂרָאֵל: לא

4  א

| | | |
|---|---|---|
| 1 | The Israelites again did what was offensive to GOD —Ehud now being dead. | *va-yo-SI-fu b'-NAY yis-ra-AYL la-a-SOT ha-RA b'-ay-NAY a-do-NAI v'-ay-HUD MAYT* | וַיֹּסִפוּ בְּנֵי יִשְׂרָאֵל לַעֲשׂוֹת הָרַע בְּעֵינֵי יְהֹוָה וְאֵהוּד מֵת: | א |

וַיִּמְכְּרֵם יְהֹוָה בְּיַד יָבִין מֶלֶךְ־כְּנַעַן אֲשֶׁר מָלַךְ בְּחָצוֹר וְשַׂר־צְבָאוֹ סִיסְרָא וְהוּא יוֹשֵׁב בַּחֲרֹשֶׁת הַגּוֹיִם: ב

And GOD surrendered them to King Jabin of Canaan, who reigned in Hazor. His army commander was Sisera, whose base was Harosheth-goiim.

*va-yim-k'-RAYM a-do-NAI b'-YAD ya-VEEN me-lekh k'-NA-an a-SHER ma-LAKH b'-kha-TZOR v'-sar tz'-va-O see-s'-RA v'-HU yo-SHAYV ba-kha-RO-shet ha-go-YIM*

וַיִּצְעֲקוּ בְנֵי־יִשְׂרָאֵל אֶל־יְהֹוָה כִּי תְּשַׁע מֵאוֹת רֶכֶב־בַּרְזֶל לוֹ וְהוּא לָחַץ אֶת־בְּנֵי יִשְׂרָאֵל בְּחָזְקָה עֶשְׂרִים שָׁנָה: ג

The Israelites cried out to GOD; for he had nine hundred iron chariots, and he had oppressed Israel ruthlessly for twenty years.

*va-yitz-a-KU v'-NAY yis-ra-AYL el a-do-NAI KEE t'-SHA may-OT re-khev bar-ZEL LO v'-HU la-KHATZ et b'-NAY yis-ra-AYL b'-khoz-KAH es-REEM sha-NAH*

וּדְבוֹרָה אִשָּׁה נְבִיאָה אֵשֶׁת לַפִּידוֹת הִיא שֹׁפְטָה אֶת־יִשְׂרָאֵל בָּעֵת הַהִיא: ד

Deborah, wife of Lappidoth, was a prophet; she led Israel at that time.

*ud-vo-RAH i-SHAH n'-vee-AH AY-shet la-pi-DOT HEE sho-f'-TAH et yis-ra-AYL ba-AYT ha-HEE*

5 She used to sit under the Palm of Deborah, between Ramah and Bethel in the hill country of Ephraim, and the Israelites would come to her for decisions.

*v'-HEE yo-SHE-vet ta-khat TO-mer d'-vo-RAH BAYN ha-ra-MAH u-VAYN bayt AYL b'-HAR ef-RA-yim va-ya-a-LU ay-LE-ha b'-NAY yis-ra-AYL la-mish-PAT*

וְהִיא יוֹשֶׁבֶת תַּחַת־תֹּמֶר דְּבוֹרָה בֵּין הָרָמָה וּבֵין בֵּית־אֵל בְּהַר אֶפְרָיִם וַיַּעֲלוּ אֵלֶיהָ בְּנֵי יִשְׂרָאֵל לַמִּשְׁפָּט:

ה

6 She summoned Barak son of Abinoam, of Kedesh in Naphtali, and said to him, "The ETERNAL, the God of Israel, has commanded: Go, march up to Mount Tabor, and take with you ten thousand men of Naphtali and Zebulun.

*va-tish-LAKH va-tik-RA l'-va-RAK ben a-vee-NO-am mi-KE-desh naf-ta-LEE va-TO-mer ay-LAV ha-LO tzi-VAH a-do-NAI e-lo-hay yis-ra-AYL LAYKH u-ma-shakh-TA b'-HAR ta-VOR v'-la-kakh-TA i-m'-KHA a-SE-ret a-la-FEEM EESH mi-b'-NAY naf-ta-LEE u-mi-b'-NAY z'-vu-LUN*

וַתִּשְׁלַח וַתִּקְרָא לְבָרָק בֶּן־אֲבִינֹעַם מִקֶּדֶשׁ נַפְתָּלִי וַתֹּאמֶר אֵלָיו הֲלֹא צִוָּה יְהֹוָה אֱלֹהֵי־יִשְׂרָאֵל לֵךְ וּמָשַׁכְתָּ בְּהַר תָּבוֹר וְלָקַחְתָּ עִמְּךָ עֲשֶׂרֶת אֲלָפִים אִישׁ מִבְּנֵי נַפְתָּלִי וּמִבְּנֵי זְבֻלוּן:

ו

7 And I will draw Sisera, Jabin's army commander, with his chariots and his troops, toward you up to the Wadi Kishon; and I will deliver him into your hands."

*u-ma-shakh-TEE ay-LE-kha el NA-khal kee-SHON et see-s'-RA sar tz'-VA ya-VEEN v'-et rikh-BO v'-et ha-mo-NO un-ta-TEE-hu b'-ya-DE-kha*

וּמָשַׁכְתִּי אֵלֶיךָ אֶל־נַחַל קִישׁוֹן אֶת־סִיסְרָא שַׂר־צְבָא יָבִין וְאֶת־רִכְבּוֹ וְאֶת־הֲמוֹנוֹ וּנְתַתִּיהוּ בְּיָדֶךָ:

ז

8 But Barak said to her, "If you will go with me, I will go; if not, I will not go."

*va-YO-mer ay-LE-ha ba-RAK im tay-l'-KHEE i-MEE v'-ha-lakh-TEE v'-im LO tay-l'-KHEE i-MEE LO ay-LAYKH*

וַיֹּאמֶר אֵלֶיהָ בָּרָק אִם־תֵּלְכִי עִמִּי וְהָלָכְתִּי וְאִם־לֹא תֵלְכִי עִמִּי לֹא אֵלֵךְ:

ח

9
"Very well, I will go with you," she answered. "However, there will be no glory for you in the course you are taking, for then GOD will deliver Sisera into the hands of a woman." So Deborah went with Barak to Kedesh.

*va-TO-mer ha-LOKH ay-LAYKH i-MAKH E-fes KEE LO tih-YEH tif-art'-KHA al ha-DE-rekh a-SHER a-TAH ho-LAYKH KEE v'-YAD i-SHAH yim-KOR a-do-NAI et sees-RA va-TA-kom d'-vo-RAH va-TAY-lekh im ba-RAK KED-shah*

וַתֹּאמֶר הָלֹךְ אֵלֵךְ עִמָּךְ אֶפֶס כִּי לֹא תִהְיֶה תִּפְאַרְתְּךָ עַל־הַדֶּרֶךְ אֲשֶׁר אַתָּה הוֹלֵךְ כִּי בְיַד־אִשָּׁה יִמְכֹּר יְהוָה אֶת־סִיסְרָא וַתָּקָם דְּבוֹרָה וַתֵּלֶךְ עִם־בָּרָק קֶדְשָׁה:

10
Barak then mustered Zebulun and Naphtali at Kedesh; ten thousand men marched up after him; and Deborah also went up with him.

*va-yaz-AYK ba-RAK et z'-vu-LUN v'-et naf-ta-LEE KED-shah va-YA-al b'-rag-LAV a-SE-ret al-FAY EESH va-TA-al i-MO d'-vo-RAH*

וַיַּזְעֵק בָּרָק אֶת־זְבוּלֻן וְאֶת־נַפְתָּלִי קֶדְשָׁה וַיַּעַל בְּרַגְלָיו עֲשֶׂרֶת אַלְפֵי אִישׁ וַתַּעַל עִמּוֹ דְּבוֹרָה:

11
Now Heber the Kenite had separated from the other Kenites, descendants of Hobab, father-in-law of Moses, and had pitched his tent at Elon-bezaanannim, which is near Kedesh.

*v'-KHE-ver ha-kay-NEE nif-RAD mi-KA-yin mi-b'-NAY kho-VAV kho-TAYN mo-SHEH va-YAYT ad ay-LON b'-tza-a-na-NEEM a-SHER et KE-desh*

וְחֶבֶר הַקֵּינִי נִפְרָד מִקַּיִן מִבְּנֵי חֹבָב חֹתֵן מֹשֶׁה וַיֵּט אָהֳלוֹ עַד־אֵילוֹן (בצענים) [בְּצַעֲנַנִּים] אֲשֶׁר אֶת־קֶדֶשׁ:

12
Sisera was informed that Barak son of Abinoam had gone up to Mount Tabor.

*va-ya-GI-du l'-sees-RA KEE a-LAH ba-RAK ben a-vee-NO-am har ta-VOR*

וַיַּגִּדוּ לְסִיסְרָא כִּי עָלָה בָּרָק בֶּן־אֲבִינֹעַם הַר־תָּבוֹר:

| | | | |
|---|---|---|---|
| 13 | So Sisera ordered all his chariots—nine hundred iron chariots—and all the troops he had to move from Haroshcth-goiim to the Wadi Kishon. | *va-yaz-AYK sees-RA et kol rikh-BO t'-SHA may-OT RE-khev bar-ZEL v'-et kol ha-AM a-SHER i-TO may-kha-RO-shet ha-go-YIM el NA-khal kee-SHON* | וַיַּזְעֵק סִיסְרָא אֶת־כָּל־ רִכְבּוֹ תְּשַׁע מֵאוֹת רֶכֶב בַּרְזֶל וְאֶת־כָּל־הָעָם אֲשֶׁר אִתּוֹ מֵחֲרֹשֶׁת הַגּוֹיִם אֶל־נַחַל קִישׁוֹן׃ יג |
| 14 | Then Deborah said to Barak, "Up! This is the day on which GOD will deliver Sisera into your hands: GOD is marching before you." Barak charged down Mount Tabor, followed by the ten thousand men, | *va-TO-mer d'-vo-RAH el ba-RAK KUM KEE ZEH ha-YOM a-SHER na-TAN a-do-NAI et sees-RA b'-ya-DE-kha ha-LO a-do-NAI ya-TZA l'-fa-NE-kha va-YAY-red ba-RAK may-HAR ta-VOR va-a-SE-ret a-la-FEEM EESH a-kha-RAV* | וַתֹּאמֶר דְּבֹרָה אֶל־בָּרָק קוּם כִּי זֶה הַיּוֹם אֲשֶׁר נָתַן יְהוָה אֶת־סִיסְרָא בְּיָדֶךָ הֲלֹא יְהוָה יָצָא לְפָנֶיךָ וַיֵּרֶד בָּרָק מֵהַר תָּבוֹר וַעֲשֶׂרֶת אֲלָפִים אִישׁ אַחֲרָיו׃ יד |
| 15 | and GOD threw Sisera and all his chariots and army into a panic before the onslaught of Barak. Sisera leaped from his chariot and fled on foot | *va-YA-hom a-do-NAI et sees-RA v'-et kol ha-RE-khev v'-et kol ha-ma-kha-NEH l'-fee KHE-rev lif-NAY va-RAK va-YAY-red sees-RA may-AL ha-mer-ka-VAH va-YA-nos b'-rag-LAV* | וַיָּהָם יְהוָה אֶת־סִיסְרָא וְאֶת־כָּל־הָרֶכֶב וְאֶת־כָּל־ הַמַּחֲנֶה לְפִי־חֶרֶב לִפְנֵי בָרָק וַיֵּרֶד סִיסְרָא מֵעַל הַמֶּרְכָּבָה וַיָּנָס בְּרַגְלָיו׃ טו |
| 16 | as Barak pursued the chariots and the soldiers as far as Harosheth-goiim. All of Sisera's soldiers fell by the sword; not one was left. | *u-va-RAK ra-DAF a-kha-RAY ha-RE-khev v'-a-kha-RAY ha-ma-kha-NEH AD kha-RO-shet ha-go-YIM va-yi-POL kol ma-kha-NAY sees-RA l'-fee KHE-rev LO nish-AR ad e-KHAD* | וּבָרָק רָדַף אַחֲרֵי הָרֶכֶב וְאַחֲרֵי הַמַּחֲנֶה עַד חֲרֹשֶׁת הַגּוֹיִם וַיִּפֹּל כָּל־מַחֲנֵה סִיסְרָא לְפִי־חֶרֶב לֹא נִשְׁאַר עַד־אֶחָד׃ טז |

17 | Sisera, meanwhile, had fled on foot to the tent of Jael, wife of Heber the Kenite; for there was friendship between King Jabin of Hazor and the family of Heber the Kenite. | *v'-sees-RA NAS b'-rag-LAV el O-hel ya-AYL AY-shet KHE-ver ha-kay-NEE KEE sha-LOM BAYN ya-VEEN ME-lekh kha-TZOR u-VAYN BAYT KHE-ver ha-kay-NEE* | וְסִיסְרָא נָס בְּרַגְלָיו אֶל־אֹהֶל יָעֵל אֵשֶׁת חֶבֶר הַקֵּינִי כִּי שָׁלוֹם בֵּין יָבִין מֶלֶךְ־חָצוֹר וּבֵין בֵּית חֶבֶר הַקֵּינִי: | יז

18 | Jael came out to greet Sisera and said to him, "Come in, my lord, come in here, do not be afraid." So he entered her tent, and she covered him with a blanket. | *va-tay-TZAY ya-AYL lik-RAT sees-RA va-TO-mer ay-LAV su-RAH a-do-NEE su-RAH ay-LAI al tee-RA va-YA-sar ay-LE-ha ha-O-he-lah va-t'-kha-SAY-hu ba-s'-mee-KHAH* | וַתֵּצֵא יָעֵל לִקְרַאת סִיסְרָא וַתֹּאמֶר אֵלָיו סוּרָה אֲדֹנִי סוּרָה אֵלַי אַל־תִּירָא וַיָּסַר אֵלֶיהָ הָאֹהֱלָה וַתְּכַסֵּהוּ בַּשְּׂמִיכָה: | יח

19 | He said to her, "Please let me have some water; I am thirsty." She opened a skin of milk and gave him some to drink; and she covered him again. | *va-YO-mer ay-LE-ha hash-kee-nee NA m'-at MA-yim KEE tza-MAY-tee va-tif-TAKH et NOD he-kha-LAV va-tash-KAY-hu va-t'-kha-SAY-hu* | וַיֹּאמֶר אֵלֶיהָ הַשְׁקִינִי־נָא מְעַט־מַיִם כִּי צָמֵאתִי וַתִּפְתַּח אֶת־נֹאוד הֶחָלָב וַתַּשְׁקֵהוּ וַתְּכַסֵּהוּ: | יט

20 | He said to her, "Stand at the entrance of the tent. If anybody comes and asks you if there is anybody here, say 'No.'" | *va-YO-mer ay-LE-ha a-MOD PE-takh ha-O-hel v'-ha-YAH im EESH ya-VO ush-ay-LAYKH v'-a-MAR ha-yaysh POH EESH v'-a-MAR-t' A-yin* | וַיֹּאמֶר אֵלֶיהָ עֲמֹד פֶּתַח הָאֹהֶל וְהָיָה אִם־אִישׁ יָבֹא וּשְׁאֵלֵךְ וְאָמַר הֲיֵשׁ־פֹּה אִישׁ וְאָמַרְתְּ אָיִן: | כ

| 21 | Then Jael wife of Heber took a tent pin and grasped the mallet. When he was fast asleep from exhaustion, she approached him stealthily and drove the pin through his temple till it went down to the ground. Thus he died. | *va-ti-KAKH ya-AYL ay-shet KHE-ver et y'-TAD ha-O-hel va-TA-sem et ha-ma-KE-vet b'-ya-DAH va-ta-VO ay-LAV ba-LAT va-tit-KA et ha-ya-TAYD b'-ra-ka-TO ta-titz-NAKH ba-A-retz v'-hu nir-DAM va-YA-af va-ya-MOT* | וַתִּקַּח יָעֵל אֵשֶׁת־חֶבֶר אֶת־יְתַד הָאֹהֶל וַתָּשֶׂם אֶת־הַמַּקֶּבֶת בְּיָדָהּ וַתָּבוֹא אֵלָיו בַּלָּאט וַתִּתְקַע אֶת־הַיָּתֵד בְּרַקָּתוֹ וַתִּצְנַח בָּאָרֶץ וְהוּא־נִרְדָּם וַיָּעַף וַיָּמֹת׃ | כא |

| 22 | Now Barak appeared in pursuit of Sisera. Jael went out to greet him and said, "Come, I will show you the man you are looking for." He went inside with her, and there Sisera was lying dead, with the pin in his temple. | *v'-hi-NAY va-RAK ro-DAYF et sees-RA va-TAY-tzay ya-AYL lik-ra-TO va-TO-mer LO LAYKH v'-ar-AYKH et ha-EESH a-sher a-TAH m'-va-KAYSH va-ya-VO ay-LE-ha v'-hi-NAY sees-RA no-FAYL MAYT v'-ha-ya-TAYD b'-ra-ka-TO* | וְהִנֵּה בָרָק רֹדֵף אֶת־סִיסְרָא וַתֵּצֵא יָעֵל לִקְרָאתוֹ וַתֹּאמֶר לוֹ לֵךְ וְאַרְאֶךָּ אֶת־הָאִישׁ אֲשֶׁר־אַתָּה מְבַקֵּשׁ וַיָּבֹא אֵלֶיהָ וְהִנֵּה סִיסְרָא נֹפֵל מֵת וְהַיָּתֵד בְּרַקָּתוֹ׃ | כב |

| 23 | On that day God subdued King Jabin of Canaan before the Israelites. | *va-yakh-NA e-lo-HEEM ba-YOM ha-HU AYT ya-VEEN me-lekh k'-NA-an lif-NAY b'-NAY yis-ra-AYL* | וַיַּכְנַע אֱלֹהִים בַּיּוֹם הַהוּא אֵת יָבִין מֶלֶךְ כְּנָעַן לִפְנֵי בְּנֵי יִשְׂרָאֵל׃ | כג |

| 24 | The hand of the Israelites bore harder and harder on King Jabin of Canaan, until they destroyed King Jabin of Canaan. | *va-TAY-lekh YAD b'-NAY yis-ra-AYL ha-LOKH v'-ka-SHAH AL ya-VEEN me-lekh k'-NA-an AD a-SHER hikh-REE-tu AYT ya-VEEN me-lekh k'-NA-an* | וַתֵּלֶךְ יַד בְּנֵי־יִשְׂרָאֵל הָלוֹךְ וְקָשָׁה עַל יָבִין מֶלֶךְ־כְּנַעַן עַד אֲשֶׁר הִכְרִיתוּ אֵת יָבִין מֶלֶךְ־כְּנָעַן׃ | כד |

# God is Not a Sexist

The Book of Judges has a standard playbook: the people of Israel drift away from God, God sends enemies to persecute them, the people cry out to God, and then God sends a heroic warrior to save them. As you would expect, the heroic warriors are invariably men - with one exception:

"Deborah, wife of Lappidoth, was a prophetess; she led Israel at that time." (Judges, 4:4)

Remarkably, thousands of years before modern feminism and the #MeToo movement, at a time when women were treated as chattel in other societies, the people of Israel were judged and led by a woman.

As a leader, Deborah was no pushover, summoning the leading Israelite general of the time and ordering him to attack the enemies of Israel:

"She summoned Barak son of Abinoam… and said to him, "The ETERNAL, the God of Israel, has commanded: Go, march up to Mount Tabor, and take with you ten thousand men of Naphtali and Zebulun. And I will draw Sisera, Jabin's army commander, with his chariots and his troops, toward you up to the Wadi Kishon; and I will deliver him into your hands." (Judges 4:6-7)

The sages explain that Deborah's husband was not actually named "Lappidoth," but that the word is hinting that Deborah would spend her time preparing wicks - known in Hebrew as "Lappidoth" - for the Tabernacle in Shiloh. Who, then, was Deborah's husband?

The medieval scholar Rabbi David Kimchi (1160–1235) explains that Deborah's husband was none other than Barak, the general of the army! Interestingly, Deborah's husband is not identified by name. The Bible, it seems, purposely downplays his role, emphasizing that Deborah was the leader of her family, possessing the courage, strength and faith that her husband lacked. As Barak admits in fear to his fearless wife: "If you will go with me, I will go; if not, I will not go" (Judges 4:8).

How did Deborah buck the trend of ancient times to become the only female leader of Israel in the entire Book of Judges?

The sages ask precisely this question, and offer an astonishing explanation:

"What was it about Deborah's character that allowed her to be a prophetess over Israel and to judge them? After all, wasn't Phineas the son of Elazar still alive at the time? Calling heaven and earth as witness, I hereby testify that whether gentile or Jew, man or woman, slave or maidservant, the spirit of God rests upon a person only in accordance with their deeds!" (Tanna Dvei Eliyahu Rabba 9)

Deborah the prophetess teaches us a critically important life lesson. Every human being, regardless of gender, skin color or nationality, is judged by God according to his or her individual merits. Every one of us can choose to dedicate our lives to serving God, and every one of us can become a leader.

Men and women are different, of course, and so are Jews and Gentiles. God has given each of us a unique role to play. But as Deborah proves, every human being can draw close to God; it's up to us to make it happen.

# Jael: Sacrificing Morality for God

Would you consider a woman who seduces an army general, lulls him to sleep, and then murders him to be a religious hero? Incredibly, the Bible does!

"...Jael came out to greet Sisera... he entered her tent... she opened a skin of milk and gave him some to drink, and she covered him.... Jael, wife of Heber, took a tent pin and grasped the mallet. When he was fast asleep from exhaustion, she approached him stealthily and drove the pin through his temple till it went down to the ground. Thus he died." (Judges 4:17-21).

The sages explain that Jael seduced the evil general Sisera in order to kill him (Talmud Yevamot 103a), sacrificing her morality in order to kill a great enemy of the people of Israel. Did Jael make the right choice? In the next chapter, Deborah makes clear that Jael is to be praised for her deed:

"Most blessed of women is Jael, wife of Heber the Kenite; above women of the tent she shall be blessed... Her [left] hand reached for the tent pin, her right for the workman's hammer. She struck Sisera, crushed his head, smashed and pierced his temple." (Judges 5:24-26)

How can Deborah the prophetess praise Jael for her actions, which came at the cost of her modesty?

Deborah says that Jael is blessed "above women of the tents," an unusual phrase. The sages explain that "women of the tents" alludes to the holy foremothers of Israel - Sarah, Rebecca, Rachel and Leah - women who are associated with the image of the tent, for they modestly avoided the public attention that was available to them "outside of the tent." Incredibly, Deborah says that Jael is blessed even more than the modest foremothers of Israel! How can this be?

Though often unappreciated in our modern secular culture, modesty is unquestionably a fundamental value of the Bible. But modesty, however, does not mean passivity. Though modesty is the virtuous standard for religiously committed women, the Bible is telling us that there are moments in history when women must leave their comfort zone and take action, even at the expense of their own virtue.

During times of upheaval and war, women are sometimes called upon to leave their tents and temporarily set aside their modesty to fight for what is good and righteous.

Truus and Freddie Oversteegen, Dutch sisters living through the nightmare of Nazi occupation, bravely joined the Dutch resistance. Their job was to seduce Nazis, applying makeup and bright red lipstick to pick up soldiers at bars and lure them to their deaths. "Ha Heinz, come here," they would call to the soldiers, pretending to be drunk when they approached their targets. They would then lure the men to the woods, where their comrades were lying in wait to kill the soldiers (Sophie Poldermans, Seducing and Killing Nazis: Hannie, Truus and Freddie: Dutch Resistance Heroines of WWII). Truus was later honored by Yad Vashem, Israel's Holocaust museum, for her bravery in protecting Jews during the Holocaust.

Though we pray for peace, war and crisis will be a part of our lives until the final redemption arrives. And in moments of crisis, we are deeply thankful that there are righteous women who are willing to sacrifice everything in the battle of good versus evil.

5

| | | |
|---|---|---|
| 1 | On that day Deborah and Barak son of Abinoam sang: | *va-TA-shar d'-vo-RAH u-va-RAK ben a-vee-NO-am ba-YOM ha-HU lay-MOR* | וַתָּשַׁר דְּבוֹרָה וּבָרָק בֶּן־אֲבִינֹעַם בַּיּוֹם הַהוּא לֵאמֹר: | א |

| 2 | When locks go untrimmed in Israel, When people dedicate themselves—Bless GOD! | *bif-RO-a p'-ra-OT b'-yis-ra-AYL b'-hit-na-DAYV AM ba-r'-KHU a-do-NAI* | בִּפְרֹעַ פְּרָעוֹת בְּיִשְׂרָאֵל בְּהִתְנַדֵּב עָם בָּרְכוּ יְהֹוָה: | ב |

| 3 | "Hear, O kings! Give ear, O potentates! I will sing, will sing to GOD, Will hymn the ETERNAL, the God of Israel." | *shim-U m'-la-KHEEM ha-a-ZEE-nu ro-z'-NEEM a-no-KHEE a-SHEE-rah a-za-MAYR la-do-NAI e-lo-HAY yis-ra-AYL* | שִׁמְעוּ מְלָכִים הַאֲזִינוּ רֹזְנִים אָנֹכִי לַיהֹוָה אָנֹכִי אָשִׁירָה אֲזַמֵּר לַיהֹוָה אֱלֹהֵי יִשְׂרָאֵל: | ג |

| 4 | O GOD, when You came forth from Seir, Advanced from the country of Edom, The earth trembled; The heavens dripped, Yea, the clouds dripped water, | *a-do-NAI b'-tzay-t'-KHA mi-say-EER b'-tza-d'-KHA mis-DAY e-DOM E-retz ra-A-shah gam sha-MA-yim na-TA-fu gam a-VEEM na-t'-FU MA-yim* | יְהֹוָה בְּצֵאתְךָ מִשֵּׂעִיר בְּצַעְדְּךָ מִשְּׂדֵה אֱדוֹם אֶרֶץ רָעָשָׁה גַּם־שָׁמַיִם נָטָפוּ גַּם־עָבִים נָטְפוּ מָיִם: | ד |

| 5 | The mountains quaked because of GOD, Yon Sinai, because of GOD — the God of Israel | *ha-REEM na-z'-LU mi-p'-NAY a-do-NAI ZEH see-NAI mi-p'-NAY a-do-NAI e-lo-HAY yis-ra-AYL* | הָרִים נָזְלוּ מִפְּנֵי יְהֹוָה זֶה סִינַי מִפְּנֵי יְהֹוָה אֱלֹהֵי יִשְׂרָאֵל: | ה |

| | | | |
|---|---|---|---|
| 6 | In the days of Shamgar son of Anath, In the days of Jael, caravans ceased, And wayfarers went By roundabout paths. | *bee-MAY sham-GAR ben a-NAT bee-MAY ya-AYL kha-d'-LU a-ra-KHOT v'-ho-l'-KHAY n'-tee-VOT yay-l'-KHU a-ra-KHOT a-kal-ka-LOT* | ו בִּימֵי שַׁמְגַּר בֶּן־עֲנָת בִּימֵי יָעֵל חָדְלוּ אֳרָחוֹת וְהֹלְכֵי נְתִיבוֹת יֵלְכוּ אֳרָחוֹת עֲקַלְקַלּוֹת: |
| 7 | "Deliverance ceased, Ceased in Israel, Till you arose, O Deborah, Arose, O mother, in Israel!" | *kha-d'-LU f'-ra-ZON b'-yis-ra-AYL kha-DAY-lu AD sha-KAM-tee d'-vo-RAH sha-KAM-tee AYM b'-yis-ra-AYL* | ז חָדְלוּ פְרָזוֹן בְּיִשְׂרָאֵל חָדֵלּוּ עַד שַׁקַּמְתִּי דְּבוֹרָה שַׁקַּמְתִּי אֵם בְּיִשְׂרָאֵל: |
| 8 | When they chose new gods, Was there a fighter then in the gates? No shield or spear was seen Among forty thousand in Israel! | *yiv-KHAR a-lo-HEEM kha-da-SHEEM AZ la-KHEM sh'-a-REEM ma-GAYN im yay-ra-EH va-RO-makh b'-ar-ba-EEM E-lef b'-yis-ra-AYL* | ח יִבְחַר אֱלֹהִים חֲדָשִׁים אָז לָחֶם שְׁעָרִים מָגֵן אִם־יֵרָאֶה וָרֹמַח בְּאַרְבָּעִים אֶלֶף בְּיִשְׂרָאֵל: |
| 9 | "My heart is with Israel's leaders, With the dedicated of the people—Bless GOD!" | *li-BEE l'-kho-k'-KAY yis-ra-AYL ha-mit-na-d'-VEEM ba-AM ba-r'-KHU a-do-NAI* | ט לִבִּי לְחוֹקְקֵי יִשְׂרָאֵל הַמִּתְנַדְּבִים בָּעָם בָּרְכוּ יְהֹוָה: |
| 10 | "You riders on tawny jennies, You who sit on saddle rugs, And you wayfarers, declare it!" | *ro-kh'-VAY a-to-NOT tz'-kho-ROT yo-sh'-VAY al mi-DEEN v'-ho-l'-KHAY al DE-rekh SEE-khu* | י רֹכְבֵי אֲתֹנוֹת צְחֹרוֹת יֹשְׁבֵי עַל־מִדִּין וְהֹלְכֵי עַל־דֶּרֶךְ שִׂיחוּ: |

11 "Louder than the sound of archers, There among the watering places Let them chant GOD's gracious acts—The gracious deliverance of Israel.Then did GOD's people March down to the gates!"

*mi-KOL m'-kha-tz'-TZEEM BAYN mash-a-BEEM SHAM y'-ta-NU tzid-KOT a-do-NAI tzid-KOT pir-zo-NO b'-yis-ra-AYL AZ ya-r'-DU la-sh'-a-REEM am a-do-NAI*

מִקּוֹל מְחַצְצִים בֵּין מַשְׁאַבִּים שָׁם יְתַנּוּ צִדְקוֹת יְהוָה צִדְקֹת פִּרְזוֹנוֹ בְּיִשְׂרָאֵל אָז יָרְדוּ לַשְּׁעָרִים עַם־יְהוָה: יא

12 "Awake, awake, O Deborah! Awake, awake, strike up the chant! Arise, O Barak; Take your captives, O son of Abinoam!"

*u-REE u-REE d'-vo-RAH u-REE u-REE da-b'-ree SHEER KUM ba-RAK u-sha-VAY shev-y'-KHA ben a-vee-NO-am*

עוּרִי עוּרִי דְּבוֹרָה עוּרִי עוּרִי דַּבְּרִי־שִׁיר קוּם בָּרָק וּשֲׁבֵה שֶׁבְיְךָ בֶּן־אֲבִינֹעַם: יב

13 "Then was the remnant made victor over the mighty, GOD's people won my victory over the warriors."

*AZ y'-RAD sa-REED l'-a-dee-REEM AM a-do-NAI y'-rad LEE ba-gi-bo-REEM*

אָז יְרַד שָׂרִיד לְאַדִּירִים עָם יְהוָה יְרַד־לִי בַּגִּבּוֹרִים: יג

14 "From Ephraim came they whose roots are in Amalek; After you, your kin Benjamin; From Machir came down leaders, From Zebulun such as hold the marshal's staff."

*mi-NEE ef-RA-yim sha-r'-SHAM ba-a-ma-LAYK a-kha-RE-kha vin-ya-MEEN ba-a-ma-ME-kha mi-NEE ma-KHEER ya-r'-DU m'-kho-k'-KEEM u-mi-z'-vu-LUN mo-sh'-KHEEM b'-SHAY-vet so-FAYR*

מִנִּי אֶפְרַיִם שָׁרְשָׁם בַּעֲמָלֵק אַחֲרֶיךָ בִנְיָמִין בַּעֲמָמֶיךָ מִנִּי מָכִיר יָרְדוּ מְחֹקְקִים וּמִזְּבוּלֻן מֹשְׁכִים בְּשֵׁבֶט סֹפֵר: יד

| | | | |
|---|---|---|---|
| 15 | "And Issachar's chiefs were with Deborah; As Barak, so was Issachar—Rushing after him into the valley. Among the clans of Reuben Were great decisions of heart." | *v'-sa-RAI b'-yi-sa-KHAR im d'-vo-RAH v'-yi-sa-KHAR KAYN ba-RAK ba-AY-mek shu-LAKH b'-rag-LAV bif-la-GOT r'-u-VAYN g'-do-LEEM khi-k'-kay LAYV* | וְשָׂרַי בְּיִשָּׂשכָר עם־דְּבֹרָה וְיִשָּׂשכָר כֵּן בָּרָק בָּעֵמֶק שֻׁלַּח בְּרַגְלָיו בִּפְלַגּוֹת רְאוּבֵן גְּדֹלִים חִקְקֵי־לֵב: |
| 16 | "Why then did you stay among the sheepfolds And listen as they pipe for the flocks? Among the clans of Reuben Were great searchings of heart!" | *LA-mah ya-SHAV-ta BAYN ha-mish-p'-TA-yim lish-MO-a sh'-ri-KOT a-da-REEM lif-la-GOT r'-u-VAYN g'-do-LEEM khik-ray LAYV* | לָמָּה יָשַׁבְתָּ בֵּין הַמִּשְׁפְּתַיִם לִשְׁמֹעַ שְׁרִקוֹת עֲדָרִים לִפְלַגּוֹת רְאוּבֵן גְּדוֹלִים חִקְרֵי־לֵב: |
| 17 | "Gilead tarried beyond the Jordan; And Dan—why did he linger by the ships? Asher remained at the seacoast And tarried at his landings." | *gil-AD b'-AY-ver ha-yar-DAYN sha-KHAYN v'-DAN LA-mah ya-GUR o-ni-YOT a-SHAYR ya-SHAV l'-KHOF ya-MEEM v'-AL mif-ra-TZAV yish-KON* | גִּלְעָד בְּעֵבֶר הַיַּרְדֵּן שָׁכֵן וְדָן לָמָּה יָגוּר אֳנִיּוֹת אָשֵׁר יָשַׁב לְחוֹף יַמִּים וְעַל מִפְרָצָיו יִשְׁכּוֹן: |
| 18 | "Zebulun is a people that mocked at death, Naphtali—on the open heights." | *z'-vu-LUN AM khay-RAYF naf-SHO la-MUT v'-naf-ta-LEE AL m'-ro-MAY sa-DEH* | זְבֻלוּן עַם חֵרֵף נַפְשׁוֹ לָמוּת וְנַפְתָּלִי עַל מְרוֹמֵי שָׂדֶה: |
| 19 | "Then the kings came, they fought: The kings of Canaan fought At Taanach, by Megiddo's waters—They got no spoil of silver." | *BA-u m'-la-KHEEM nil-KHA-mu AZ nil-kha-MU mal-KHAY kh'-NA-an b'-ta-NAKH al MAY m'-gi-DO BE-tza KE-sef LO la-KA-khu* | בָּאוּ מְלָכִים נִלְחָמוּ אָז נִלְחֲמוּ מַלְכֵי כְנַעַן בְּתַעְנַךְ עַל־מֵי מְגִדּוֹ בֶּצַע כֶּסֶף לֹא לָקָחוּ: |

| | | | |
|---|---|---|---|
| 20 | The stars fought from heaven, From their courses they fought against Sisera. | *min sha-MA-yim nil-KHA-mu ha-ko-kha-VEEM mi-m'-si-lo-TAM nil-kha-MU im sees-RA* | מִן־שָׁמַיִם נִלְחָמוּ הַכּוֹכָבִים מִמְּסִלּוֹתָם נִלְחֲמוּ עִם־סִיסְרָא: כ |
| 21 | The torrent Kishon swept them away, The raging torrent, the torrent Kishon. March on, my soul, with courage! | *NA-khal kee-SHON g'-ra-FAM NA-khal k'-du-MEEM NA-khal kee-SHON tid-r'-KHEE naf-SHEE OZ* | נַחַל קִישׁוֹן גְּרָפָם נַחַל קְדוּמִים נַחַל קִישׁוֹן תִּדְרְכִי נַפְשִׁי עֹז: כא |
| 22 | "Then the horses' hoofs pounded As headlong galloped the steeds." | *AZ ha-l'-MU i-k'-vay SUS mi-da-ha-ROT da-ha-ROT a-bee-RAV* | אָז הָלְמוּ עִקְּבֵי־סוּס מִדַּהֲרוֹת דַּהֲרוֹת אַבִּירָיו: כב |
| 23 | ""Curse Meroz!" said the angel of GOD. "Bitterly curse its inhabitants, Because they came not to the aid of GOD, To the aid of GOD among the warriors."" | *O-ru may-ROZ a-MAR mal-AKH a-do-NAI O-ru a-ROR yo-sh'-VE-ha KEE lo VA-u l'-ez-RAT a-do-NAI l'-ez-RAT a-do-NAI ba-gi-bo-REEM* | אוֹרוּ מֵרוֹז אָמַר מַלְאַךְ יְהֹוָה אֹרוּ אָרוֹר יֹשְׁבֶיהָ כִּי לֹא־בָאוּ לְעֶזְרַת יְהֹוָה לְעֶזְרַת יְהֹוָה בַּגִּבּוֹרִים: כג |
| 24 | "Most blessed of women be Jael, Wife of Heber the Kenite, Most blessed of women in tents." | *t'-vo-RAKH mi-na-SHEEM ya-AYL AY-shet KHE-ver ha-kay-NEE mi-na-SHEEM ba-O-hel t'-vo-RAKH* | תְּבֹרַךְ מִנָּשִׁים יָעֵל אֵשֶׁת חֶבֶר הַקֵּינִי מִנָּשִׁים בָּאֹהֶל תְּבֹרָךְ: כד |
| 25 | "He asked for water, she offered milk; In a princely bowl she brought him curds." | *MA-yim sha-AL kha-LAV na-TA-nah b'-SAY-fel a-dee-REEM hik-REE-vah khem-AH* | מַיִם שָׁאַל חָלָב נָתָנָה בְּסֵפֶל אַדִּירִים הִקְרִיבָה חֶמְאָה: כה |

| | | | |
|---|---|---|---|
| 26 | "Her [left] hand reached for the tent pin, Her right for the workmen's hammer. She struck Sisera, crushed his head, Smashed and pierced his temple." | *ya-DAH la-ya-TAYD tish-LAKH-nah vee-mee-NAH l'-hal-MUT a-may-LEEM v'-ha-l'-MAH sees-RA ma-kha-KAH ro-SHO u-ma-kha-TZAH v'-kha-l'-FAH ra-ka-TO* | יָדָהּ לַיָּתֵד תִּשְׁלַחְנָה וִימִינָהּ לְהַלְמוּת עֲמֵלִים וְהָלְמָה סִיסְרָא מָחֲקָה רֹאשׁוֹ וּמָחֲצָה וְחָלְפָה רַקָּתוֹ: | כו |
| 27 | "At her feet he sank, lay outstretched, At her feet he sank, lay still; Where he sank, there he lay— destroyed." | *BAYN rag-LE-ha ka-RA na-FAL sha-KHAV BAYN rag-LE-ha ka-RA na-FAL ba-a-SHER ka-RA SHAM na-FAL sha-DUD* | בֵּין רַגְלֶיהָ כָּרַע נָפַל שָׁכָב בֵּין רַגְלֶיהָ כָּרַע נָפַל בַּאֲשֶׁר כָּרַע שָׁם נָפַל שָׁדוּד: | כז |
| 28 | "Through the window peered Sisera's mother, Behind the lattice she whined: "Why is his chariot so long in coming? Why so late the clatter of his wheels?"" | *b'-AD ha-kha-LON nish-k'-FAH va-t'-ya-BAYV AYM sees-RA b'-AD ha-esh-NAV ma-DU-a bo-SHAYSH rikh-BO la-VO ma-DU-a e-khe-RU pa-a-MAY mar-k'-vo-TAV* | בְּעַד הַחַלּוֹן נִשְׁקְפָה וַתְּיַבֵּב אֵם סִיסְרָא בְּעַד הָאֶשְׁנָב מַדּוּעַ בֹּשֵׁשׁ רִכְבּוֹ לָבוֹא מַדּוּעַ אֶחֱרוּ פַּעֲמֵי מַרְכְּבוֹתָיו: | כח |
| 29 | The wisest of her ladies give answer; She, too, replies to herself: | *khakh-MOT sa-ro-TE-ha ta-a-NE-ha af HEE ta-SHEEV a-ma-RE-ha LAH* | חַכְמוֹת שָׂרוֹתֶיהָ תַּעֲנֶינָּה אַף־הִיא תָּשִׁיב אֲמָרֶיהָ לָהּ: | כט |
| 30 | ""They must be dividing the spoil they have found: A woman or two for each man, Spoil of dyed cloths for Sisera, Spoil of embroidered cloths, A couple of embroidered cloths Round every neck as spoil."" | *ha-LO yim-tz'-U y'-kha-l'-KU sha-LAL RA-kham ra-kha-ma-TA-yim l'-ROSH GE-ver sh'-LAL tz'-va-EEM l'-sees-RA sh'-LAL tz'-va-EEM rik-MAH TZE-va rik-ma-TA-yim l'-tza-v'-RAY sha-LAL* | הֲלֹא יִמְצְאוּ יְחַלְּקוּ שָׁלָל רַחַם רַחֲמָתַיִם לְרֹאשׁ גֶּבֶר שְׁלַל צְבָעִים לְסִיסְרָא שְׁלַל צְבָעִים רִקְמָה צֶבַע רִקְמָתַיִם לְצַוְּארֵי שָׁלָל: | ל |

31

"So may all Your enemies perish, O GOD ! But may Your friends be as the sun rising in might!And the land was tranquil forty years."

*KAYN yo-v'-DU khol o-y'-VE-kha a-do-NAI v'-o-ha-VAV k'-TZAYT ha-SHE-mesh big-vu-ra-TO va-tish-KOT ha-A-retz ar-ba-EEM sha-NAH*

כֵּן יֹאבְדוּ כָל־אוֹיְבֶיךָ
יְהֹוָה וְאֹהֲבָיו כְּצֵאת
הַשֶּׁמֶשׁ בִּגְבֻרָתוֹ
וַתִּשְׁקֹט הָאָרֶץ
אַרְבָּעִים שָׁנָה:

לא

# The Palm-Tree Prophetess

Throughout the Book of Judges, the people of Israel's greatest enemy was looking at them in the mirror. Though they were plagued by many dangerous external enemies, Israel suffered most from internal division and infighting. The tribes, by and large, did not feel obligated to come to each other's aid in times of war, and even periodically descended into civil war. It's no wonder the fractured nation was so susceptible to foreign attackers.

Throughout the 400-year era of the book of Judges, few leaders succeeded in uniting the people like the prophetess Deborah. When the evil general Sisera led a terrifying army of 900 iron chariots - the equivalent of tanks in the ancient era - Deborah succeeded in unifying several of the Israelite tribes, who miraculously defeated their oppressors. As Deborah sings in her song of thanks to God:

"From Ephraim came they... your kin Benjamin; From Machir [Manasseh] came down leaders, From Zebulun such as hold the marshal's staff... And Issachar's chiefs were with Deborah..." (Judges 5:14-15)

How did Deborah succeed in overcoming the tribes' mutual distrust and uniting the nation of Israel?

The Bible hints to Deborah's unique ability to unify the nation in its description of her governing style:

"She used to sit under the Palm of Deborah, between Ramah and Bethel in the hill country of Ephraim, and the Israelites would come to her for decisions." (Judges 4:5)

What is the significance of the palm tree? Why did Deborah choose to judge the tribes of Israel while sitting under this particular tree?

The palm tree is large and gives off significant shade, allowing many people to take refuge under its branches from the sun. Its fruit is sweet; in the Bible, "honey" refers to date honey, which comes from the palm tree. For this reason, in Jewish tradition, the palm tree symbolizes unity:

"Just as this date tree only has one heart, so too do the people of Israel only have one heart for their Father in heaven" (Talmud Megillah 14a).

These qualities of the palm tree are shared by Deborah and her entire tribe. Deborah was a descendant of the tribe of Naphtali, a tribe that succeeded in forming warm relationships with all of the other tribes of Israel. Like her warm and friendly forefather Naphtali, and like the palm tree she chose as her defining symbol, Deborah was deeply loved and respected by all who met her. She was welcoming and humble, making room for all kinds of people to feel comfortable in the shade of her palm tree. Through love and kindness, she inspired devotion. And with her encouragement, the people of Israel were able to overlook their differences and fight together against the evil Sisera.

In modern Israel, the many "tribes" of the nation - religious, secular, Russian, Ethiopian, American, etc. - are deeply divided, just as they were during Deborah's generation. Fortunately, we are blessed in our own generation with an extraordinary woman who follows the path of Deborah the prophetess: Miriam Peretz.

Miriam Peretz has made the most painful sacrifice of all. Two of her sons - Uriel and Eliraz - were killed by Arab terrorists while serving in the Israel Defense Forces. She also lost her husband at a young age. Somehow, she has not been broken by her terrible losses, but has become one of the most beloved figures in modern Israel. In her current role, she works to inspire Israeli teenagers who are preparing to serve in Israel's army. Like the Deborah of old, she unifies the nation and gives strength to the brave soldiers who must stand up in defense of Israel.

In her memoir, Miriam describes her work with the many "tribes" of Israel: "As part of my new job, I meet with youth, recount my personal story to them, and talk with them about coping during crises. I talk about spiritual strength, love for the Land of Israel, giving, and other values. I meet wonderful youngsters who connect to the pain, and through it understand the price of our existence in our country. My work in the department also enables me to focus on raising motivation for performing meaningful military service."

"The feedback I receive from schools regarding my meetings with youth encourages me tremendously. I often ask myself, as Eliraz did, why I came into this world. What is my mission? What am I supposed to do? I have no answer. But when a student comes up to me at the end of the meeting and says, "Miriam, you inspired me, you gave me strength and direction," I feel that I gained from this student as much as he gained from me. Each of us in turn both gave and received."

Through love and respect for others who are different from us, we can do our part to unify our society. Like Deborah the prophetess and Miriam Peretz, we can, and must, invite others to join us under the palm tree - together.

# Celebrating Life – or Death?

On January 27th, 2023, a Palestinian terrorist murdered seven Israelis, including a 14-year-old boy, at a synagogue in Jerusalem. Incredibly, the terrorist chose to carry out his cruel and heinous murder of innocent Jews on International Holocaust Remembrance Day - a stark reminder that evil is alive and well in our generation.

When news of the murders became public, Arabs throughout Judea, Samaria and Gaza shamelessly celebrated. Thousands of Arabs in the Balata "refugee camp" (Balata is not actually a refugee camp; it was founded 73 years ago and currently has over 30,000 residents) celebrated in the streets, screaming "God is great," setting off fireworks, firing guns, honking car horns and giving out sweets to children.

The sickening cruelty and murderous culture of Palestinian Arab society are deeply jarring. But a close study of Israel's Biblical enemies shows that they are far from the first society to celebrate murder.

The prophets who authored the books of the Bible often draw parallels that we are meant to notice and reflect upon. One of these easy-to-miss parallels is found in Deborah's song of thanks to God after the people of Israel's miraculous victory over the evil general Sisera and his army.

"Deliverance ceased, ceased in Israel, till you arose, O Deborah, arose a mother in Israel!" (Judges 5:7)

In this verse, Deborah is described as a "mother" of the people of Israel - an unusual description given that Deborah was a judge, prophetess and leader of Israel! Why is Deborah described as a "mother" of the nation?

I believe that the prophet intended to contrast Deborah with another mother mentioned in chapter 5 of Judges - the mother of the evil general Sisera.

"Through the window peered Sisera's mother; behind the lattice she whined: "Why is his chariot so long in coming? Why so late the clatter of his wheels?" The wisest of her ladies give answer; she, too, replies to herself: "They must be dividing the spoil they have found: A damsel or two for each man, spoil of dyed cloth for Sisera, spoil of embroidered cloth, a couple of embroidered cloths round every neck as spoil." (Judges 5:28-30)

The contrast between Deborah and Sisera's mother is stark. Deborah is the loving mother of the people of Israel, a woman who dedicated her life to caring for and encouraging her people. She welcomed all of her "children" to sit under her palm tree, where she judged them with mercy and love.

By contrast, Sisera's mother, waiting for her son to return home from war, comforts herself by imagining her son and his soldiers raping Jewish women, "a damsel or two for each man." She smiles as she convinces herself that he is late in returning home because he is plundering Israelite towns and enjoying his spoils.

As the mother of Israel proclaims life's inherent sanctity and celebrates her people's salvation from servitude and suffering, the mother of Israel's enemy dreams of bloodshed. How little has changed since the time of Judges!

Magda Faul, a Christian children's book writer in South Africa, writes about Rachelle Fraenkel, the Israeli mother of one of three teenage boys murdered by Palestinian terrorists in 2014:

"An emotional and spiritual turning point came one morning while I watched a video interview with Rachelle Fraenkel, the bereaved mother of late Naftali Fraenkel. It was clear that Mrs. Fraenkel was emotionally very vulnerable, but nevertheless courageous. At one stage, the interviewer asked her how she felt about the fact that the mother of the alleged kidnapper and murderer of her son encouraged feasting and partying to celebrate the murders and that this mother regarded her son, the killer, as a hero. Rachelle Fraenkel's reply came with no bitterness or hate. As far as I remember, she simply said she couldn't relate to it, to a people obsessed with death. And that Judaism is all about life" (Magda Faul, Glimpses of My Personal Torah Awakening, in Rivka Adler, Ten From the Nations: Torah Awakening Among Non-Jews, 73).

Sometimes the battle between good and evil is not complicated. May the people who celebrate life overcome the hatred and evil of the people obsessed with death. And may God comfort His people, the people who "choose life" (Deuteronomy 30:19).

# An Obligation to Serve?

When I graduated from my Boston-area high school about 25 years ago, I chose to spend a year and a half in Israel, where I studied the Bible and Jewish wisdom at a yeshiva (a school for Jewish studies). As I came to the end of my studies, I had to make a decision: would I return to the United States and go to college, or volunteer to serve for one year in the Israel Defence Forces?

Not particularly brave or athletic, I didn't dwell very long on the decision - I would go back to the United States to earn my college degree. But over the last twenty-five years, I've often looked back at my decision to forgo the army with discomfort and more than a little guilt. Young men and women in Israel put their lives at risk and dedicate three years of their lives to serving their country, and I chose not to serve for one? As an American citizen, I was not legally required to serve in Israel's army, but I couldn't shake the feeling that I had shirked my obligation.

This year, as I studied the book of Judges in-depth, it all became clear to me.

After Deborah and her trusted general Barak led the people of Israel to victory over the evil Sisera and his army, Deborah and Barak sang a song of thanks to God. But the song is more than just a song of thanks; it also contains a powerful rebuke of several of the tribes of Israel:

"Why then did you stay among the sheepfolds and listen as they pipe for the flocks? Among the clans of Reuben were great searchings of heart! Gilad tarried beyond the Jordan River; and Dan - why did he linger by the ships? Asher remained at the seacoast and tarried at his landings." (Judges 5:16-17)

Though Deborah succeeded in inspiring many of the Israelite tribes to come to the defense of the tribes of Zebulun and Naphtali, several tribes refused to join the fight. The tribe of Reuben waited nearby to see which way the battle would go, while the men of Gilad of the tribe of Manasseh remained on the other side of the Jordan River. The tribes of Dan and Asher, fearing the wrath of the powerful Sisera, remained at the shores of the Mediterranean Sea, ready to sail away and save their own skins.

Though their fears were real and warranted, Deborah aimed her prophetic anger toward the tribes who refused to help their brothers during a time of crisis. While the people of Israel achieved a great miraculous victory, there were certainly many Israelite soldiers who died defending their nation - even as other tribes sat out the war and protected themselves. Deborah's anger was justified. Why should some mothers bear sleepless nights as their sons battle the enemy, while others sleep soundly because their sons shirk their duty to serve?

As I studied her song, Deborah's anger hit me like a ton of bricks. Technically, as an American citizen, I did not have an obligation to serve in Israel's army. But as a Jew, as a descendant of Abraham, Isaac and Jacob, how could I have shirked my duty to defend my people?

Rabbi Aaron Rakeffet-Rothkoff, a leading American rabbi who moved to Israel many years ago, forcefully restates Deborah's point for the people of our generation:

"Army service is the touchstone issue [in Israel today]. According to Jewish law, no Jew in the world, no one living in New Jersey or Florida or anywhere else in the world, is exempt from the army; every Jew must come and fight. It's a milchemet mitzvah, an obligatory, defensive war in which every Jew is obligated to fight to defend our people."

For the last 75 years, Israel has been subjected to a constant state of war, surrounded by enemy nations and terrorists who seek nothing less than its destruction. Though I am now too old to serve as a soldier, it is incumbent upon me, and every one of us who identifies with God's chosen people, to serve the nation of Israel in any way that we can. As Nadia Matar, one of Israel's modern heroines, recently wrote: "We can choose to be players on the soccer field, or spectators who watch the game from the stands. Come and be part of those who are playing on the field; don't just be a spectator!"

During these difficult days before our final redemption, may each of us find our own way to strengthen the State of Israel. And may there soon be peace in the Holy Land, so that everyone may "beat their swords into plowshares and their spears into pruning hooks," a time when "nation shall not take up sword against nation and they shall never again know war" (Isaiah 2:4).

# 6

ו

| | Then the Israelites did what was offensive to GOD, and GOD delivered them into the hands of the Midianites for seven years. | *va-ya-a-SU v'-nay yis-ra-AYL ha-RA b'-ay-NAY a-do-NAI va-yi-t'-NAYM a-do-NAI b'-yad mid-YAN SHE-va sha-NEEM.* | וַיַּעֲשׂוּ בְנֵי־יִשְׂרָאֵל הָרַע בְּעֵינֵי יְהֹוָה וַיִּתְּנֵם יְהֹוָה בְּיַד־מִדְיָן שֶׁבַע שָׁנִים: |
|---|---|---|---|
| 1 | | | א |

| 2 | The hand of the Midianites prevailed over Israel; and because of Midian, the Israelites provided themselves with refuges in the caves and strongholds of the mountains. | *va-TA-az yad mid-YAN al yis-ra-AYL mi-p'-NAY mid-YAN a-SU la-HEM b'-NAY yis-ra-AYL et ha-min-ha-ROT a-SHER be-ha-REEM v'-et ha-m'-a-ROT v'-et ha-mitz-DOT.* | וַתָּעׇז יַד־מִדְיָן עַל־יִשְׂרָאֵל מִפְּנֵי מִדְיָן עָשׂוּ לָהֶם בְּנֵי יִשְׂרָאֵל אֶת־הַמִּנְהָרוֹת אֲשֶׁר בֶּהָרִים וְאֶת־הַמְּעָרוֹת וְאֶת־הַמְּצָדוֹת: |
| | | | ב |

| 3 | After the Israelites had done their sowing, Midian, Amalek, and the Kedemites would come up and raid them; | *v'-ha-YAH im za-RA yis-ra-AYL v'-a-LAH mid-YAN va-a-ma-LAYK uv'-nay KE-dem v'-a-LU a-LAV.* | וְהָיָה אִם־זָרַע יִשְׂרָאֵל וְעָלָה מִדְיָן וַעֲמָלֵק וּבְנֵי־קֶדֶם וְעָלוּ עָלָיו: |
| | | | ג |

| 4 | they would attack them, destroy the produce of the land all the way to Gaza, and leave no means of sustenance in Israel, not a sheep or an ox or a donkey. | *va-ya-kha-NU a-lay-HEM va-yash-KHEE-tu et y'-VUL ha-A-retz ad bo-a-KHA a-ZAH v'-LO yash-EE-ru mikh-YAH b'-yis-ra-AYL v'-SEH va-SHOR va-kha-MOR.* | וַיַּחֲנוּ עֲלֵיהֶם וַיַּשְׁחִיתוּ אֶת־יְבוּל הָאָרֶץ עַד־בּוֹאֲךָ עַזָּה וְלֹא־יַשְׁאִירוּ מִחְיָה בְּיִשְׂרָאֵל וְשֶׂה וָשׁוֹר וַחֲמוֹר: |
| | | | ד |

5
| For they would come up with their livestock and their tents, swarming as thick as locusts; they and their camels were innumerable. Thus they would invade the land and ravage it. | *KEE HAYM u-mik-nay-HEM ya-a-LU v'-o-ha-lay-HEM u-VA-u kh'-day ar-BEH la-ROV v'-la-HEM v'-lig-ma-lay-HEM AYN mis-PAR va-ya-VO-u va-A-retz l'-sha-kha-TAH.* | כִּי הֵם וּמִקְנֵיהֶם יַעֲלוּ וְאׇהֳלֵיהֶם (יבאו) [וּבָאוּ] כְדֵי־אַרְבֶּה לָרֹב וְלָהֶם וְלִגְמַלֵּיהֶם אֵין מִסְפָּר וַיָּבֹאוּ בָאָרֶץ לְשַׁחֲתָהּ: ה |

6
| Israel was reduced to utter misery by the Midianites, and the Israelites cried out to GOD. | *va-yi-DAL yis-ra-AYL m'-OD mi-p'-NAY mid-YAN va-yiz-a-KU v'-NAY yis-ra-AYL el a-do-NAI.* | וַיִּדַּל יִשְׂרָאֵל מְאֹד מִפְּנֵי מִדְיָן וַיִּזְעֲקוּ בְנֵי־ יִשְׂרָאֵל אֶל־יְהֹוָה: ו |

7
| When the Israelites cried to GOD on account of Midian, | *vai-HEE kee za-a-KU v'-NAY yis-ra-AYL el a-do-NAI AL o-DOT mid-YAN.* | וַיְהִי כִּי־זָעֲקוּ בְנֵי־ יִשְׂרָאֵל אֶל־יְהֹוָה עַל אֹדוֹת מִדְיָן: ז |

8
| GOD sent a certain prophet to the Israelites. He said to them, "Thus said the ETERNAL, the God of Israel: I brought you up out of Egypt and freed you from the house of bondage. | *va-yish-LAKH a-do-NAI EESH na-VEE el b'-NAY yis-ra-AYL va-YO-mer la-HEM koh AMAR a-do-NAI e-lo-HAY yis-ra-AYL a-no-KHEE he-e-LAY-tee et-KHEM mi-mitz-RA-yim va-o-TZEE et-KHEM mi-BAYT a-va-DEEM.* | וַיִּשְׁלַח יְהֹוָה אִישׁ נָבִיא אֶל־בְּנֵי יִשְׂרָאֵל וַיֹּאמֶר לָהֶם כֹּה־אָמַר יְהֹוָה אֱלֹהֵי יִשְׂרָאֵל אָנֹכִי הֶעֱלֵיתִי אֶתְכֶם מִמִּצְרַיִם וָאֹצִיא אֶתְכֶם מִבֵּית עֲבָדִים: ח |

9
| I rescued you from the Egyptians and from all your oppressors; I drove them out before you, and gave you their land. | *va-a-TZIL et-KHEM mi-YAD mitz-RA-yim u-mi-YAD kol lo-kha-tzay-KHEM va-a-ga-RAYSH o-TAM mi-p'-nay-KHEM va-e-t'-NAH la-KHEM et ar-TZAM.* | וָאַצִּל אֶתְכֶם מִיַּד מִצְרַיִם וּמִיַּד כׇּל־ לֹחֲצֵיכֶם וָאֲגָרֵשׁ אוֹתָם מִפְּנֵיכֶם וָאֶתְּנָה לָכֶם אֶת־אַרְצָם: ט |

| | | | |
|---|---|---|---|
| 10 | And I said to you, 'I the ETERNAL One am your God. You must not worship the gods of the Amorites in whose land you dwell.' But you did not obey Me." | *va-o-m'-RAH la-KHEM a-NEE a-do-NAI e-lo-hay-KHEM LO teer-U et e-lo-HAY ha-e-mo-REE a-sher a-TEM yo-sh'-VEEM b'-ar-TZAM v'-LO sh'-ma-TEM b'-KO-lee.* | וָאֹמְרָה לָכֶם אֲנִי יְהֹוָה אֱלֹהֵיכֶם לֹא תִירְאוּ אֶת־אֱלֹהֵי הָאֱמֹרִי אֲשֶׁר אַתֶּם יוֹשְׁבִים בְּאַרְצָם וְלֹא שְׁמַעְתֶּם בְּקוֹלִי: |
| 11 | An angel of GOD came and sat under the terebinth at Ophrah, which belonged to Joash the Abiezrite. His son Gideon was then beating out wheat inside a winepress in order to keep it safe from the Midianites. | *va-ya-VO mal-AKH a-do-NAI, va-YAY-shev TA-khat ha-ay-LAH a-SHER b'-of-RAH a-SHER l'-yo-ASH a-vee ha-ez-REE v'-gid-ON b'-NO cho-VAYT khi-TEEM ba-GAT l'-ha-NEES mi-p'-NAY mid-YAN.* | וַיָּבֹא מַלְאַךְ יְהֹוָה וַיֵּשֶׁב תַּחַת הָאֵלָה אֲשֶׁר בְּעָפְרָה אֲשֶׁר לְיוֹאָשׁ אֲבִי הָעֶזְרִי וְגִדְעוֹן בְּנוֹ חֹבֵט חִטִּים בַּגַּת לְהָנִיס מִפְּנֵי מִדְיָן: |
| 12 | The angel of GOD appeared to him and said to him, "GOD is with you, valiant warrior!" | *va-yay-RA ay-LAV mal-AKH a-do-NAI va-YO-mer ay-LAV a-do-NAI i-m'-KHA gi-BOR he-KHA-yil.* | וַיֵּרָא אֵלָיו מַלְאַךְ יְהֹוָה וַיֹּאמֶר אֵלָיו יְהֹוָה עִמְּךָ גִּבּוֹר הֶחָיִל: |
| 13 | Gideon said to him, "Please, my lord, if GOD is with us, why has all this befallen us? Where are all those wondrous deeds about which our ancestors told us, saying, 'Truly GOD brought us up from Egypt'? Now GOD has abandoned us and delivered us into the hands of Midian!" | *va-YO-mer ay-LAV gid-ON BEE a-do-NEE v'-YAYSH a-do-NAI i-MA-nu v'-LA-mah m'-tza-AT-nu kol ZOT v'-a-YAY khol nif-l'-o-TAV a-SHER si-p'-RU LA-nu a-vo-TAY-nu lay-MOR ha-LO mi-mitz-RA-yim he-e-LA-nu a-do-NAI v'-a-TAH n'-ta-SHA-nu a-do-NAI va-yi-t'-NAY-nu b'-KHAF mid-YAN.* | וַיֹּאמֶר אֵלָיו גִּדְעוֹן בִּי אֲדֹנִי וְיֵשׁ יְהֹוָה עִמָּנוּ וְלָמָּה מְצָאַתְנוּ כָּל־זֹאת וְאַיֵּה כָל־נִפְלְאֹתָיו אֲשֶׁר סִפְּרוּ־לָנוּ אֲבוֹתֵינוּ לֵאמֹר הֲלֹא מִמִּצְרַיִם הֶעֱלָנוּ יְהֹוָה וְעַתָּה נְטָשָׁנוּ יְהֹוָה וַיִּתְּנֵנוּ בְּכַף־מִדְיָן: |

| | |
|---|---|
| י | 10 |
| יא | 11 |
| יב | 12 |
| יג | 13 |

| |  |  |  |
|---|---|---|---|
| 14 | GOD turned to him and said, "Go in this strength of yours and deliver Israel from the Midianites. I herewith make you My messenger." | *va-YI-fen ay-LAV a-do-NAI va-YO-mer LAYKH b'-kho-kha-KHA ZEH v'-ho-sha-TAH et-yis-ra-AYL mi-KAF mid-YAN ha-LO sh'-lakh-TEE-kha.* | וַיִּפֶן אֵלָיו יְהוָה וַיֹּאמֶר לֵךְ בְּכֹחֲךָ זֶה וְהוֹשַׁעְתָּ אֶת־יִשְׂרָאֵל מִכַּף מִדְיָן הֲלֹא שְׁלַחְתִּיךָ׃ |
| 15 | He said to him, "Please, my Sovereign, how can I deliver Israel? Why, my clan is the humblest in Manasseh, and I am the youngest in my father's household." | *va-YO-mer ay-LAV BEE a-do-NAI ba-MAH o-SHEE-a et yis-ra-AYL hi-NAY al-FAY ha-DAL bim-na-SHEH v'-a-no-KHEE ha-tza-EER b'-vayt a-vee.* | וַיֹּאמֶר אֵלָיו בִּי אֲדֹנָי בַּמָּה אוֹשִׁיעַ אֶת־יִשְׂרָאֵל הִנֵּה אַלְפִּי הַדַּל בִּמְנַשֶּׁה וְאָנֹכִי הַצָּעִיר בְּבֵית אָבִי׃ |
| 16 | GOD replied, "I will be with you, and you shall defeat Midian all at once." | *va-YO-mer ay-LAV a-do-NAI kee eh-YEH i-MAKH v'-hi-kee-TAH et mid-YAN k'-eesh e-KHAD.* | וַיֹּאמֶר אֵלָיו יְהוָה כִּי אֶהְיֶה עִמָּךְ וְהִכִּיתָ אֶת־מִדְיָן כְּאִישׁ אֶחָד׃ |
| 17 | And he said to him, "If I have gained Your favor, give me a sign that it is You who are speaking to me. | *va-YO-mer ay-LAV im NA ma-TZA-tee KHAYN b'-ay-NE-kha v'-a-SEE-ta LEE OT sha-a-TAH m'-da-BAYR i-MEE.* | וַיֹּאמֶר אֵלָיו אִם־נָא מָצָאתִי חֵן בְּעֵינֶיךָ וְעָשִׂיתָ לִּי אוֹת שָׁאַתָּה מְדַבֵּר עִמִּי׃ |
| 18 | Do not leave this place until I come back to you and bring out my offering and place it before you." And he answered, "I will stay until you return." | *al NA ta-MUSH mi-ZEH ad bo-EE ay-LE-kha v'-ho-tzay-TEE et min-KHA-tee v'-hi-nakh-TEE l'-fa-NE-kha va-yo-MAR a-no-KHEE ay-SHAYV AD shu-VE-kha.* | אַל־נָא תָמֻשׁ מִזֶּה עַד־בֹּאִי אֵלֶיךָ וְהֹצֵאתִי אֶת־מִנְחָתִי וְהִנַּחְתִּי לְפָנֶיךָ וַיֹּאמַר אָנֹכִי אֵשֵׁב עַד שׁוּבֶךָ׃ |

19 So Gideon went in and prepared a kid, and [baked] unleavened bread from an ephah of flour. He put the meat in a basket and poured the broth into a pot, and he brought them out to him under the terebinth. As he presented them,

*va-gid-ON BA va-YA-as g'-DEE i-ZEEM v'-ay-fat KE-makh ma-TZOT ha-ba-SAR SAM ba-SAL v'-ha-ma-RAK SAM ba-pa-RUR; va-yo-TZAY ay-LAV el TA-khat ha-ay-LAH va-ya-GASH.*

וְגִדְעוֹן בָּא וַיַּעַשׂ גְּדִי־
עִזִּים וְאֵיפַת־קֶמַח
מַצּוֹת הַבָּשָׂר שָׂם בַּסַּל
וְהַמָּרַק שָׂם בַּפָּרוּר
וַיּוֹצֵא אֵלָיו אֶל־תַּחַת
הָאֵלָה וַיַּגַּשׁ: יט

20 the angel of God said to him, "Take the meat and the unleavened bread, put them on yonder rock, and spill out the broth." He did so.

*va-YO-mer ay-LAV mal-AKH ha-e-lo-HEEM KAKH et ha-ba-SAR v'-ET ha-ma-TZOT v'-ha-NAKH el ha-SE-la ha-LAZ v'-et ha-ma-RAK sh'-FOKH va-YA-as KAYN*

וַיֹּאמֶר אֵלָיו מַלְאַךְ
הָאֱלֹהִים קַח אֶת־
הַבָּשָׂר וְאֶת־הַמַּצּוֹת
וְהַנַּח אֶל־הַסֶּלַע הַלָּז
וְאֶת־הַמָּרַק שְׁפוֹךְ
וַיַּעַשׂ כֵּן: כ

21 The angel of GOD held out the staff that he carried, and touched the meat and the unleavened bread with its tip. A fire sprang up from the rock and consumed the meat and the unleavened bread. And the angel of GOD vanished from his sight.

*va-yish-LAKH mal-AKH a-do-NAI et k'-TZAY ha-mish-E-net a-SHER b'-ya-DO va-yi-GA ba-ba-SAR u-va-ma-TZOT va-TA-al ha-AYSH min ha-TZUR va-TO-khal et ha-ba-SAR v'-et ha-ma-TZOT u-mal-AKH a-do-NAI ha-LAKH may-ay-NAV*

וַיִּשְׁלַח מַלְאַךְ יְהוָה
אֶת־קְצֵה הַמִּשְׁעֶנֶת
אֲשֶׁר בְּיָדוֹ וַיִּגַּע בַּבָּשָׂר
וּבַמַּצּוֹת וַתַּעַל הָאֵשׁ
מִן־הַצּוּר וַתֹּאכַל אֶת־
הַבָּשָׂר וְאֶת־הַמַּצּוֹת
וּמַלְאַךְ יְהוָה הָלַךְ
מֵעֵינָיו: כא

| | | | |
|---|---|---|---|
| 22 | Then Gideon realized that indeed it was an angel of GOD; and Gideon said, "Alas, O Sovereign GOD ! For I have seen an angel of GOD face to face." | *va-YAR gid-ON kee mal-AKH a-do-NAI HU va-YO-mer gid-ON a-HAH a-do-NAI e-lo-HEEM kee al KAYN ra-EE-tee mal-AKH a-do-NAI pa-NEEM el pa-NEEM* | וַיַּרְא גִּדְעוֹן כִּי־מַלְאַךְ יְהוָה הוּא וַיֹּאמֶר גִּדְעוֹן אֲהָהּ אֲדֹנָי יֱהֹוִה כִּי־עַל־כֵּן רָאִיתִי מַלְאַךְ יְהוָה פָּנִים אֶל־פָּנִים: | כב |
| 23 | But GOD said to him, "All is well; have no fear, you shall not die." | *va-YO-mer LO a-do-NAI sha-LOM l'-KHA al tee-RA LO ta-MUT* | וַיֹּאמֶר לוֹ יְהוָה שָׁלוֹם לְךָ אַל־תִּירָא לֹא תָּמוּת: | כג |
| 24 | So Gideon built there an altar to GOD and called it Adonai-shalom. To this day it stands in Ophrah of the Abiezrites. | *va-YI-ven SHAM gid-ON miz-BAY-akh la-do-NAI va-yik-ra LO a-do-NAI sha-LOM AD ha-YOM ha-ZEH o-DE-nu b'-of-RAT a-VEE ha-ez-REE* | וַיִּבֶן שָׁם גִּדְעוֹן מִזְבֵּחַ לַיהוָה וַיִּקְרָא־לוֹ יְהוָה שָׁלוֹם עַד הַיּוֹם הַזֶּה עוֹדֶנּוּ בְּעָפְרָת אֲבִי הָעֶזְרִי: | כד |
| 25 | That night GOD said to him: "Take the young bull belonging to your father and another bull seven years old; pull down the altar of Baal that belongs to your father, and cut down the sacred post that is beside it. | *vai-HEE ba-LAI-lah ha-HU va-YO-mer LO a-do-NAI KAKH et par ha-SHOR a-SHER l'-a-VEE-kha u-FAR ha-shay-NEE SHE-va sha-NEEM v'-ha-ras-TA et miz-BAKH ha-BA-al a-SHER l'-a-VEE-kha v'-et ha-a-shay-RAH a-sher a-LAV tikh-ROT* | וַיְהִי בַּלַּיְלָה הַהוּא וַיֹּאמֶר לוֹ יְהוָה קַח אֶת־פַּר־הַשּׁוֹר אֲשֶׁר לְאָבִיךָ וּפַר הַשֵּׁנִי שֶׁבַע שָׁנִים וְהָרַסְתָּ אֶת־מִזְבַּח הַבַּעַל אֲשֶׁר לְאָבִיךָ וְאֶת־הָאֲשֵׁרָה אֲשֶׁר־עָלָיו תִּכְרֹת: | כה |

| | | |
|---|---|---|
| 26 | Then build an altar to the ETERNAL your God, on the level ground on top of this stronghold. Take the other bull and offer it as a burnt offering, using the wood of the sacred post that you have cut down." | *u-va-NEE-ta miz-BAY-akh la-do-NAI e-lo-HE-kha al ROSH ha-ma-OZ ha-ZEH ba-ma-a-ra-KHAH v'-la-kakh-TA et ha-PAR ha-shay-NEE v'-ha-a-LEE-ta o-LAH ba-a-TZAY ha-a-shay-RAH a-SHER tikh-ROT* | וּבָנִיתָ מִזְבֵּחַ לַיהוָה אֱלֹהֶיךָ עַל רֹאשׁ הַמָּעוֹז הַזֶּה בַּמַּעֲרָכָה וְלָקַחְתָּ אֶת־הַפָּר הַשֵּׁנִי וְהַעֲלִיתָ עוֹלָה בַּעֲצֵי הָאֲשֵׁרָה אֲשֶׁר תִּכְרֹת: | כו |

| | | |
|---|---|---|
| 27 | So Gideon took ten of his servants and did as GOD had told him; but as he was afraid to do it by day, on account of his father's household and the townspeople, he did it by night. | *va-yi-KAKH gid-ON a-sa-RAH a-na-SHEEM may-a-va-DAV va-YA-as ka-a-SHER di-BER ay-LAV a-do-NAI vai-HEE ka-a-SHER ya-RAY et BAYT a-VEEV v'-et an-SHAY ha-EER may-a-SOT yo-MAM va-YA-as LAI-lah* | וַיִּקַּח גִּדְעוֹן עֲשָׂרָה אֲנָשִׁים מֵעֲבָדָיו וַיַּעַשׂ כַּאֲשֶׁר דִּבֶּר אֵלָיו יְהוָה וַיְהִי כַּאֲשֶׁר יָרֵא אֶת־בֵּית אָבִיו וְאֶת־אַנְשֵׁי הָעִיר מֵעֲשׂוֹת יוֹמָם וַיַּעַשׂ לָיְלָה: | כז |

| | | |
|---|---|---|
| 28 | Early the next morning, the townspeople found that the altar of Baal had been torn down and the sacred post beside it had been cut down, and that the second bull had been offered on the newly built altar. | *va-yash-KEE-mu an-SHAY ha-EER ba-BO-ker v'-hi-NAY nu-TATZ miz-BAKH ha-BA-al v'-ha-a-shay-RAH a-sher a-LAV ko-RA-tah v'-AYT ha-PAR ha-shay-NEE ho-a-LAH al ha-miz-BAY-akh ha-ba-NUY* | וַיַּשְׁכִּימוּ אַנְשֵׁי הָעִיר בַּבֹּקֶר וְהִנֵּה נֻתַּץ מִזְבַּח הַבַּעַל וְהָאֲשֵׁרָה אֲשֶׁר־עָלָיו כֹּרָתָה וְאֵת הַפָּר הַשֵּׁנִי הֹעֲלָה עַל הַמִּזְבֵּחַ הַבָּנוּי: | כח |

| | | |
|---|---|---|
| 29 | They said to one another, "Who did this thing?" Upon inquiry and investigation, they were told, "Gideon son of Joash did this thing!" | *va-yo-m'-RU EESH el ray-AY-hu MEE a-SAH ha-da-VAR ha-ZEH va-yid-r'-SHU vai-vak-SHU va-yo-m'-RU gid-ON ben yo-ASH a-SAH ha-da-VAR ha-ZEH* | וַיֹּאמְרוּ אִישׁ אֶל־רֵעֵהוּ מִי עָשָׂה הַדָּבָר הַזֶּה וַיִּדְרְשׁוּ וַיְבַקְשׁוּ וַיֹּאמְרוּ גִּדְעוֹן בֶּן־יוֹאָשׁ עָשָׂה הַדָּבָר הַזֶּה: | כט |

| | | |
|---|---|---|
| 30 | The townspeople said to Joash, "Bring out your son, for he must die: he has torn down the altar of Baal and cut down the sacred post beside it!" | *va-YO-m'-RU an-SHAY ha-EER el yo-ASH ho-TZAY et bin-KHA v'-ya-MOT KEE na-TATZ et miz-BAKH ha-BA-al v'-KHEE kha-RAT ha-a-shay-RAH a-sher a-LAV* | וַיֹּאמְרוּ אַנְשֵׁי הָעִיר אֶל־יוֹאָשׁ הוֹצֵא אֶת־בִּנְךָ וְיָמֹת כִּי נָתַץ אֶת־מִזְבַּח הַבַּעַל וְכִי כָרַת הָאֲשֵׁרָה אֲשֶׁר־עָלָיו: | ל |
| 31 | But Joash said to all who had risen against him, "Do you have to contend for Baal? Do you have to vindicate him? Whoever fights his battles shall be dead by morning! If he is a god, let him fight his own battles, since it is his altar that has been torn down!" | *va-YO-mer yo-ASH l'-KHOL a-sher a-m'-DU a-LAV ha-a-TEM t'-ree-VUN la-BA-al im a-TEM to-shee-UN o-TO a-SHER ya-REEV LO yu-MAT ad ha-BO-ker im e-lo-HEEM HU YA-rev LO KEE na-TATZ et miz-b'-KHO* | וַיֹּאמֶר יוֹאָשׁ לְכֹל אֲשֶׁר־עָמְדוּ עָלָיו הַאַתֶּם תְּרִיבוּן לַבַּעַל אִם־אַתֶּם תּוֹשִׁיעוּן אוֹתוֹ אֲשֶׁר יָרִיב לוֹ יוּמַת עַד־הַבֹּקֶר אִם־אֱלֹהִים הוּא יָרֶב לוֹ כִּי נָתַץ אֶת־מִזְבְּחוֹ: | לא |
| 32 | That day they named him Jerubbaal, meaning "Let Baal contend with him, since he tore down his altar." | *va-yik-RA LO va-YOM ha-HU y'-ru-BA-al lay-MOR YA-rev BO ha-BA-al KEE na-TATZ et miz-b'-KHO* | וַיִּקְרָא־לוֹ בַיּוֹם־הַהוּא יְרֻבַּעַל לֵאמֹר יָרֶב בּוֹ הַבַּעַל כִּי נָתַץ אֶת־מִזְבְּחוֹ: | לב |
| 33 | All Midian, Amalek, and the Kedemites joined forces; they crossed over and encamped in the Valley of Jezreel. | *v'-khol mid-YAN va-a-ma-LAYK uv-nay KE-dem ne-es-FU yakh-DAV va-ya-av-RU va-ya-kha-NU b'-AY-mek yiz-r'-EL* | וְכָל־מִדְיָן וַעֲמָלֵק וּבְנֵי־קֶדֶם נֶאֶסְפוּ יַחְדָּו וַיַּעַבְרוּ וַיַּחֲנוּ בְּעֵמֶק יִזְרְעֶאל: | לג |

| 34 | The spirit of GOD enveloped Gideon; he sounded the horn, and the Abiezrites rallied behind him. | *v'-RU-akh a-do-NAI la-v'-SHAH et gid-ON va-yit-KA ba-sho-FAR va-yi-za-AYK a-vee-E-zer a-kha-RAV* | וְרוּחַ יְהוָה לָבְשָׁה אֶת־גִּדְעוֹן וַיִּתְקַע בַּשּׁוֹפָר וַיִּזָּעֵק אֲבִיעֶזֶר אַחֲרָיו: | לד |
| 35 | And he sent messengers throughout Manasseh, and they too rallied behind him. He then sent messengers through Asher, Zebulun, and Naphtali, and they came up to meet the Manassites. | *u-mal-a-KHEEM sha-LAKH b'-khol m'-na-SHEH va-yi-za-AYK gam HU a-kha-RAV u-mal-a-KHEEM sha-LAKH b'-a-SHAYR u-viz-vu-LUN uv-naf-ta-LEE va-ya-a-LU lik-ra-TAM* | וּמַלְאָכִים שָׁלַח בְּכָל־מְנַשֶּׁה וַיִּזָּעֵק גַּם־הוּא אַחֲרָיו וּמַלְאָכִים שָׁלַח בְּאָשֵׁר וּבִזְבֻלוּן וּבְנַפְתָּלִי וַיַּעֲלוּ לִקְרָאתָם: | לה |
| 36 | And Gideon said to God, "If You really intend to deliver Israel through me as You have said— | *va-YO-mer gid-ON el ha-e-lo-HEE im yesh-KHA mo-SHEE-a b'-ya-DEE et yis-ra-AYL ka-a-SHER di-BAR-ta* | וַיֹּאמֶר גִּדְעוֹן אֶל־הָאֱלֹהִים אִם־יֶשְׁךָ מוֹשִׁיעַ בְּיָדִי אֶת־יִשְׂרָאֵל כַּאֲשֶׁר דִּבַּרְתָּ: | לו |
| 37 | here I place a fleece of wool on the threshing floor. If dew falls only on the fleece and all the ground remains dry, I shall know that You will deliver Israel through me, as You have said." | *hi-NAY a-no-KHEE ma-TZEEG et gi-ZAT ha-TZE-mer ba-GO-ren IM TAL yih-YEH al ha-gi-ZAH l'-va-DAH v'-al kol ha-A-retz KHO-rev v'-ya-da-TEE kee to-SHEE-a b'-ya-DEE et yis-ra-AYL ka-a-SHER di-BAR-ta* | הִנֵּה אָנֹכִי מַצִּיג אֶת־גִּזַּת הַצֶּמֶר בַּגֹּרֶן אִם טַל יִהְיֶה עַל־הַגִּזָּה לְבַדָּהּ וְעַל־כָּל־הָאָרֶץ חֹרֶב וְיָדַעְתִּי כִּי־תוֹשִׁיעַ בְּיָדִי אֶת־יִשְׂרָאֵל כַּאֲשֶׁר דִּבַּרְתָּ: | לז |

| | | | |
|---|---|---|---|
| 38 | And that is what happened. Early the next day, he squeezed the fleece and wrung out the dew from the fleece, a bowlful of water. | *vai-hee KHAYN va-yash-KAYM mi-ma-kho-RAT va-YA-zar et ha-gi-ZAH va-YI-metz TAL min ha-gi-ZAH m'-LO ha-SAY-fel MA-yim* | וַיְהִי־כֵן וַיַּשְׁכֵּם מִמָּחֳרָת וַיָּזַר אֶת־הַגִּזָּה וַיִּמֶץ טַל מִן־הַגִּזָּה מְלוֹא הַסֵּפֶל מָיִם: | לח |
| 39 | Then Gideon said to God, "Do not be angry with me if I speak just once more. Let me make just one more test with the fleece: let the fleece alone be dry, while there is dew all over the ground." | *va-YO-mer gid-ON el ha-e-lo-HEEM al YI-khar a-p'-KHA BEE va-a-da-b'-RAH AKH ha-PA-am a-na-SEH na rak ha-PA-am ba-gi-ZAH y'-hee NA KHO-rev el ha-gi-ZAH l'-va-DAH v'-al kol ha-A-retz yih-yeh TAL* | וַיֹּאמֶר גִּדְעוֹן אֶל־הָאֱלֹהִים אַל־יִחַר אַפְּךָ בִּי וַאֲדַבְּרָה אַךְ הַפָּעַם אֲנַסֶּה נָּא־רַק־הַפַּעַם בַּגִּזָּה יְהִי־נָא חֹרֶב אֶל־הַגִּזָּה לְבַדָּהּ וְעַל־כָּל־הָאָרֶץ יִהְיֶה־טָּל: | לט |
| 40 | God did so that night: only the fleece was dry, while there was dew all over the ground. | *va-YA-as e-lo-HEEM KAYN ba-LAI-lah ha-HU vay-hee KHO-rev el ha-gi-ZAH l'-va-DAH v'-al kol ha-A-retz HA-yah TAL* | וַיַּעַשׂ אֱלֹהִים כֵּן בַּלַּיְלָה הַהוּא וַיְהִי־חֹרֶב אֶל־הַגִּזָּה לְבַדָּהּ וְעַל־כָּל־הָאָרֶץ הָיָה טָל: | מ |

# A Legacy of Respect

The Hebrew Bible is careful with its words. When introducing a new protagonist, the Bible rarely tells us about their background. Famously, the story of Abraham begins when he is already 75 years old, forcing the reader to speculate about the great man's beginnings and the road that led him to God. At the same time, a close study of the Biblical text will often reveal telling insights into the lives of its heroes.

When introducing us to Gideon, the Bible shares very little about his background and what makes him unique. A careful reading, however, reveals some essential details.

"An angel of GOD came and sat under the terebinth at Ophrah, which belonged to Joash the Abiezrite. His son Gideon was then beating out wheat inside a winepress in order to keep it safe from the Midianites." (Judges 6:11)

Though this appears to be a mundane verse with little interesting information, it is actually the key to understanding Gideon's personality and motivations.

Gideon was the son of Joash the Abiezrite, meaning his family descended from Abiezer. Abiezer was the son of Gilead, who was the son of Machir and the grandson of Manasseh, the firstborn son of Joseph. Why is this significant?

While Ephraim, Joseph's second son, spent time learning with his grandfather Jacob, Manasseh was Joseph's right-hand man, living and working with him in the Egyptian capital. The sages say that he served as Joseph's "interpreter" when Joseph pretended not to recognize his brothers. Manasseh, more than any other son of Jacob, was exceptionally dedicated to honoring his father.

And so it is not surprising that Manasseh and his children and grandchildren were particularly close to Joseph and honored him greatly:

"Joseph lived to see children of the third generation of Ephraim; the children of Machir son of Manasseh were likewise born upon Joseph's knees." (Genesis 50:23)

By going above and beyond to honor his father, Manasseh left a powerful legacy for his own descendants. The children of Manasseh became known for going above and beyond to honor their elders. After forty years of wandering in the wilderness and as the people of Israel prepared to enter the Land of Israel, the daughters of Zelophehad, a man of Manasseh who had died in the wilderness, approached Moses with a request:

"Our father died in the wilderness. He was not one of the faction, Korah's faction, which banded together against Hashem, but died for his own sin; and he has left no sons. Let not our father's name be lost to his clan just because he had no son! Give us a holding among our father's kinsmen!" (Numbers 27:3-4)

Though there were likely thousands of men who died in the wilderness without any sons, it was only the daughters of Zelophehad – the descendants of Manasseh – who petitioned Moses for an inheritance to remember the legacy of their father.

Gideon continued his forefather Manasseh's legacy of honoring his parents. The verse states that Joash's son Gideon "was then beating out wheat inside a winepress in order to keep it safe from the Midianites." The medieval commentator, Rabbi David Kimche, explains that initially, Joash himself was beating the wheat. But his son Gideon said to him: "My father, you have grown old; please go inside the house and allow me to beat the wheat instead of you. For if the Midianite [plunderers] come while you are beating the wheat, you won't have the strength to run from them [and hide the wheat]." In the merit of honoring his father, even in a dangerous situation, Gideon was chosen to be the savior of the people of Israel.

Modern culture is obsessed with youth. Television, movies and media all highlight young people in the prime of their lives, and generally ignore the elders of our society. But the tribe of Manasseh, and Gideon in particular, highlight the importance of honoring our parents and our elders. By following in their footsteps, we not only honor the memory of those who came before us, but we also tap into the wealth of knowledge and wisdom they have accumulated over their lifetime. When we show them respect, we acknowledge their contributions to society and the value they bring to our lives. By following in the footsteps of Gideon and his forefather Manasseh, we too can honor the legacy of our own elders and ensure that their memory and influence live on for future generations.

# The Greatness
# of Gideon

As a synagogue rabbi in New Jersey, I often thought of the classic insight that "no good deed goes unpunished." While celebrating happy events like weddings and bar mitzvahs, I would praise a particular congregant or family in the community from the pulpit, only to find out afterward that they were upset about something I said or neglected to say.

In the Book of Judges, we find a similar dynamic in an interaction between Gideon and an angel of God. When God seeks a leader to inspire the Israelites to rebel against their Midianite oppressors, He sends an angel to recruit Gideon. But Gideon's reaction is anything but kind!

The angel of GOD appeared to him and said to him, "GOD is with you, valiant warrior!" Gideon said to him, "Please, my lord, if GOD is with us, why has all this befallen us? Where are all those wondrous deeds about which our ancestors told us, saying, 'Truly GOD brought us up from Egypt'? Now GOD has abandoned us and delivered us into the hands of Midian!" (Judges 6:12-13)

Why does God choose such a rude and ungrateful man to be the savior of Israel?

Commenting on this verse, Rashi, the great medieval commentator, explains that Gideon went so far as to accuse God of being unjust:

"It was Passover, so he said, 'Last night my father recited the Hallel [songs of praise and thanks to God] and I heard him say, 'When Israel departed from Egypt, etc.' (thus recounting the miracles God performed on behalf of Israel), but now He has forsaken us. If our forefathers were righteous, let Him perform (wonders) for us in their merit, and if they were wicked, then just as He did for them undeserving wonders, so should He do for us. Where, then, are all His wonders?'"

Is Gideon truly an insolent man who does not trust in God's kindness and righteousness?

Rabbi Isaac Arama (1420 – 1494) explains that we are missing the underlying message of Gideon's response. "The angel came to Gideon to find a man who would save the people of Israel from their Midianite oppressors. This goal was etched upon Gideon's heart. Gideon did not think about his own personal concerns, and he was not concerned with saving his own crops from the Midianites [who regularly plundered Israelite farms]. Rather, Gideon turned his heart toward the suffering of his people and their salvation…" (Akeidat Yitzchak, Exodus 1:1).

Gideon's emotional outburst was not meant to be insolent nor an angry diatribe against God. On the contrary – it was a sign of his deep love for the people of Israel! While sitting at his father's Passover seder, Gideon took the message of the Exodus to heart: "God is great and all-powerful; He can save us from any enemy, no matter how frightening they might be. Why, then, does God not save us from our oppressors now?"

While other Israelites were concerned for their own lands and their own safety, Gideon felt the pain of his entire people. His emotional response to the angel was, therefore, a sign of his greatness; it was proof that God had chosen the right man to lead his people to salvation.

Rabbi Isaac Jacob Reines, one of the leading rabbis of the late 19th and early 20th century, was a man like Gideon. When he heard about acts of evil and the suffering of innocents, Rabbi Reines himself felt physical pain. His face became flushed, his body shook, and he would repeat, over and over again: "we must do something!" At times he would gather his family together and say in bitterness: "We must act, we can't sit on our hands!" Though Rabbi Reines frequently didn't know what to do – he lived at a time when Jews were often powerless to act – he felt passionately that he must do something.

In our own time, we too are confronted with great evil. Terrorists seek to murder as many Jews as they can, while anti-religious bigots hound religious believers in the United States and throughout the West. How should we respond?

Gideon must be our guide. The first critical step when responding to evil is to care! When we witness the suffering of innocent victims, we must awaken from our slumber and passivity and feel their pain! Like Gideon, we must find room in our hearts to care about them more than ourselves, our family and friends, and our personal concerns. And like Gideon, we must feel pain, anger and frustration, for these are the emotions that will propel us to genuine prayer and to fight in defense of all that is good and holy.

# Respectful Disobedience

Change or continuity? Revolution or tradition? Throughout the modern age, our society has been caught between the values of tradition and stability on the one hand, and the need for change and improvement on the other. A society that abandons its traditions will inevitably lose its way, as America has in our own generation. But at the same time, a society that refuses to address its failures and weaknesses will lose its dynamism and inevitably decline.

How can we navigate the need for both tradition and change? Gideon, the great savior of Israel, demonstrates how to walk this narrow bridge.

Gideon revered and honored his father Joash. But when God appointed him to lead the people of Israel against their Midianite oppressors, Gideon faced a thorny challenge. To bring salvation, the people of Israel would have to abandon their idolatrous ways and return to God. But Gideon's own father worshiped idols! How could Gideon destroy his community's idols while also honoring his father?

The answer can be found in the Biblical command to honor our parents:

You shall each revere your mother and your father, and keep My Sabbaths: I am Hashem your God. (Leviticus 19:3)

Rashi, the great medieval Biblical commentator, asks why the Bible juxtaposes the commandment to honor one's parents with the commandment to keep the Sabbath. What does one have to do with the other?

Rashi writes that through this juxtaposition, God is teaching us a fundamental principle: "'Although I have admonished you regarding the fear of your father, nevertheless, if he tells you to desecrate the Sabbath, do not listen to him.' And this is also the case with all the [other] commandments. 'I am the Lord, your God; both you and your father are obligated to honor Me! Therefore, do not listen to him to negate My commands.'"

Although the commandment to honor one's mother and father is included in the Ten Commandments, our obligation to God comes before our obligation to our parents. If we are forced to choose between them, we must choose to follow God!

And so Gideon does:

"That night GOD said to him: "Take the young bull belonging to your father and another bull seven years old; pull down the altar of Baal that belongs to your father, and cut down the sacred post that is beside it... So Gideon took ten of his servants and did as GOD had told him; but as he was afraid to do it by day, on account of his father's household and the townspeople, he did it by night." (Judges 6:25, 27)

How did Gideon's father react to his son's act of disobedience? To his credit, Joash was humble enough to recognize his sin:

"The townspeople said to Joash, "Bring out your son, for he must die: he has torn down the altar of Baal and cut down the sacred post beside it!" But Joash said to all who had risen against him, "Do you have to contend for Baal? Do you have to vindicate him? Whoever fights his battles shall be dead by morning! If he is a god, let him fight his own battles, since it is his altar that has been torn down!" (Judges 6:30-31)

Joash displayed great humility by publicly acknowledging that his son was correct. But much of the credit for Joash's humility is due to his son, Gideon. Gideon was not just a revolutionary; he was also a deeply respectful son! Even when Gideon was forced to reject his father's idolatry, he remained respectful and loving towards his father. Gideon was able to implement revolutionary change while remaining respectful of his elders.

We, in our own generation, must learn from Gideon and Joash. Yes, our society is imperfect and requires change. But change must always be implemented carefully, and with great respect for the traditions of our fathers.

By following the ways of Gideon, we will fulfill the prophecies concerning Elijah, another great man from the tribe of Manasseh, and bring the final redemption. As the prophet Malachi says:

"He shall reconcile parents with children and children with their parents." (Malachi 3:23)

May we soon see that day!

# 7

1    Early next day,
Jerubbaal—that is,
Gideon—and all
the troops with him
encamped above
En-harod, while the
camp of Midian was
in the plain to the
north of him, at
Gibeath-moreh.

*va-yash-KAYM y'-ru-BA-
al HU gid-ON v'-khol
ha-AM a-SHER i-TO
va-ya-kha-NU al AYN
kha-ROD u-ma-kha-NAY
mid-YAN ha-yah LO
mi-tza-FON mi-giv-AT
ha-mo-REH ba-AY-mek*

וַיַּשְׁכֵּם יְרֻבַּעַל הוּא
גִדְעוֹן וְכָל־הָעָם אֲשֶׁר
אִתּוֹ וַיַּחֲנוּ עַל־עֵין
חֲרֹד וּמַחֲנֵה מִדְיָן
הָיָה־לוֹ מִצָּפוֹן מִגִּבְעַת
הַמּוֹרֶה בָּעֵמֶק׃    א

2    GOD said to Gideon,
"You have too many
troops with you for
Me to deliver Midian
into their hands;
Israel might claim for
themselves the glory
due to Me, thinking,
'Our own hand has
brought us victory.'

*va-YO-mer a-do-NAI
el gid-ON RAV ha-
AM a-SHER i-TAKH
mi-ti-TEE et mid-YAN
b'-ya-DAM pen yit-pa-
AYR a-LAI yis-ra-AYL
lay-MOR ya-DEE ho-
SHEE-ah LEE*

וַיֹּאמֶר יְהֹוָה אֶל־גִּדְעוֹן
רַב הָעָם אֲשֶׁר אִתָּךְ
מִתִּתִּי אֶת־מִדְיָן בְּיָדָם
פֶּן־יִתְפָּאֵר עָלַי יִשְׂרָאֵל
לֵאמֹר יָדִי הוֹשִׁיעָה לִּי׃    ב

3    Therefore, announce
to the men, 'Let
anybody who is timid
and fearful turn
back, as a bird flies
from Mount Gilead.'"
Thereupon, 22,000
of the troops turned
back and 10,000
remained.

*v'-a-TAH k'-RA NA b'-
oz-NAY ha-AM lay-MOR
mee ya-RAY v'-kha-
RAYD ya-SHOV v'-yitz-
POR may-HAR ha-gil-
AD va-YA-shov min
ha-AM es-REEM ush-
NA-yim E-lef va-a-SE-ret
a-la-FEEM nish-A-ru*

וְעַתָּה קְרָא נָא בְּאָזְנֵי
הָעָם לֵאמֹר מִי־יָרֵא
וְחָרֵד יָשֹׁב וְיִצְפֹּר
מֵהַר הַגִּלְעָד וַיָּשָׁב מִן־
הָעָם עֶשְׂרִים וּשְׁנַיִם
אֶלֶף וַעֲשֶׂרֶת אֲלָפִים
נִשְׁאָרוּ׃    ג

4
"There are still too many troops," GOD said to Gideon. "Take them down to the water and I will sift them for you there. Anyone of whom I tell you, 'This one is to go with you,' that one shall go with you; and anyone of whom I tell you, 'This one is not to go with you,' that one shall not go."

*va-YO-mer a-do-NAI el gid-ON OD ha-AM RAV ho-RAYD o-TAM el ha-MA-yim v'-etz-r'-FE-nu l'-KHA SHAM v'-ha-YAH a-SHER o-MAR ay-LE-kha ZEH yay-LAYKH i-TAKH HU yay-LAYKH i-TAKH v'-KHOL a-sher o-MAR ay-LE-kha ZEH lo yay-LAYKH i-MAKH HU LO yay-LAYKH*

וַיֹּאמֶר יְהֹוָה אֶל־גִּדְעוֹן עוֹד הָעָם רָב הוֹרֵד אוֹתָם אֶל־הַמַּיִם וְאֶצְרְפֶנּוּ לְךָ שָׁם וְהָיָה אֲשֶׁר אֹמַר אֵלֶיךָ זֶה יֵלֵךְ אִתָּךְ הוּא יֵלֵךְ אִתָּךְ וְכֹל אֲשֶׁר־אֹמַר אֵלֶיךָ זֶה לֹא־יֵלֵךְ עִמָּךְ הוּא לֹא יֵלֵךְ: ד

5
So he took the troops down to the water. Then GOD said to Gideon, "Set apart all those who lap up the water with their tongues like dogs from all those who get down on their knees to drink."

*va-YO-red et ha-AM el ha-MA-yim va-YO-mer a-do-NAI el gid-ON KOL a-sher ya-LOK bil-sho-NO min ha-MA-yim ka-a-SHER ya-LOK ha-KE-lev ta-TZEEG o-TO l'-VAD v'-KHOL a-sher yikh-RA al bir-KAV lish-TOT*

וַיּוֹרֶד אֶת־הָעָם אֶל־הַמָּיִם וַיֹּאמֶר יְהֹוָה אֶל־גִּדְעוֹן כֹּל אֲשֶׁר־יָלֹק בִּלְשׁוֹנוֹ מִן־הַמַּיִם כַּאֲשֶׁר יָלֹק הַכֶּלֶב תַּצִּיג אוֹתוֹ לְבָד וְכֹל אֲשֶׁר־יִכְרַע עַל־בִּרְכָּיו לִשְׁתּוֹת: ה

6
Now those who "lapped" the water into their mouths by hand numbered three hundred; all the rest of the troops got down on their knees to drink.

*vai-HEE mis-PAR ham-la-k'-KEEM b'-ya-DAM el pee-HEM sh'-LOSH may-OT EESH v'-KHOL YE-ter ha-AM ka-r'-U al bir-khay-HEM lish-TOT MA-yim*

וַיְהִי מִסְפַּר הַמְלַקְקִים בְּיָדָם אֶל־פִּיהֶם שְׁלֹשׁ מֵאוֹת אִישׁ וְכֹל יֶתֶר הָעָם כָּרְעוּ עַל־בִּרְכֵיהֶם לִשְׁתּוֹת מָיִם: ו

7

Then GOD said to Gideon, "I will deliver you and I will put Midian into your hands through the three hundred 'lappers'; let the rest of the troops go home."

*va-YO-mer a-do-NAI el gid-ON bish-LOSH may-OT ha-EESH ham-la-k'-KEEM o-SHEE-a et-KHEM v'-na-ta-TEE et mid-YAN b'-ya-DE-kha v'-KHOL ha-AM yay-l'-KHU EESH lim-ko-MO*

וַיֹּאמֶר יְהֹוָה אֶל־גִּדְעוֹן בִּשְׁלֹשׁ מֵאוֹת הָאִישׁ הַמֲלַקְקִים אוֹשִׁיעַ אֶתְכֶם וְנָתַתִּי אֶת־מִדְיָן בְּיָדֶךָ וְכָל־הָעָם יֵלְכוּ אִישׁ לִמְקֹמוֹ: ז

8

So [the lappers] took the provisions and horns that the other men had with them, and he sent the rest of Israel's side back to their homes, retaining only the three hundred men. The Midianite camp was below him, in the plain.

*va-yik-KHU et tzay-DAH ha-AM b'-ya-DAM v'-AYT sho-f'-ro-tay-HEM v'-AYT kol EESH yis-ra-AYL shi-LAKH EESH l'-o-ha-LAV u-vish-losh may-OT ha-EESH he-khe-ZEEK u-ma-kha-NAY mid-YAN ha-YAH LO mi-TA-khat ba-AY-mek*

וַיִּקְחוּ אֶת־צֵדָה הָעָם בְּיָדָם וְאֵת שׁוֹפְרֹתֵיהֶם וְאֵת כָּל־אִישׁ יִשְׂרָאֵל שִׁלַּח אִישׁ לְאֹהָלָיו וּבִשְׁלֹשׁ־מֵאוֹת הָאִישׁ הֶחֱזִיק וּמַחֲנֵה מִדְיָן הָיָה לוֹ מִתָּחַת בָּעֵמֶק: ח

9

That night GOD said to him, "Come, attack the camp, for I have delivered it into your hands.

*vai-HEE ba-LAI-lah ha-HU va-YO-mer ay-LAV a-do-NAI KUM RAYD ba-ma-kha-NEH KEE n'-ta-TEEV b'-ya-DE-kha*

וַיְהִי בַּלַּיְלָה הַהוּא וַיֹּאמֶר אֵלָיו יְהֹוָה קוּם רֵד בַּמַּחֲנֶה כִּי נְתַתִּיו בְּיָדֶךָ: ט

10

And if you are afraid to attack, first go down to the camp with your attendant Purah

*v'-im ya-RAY a-TAH la-RE-det RAYD a-TAH u-fu-RAH na-ar-KHA el ha-ma-kha-NEH*

וְאִם־יָרֵא אַתָּה לָרֶדֶת רֵד אַתָּה וּפֻרָה נַעַרְךָ אֶל־הַמַּחֲנֶה: י

11 and listen to what they say; after that you will have the courage to attack the camp." So he went down with his attendant Purah to the outposts of the warriors who were in the camp.—

v'-sha-ma-TA mah y'-da-BAY-ru v'-a-KHAR te-khe-ZAK-nah ya-DE-kha v'-ya-rad-TA ba-ma-kha-NEH va-YAY-red HU u-fu-RAH na-a-RO el k'-TZAY ha-kha-mu-SHEEM a-SHER ba-ma-kha-NEH

וְשָׁמַעְתָּ מַה־יְדַבֵּרוּ וְאַחַר תֶּחֱזַקְנָה יָדֶיךָ וְיָרַדְתָּ בַּמַּחֲנֶה וַיֵּרֶד הוּא וּפֻרָה נַעֲרוֹ אֶל־ קְצֵה הַחֲמֻשִׁים אֲשֶׁר בַּמַּחֲנֶה: יא

12 Now Midian, Amalek, and all the Kedemites were spread over the plain, as thick as locusts; and their camels were countless, as numerous as the sands on the seashore.—

u-mid-YAN va-a-ma-LAYK v'-khol b'-nay KE-dem no-f'-LEEM ba-AY-mek ka-ar-BEH la-ROV v'-lig-ma-lay-HEM AYN mis-PAR ka-KHOL she-al s'-FAT ha-YAM la-ROV

וּמִדְיָן וַעֲמָלֵק וְכָל־ בְּנֵי־קֶדֶם נֹפְלִים בָּעֵמֶק כָּאַרְבֶּה לָרֹב וְלִגְמַלֵּיהֶם אֵין מִסְפָּר כַּחוֹל שֶׁעַל־שְׂפַת הַיָּם לָרֹב: יב

13 Gideon came there just as one man was narrating a dream to another. "Listen," he was saying, "I had this dream: There was a commotion —a loaf of barley bread was whirling through the Midianite camp. It came to a tent and struck it, and it fell; it turned it upside down, and the tent collapsed."

va-ya-VO gid-ON v'-hi-NAY EESH m'-sa-PAYR l'-ray-AY-hu kha-LOM va-YO-mer hi-NAY kha-LOM kha-LAM-tee v'-hi-NAY tz'-LEEL LE-khem s'-o-REEM mit-ha-PAYKH b'-ma-kha-NAY mid-YAN va-ya-VO ad ha-O-hel va-ya-KAY-hu va-yi-POL va-ya-haf-KHAY-hu l'-ma-LAH v'-na-FAL ha-O-hel

וַיָּבֹא גִדְעוֹן וְהִנֵּה־אִישׁ מְסַפֵּר לְרֵעֵהוּ חֲלוֹם וַיֹּאמֶר הִנֵּה חֲלוֹם חָלַמְתִּי וְהִנֵּה צְלִיל לֶחֶם שְׂעֹרִים מִתְהַפֵּךְ בְּמַחֲנֵה מִדְיָן וַיָּבֹא עַד־הָאֹהֶל וַיַּכֵּהוּ וַיִּפֹּל וַיַּהַפְכֵהוּ לְמַעְלָה וְנָפַל הָאֹהֶל: יג

14 | To this the other responded, "That can only mean the sword of the Israelite Gideon son of Joash. God is delivering Midian and the entire camp into his hands."

*va-YA-an ray-AY-hu va-YO-mer AYN ZOT bil-TEE im KHE-rev gid-ON ben yo-ASH EESH yis-ra-AYL na-TAN ha-e-lo-HEEM b'-ya-DO et mid-YAN v'-et kol ha-ma-kha-NEH*

וַיַּעַן רֵעֵהוּ וַיֹּאמֶר אֵין זֹאת בִּלְתִּי אִם־חֶרֶב גִּדְעוֹן בֶּן־יוֹאָשׁ אִישׁ יִשְׂרָאֵל נָתַן הָאֱלֹהִים בְּיָדוֹ אֶת־מִדְיָן וְאֶת־כָּל־הַמַּחֲנֶה:

יד

15 | When Gideon heard the dream told and interpreted, he bowed low. Returning to the camp of Israel, he shouted, "Come on! GOD has delivered the Midianite camp into your hands!"

*vai-HEE khish-MO-a gid-ON et mis-PAR ha-kha-LOM v'-et shiv-RO va-yish-TA-khu va-YA-shov el ma-kha-NAY yis-ra-AYL va-YO-mer KU-mu kee na-TAN a-do-NAI b'-yed-KHEM et ma-kha-NAY mid-YAN*

וַיְהִי כִשְׁמֹעַ גִדְעוֹן אֶת־מִסְפַּר הַחֲלוֹם וְאֶת־שִׁבְרוֹ וַיִּשְׁתָּחוּ וַיָּשָׁב אֶל־מַחֲנֵה יִשְׂרָאֵל וַיֹּאמֶר קוּמוּ כִּי־נָתַן יְהֹוָה בְּיֶדְכֶם אֶת־מַחֲנֵה מִדְיָן:

טו

16 | He divided the three hundred men into three columns and equipped them all with a ram's horn and an empty jar, with a torch in each jar.

*va-YA-khatz et sh'-losh may-OT ha-EESH sh'-lo-SHAH ra-SHEEM va-yi-TAYN sho-fa-ROT b'-yad ku-LAM v'-kha-DEEM ray-KEEM v'-la-pi-DEEM b'-TOKH ha-ka-DEEM*

וַיַּחַץ אֶת־שְׁלֹשׁ־מֵאוֹת הָאִישׁ שְׁלֹשָׁה רָאשִׁים וַיִּתֵּן שׁוֹפָרוֹת בְּיַד־כֻּלָּם וְכַדִּים רֵיקִים וְלַפִּדִים בְּתוֹךְ הַכַּדִּים:

טז

17 | "Watch me," he said, "and do the same. When I get to the outposts of the camp, do exactly as I do."

*va-YO-mer a-lay-HEM mi-ME-nee tir-U v'-KHAYN ta-a-SU v'-hi-NAY a-no-KHEE VA bik-TZAY ha-ma-kha-NEH v'-ha-YAH kha-a-SHER e-e-SEH KAYN ta-a-SUN*

וַיֹּאמֶר אֲלֵיהֶם מִמֶּנִּי תִרְאוּ וְכֵן תַּעֲשׂוּ וְהִנֵּה אָנֹכִי בָא בִּקְצֵה הַמַּחֲנֶה וְהָיָה כַאֲשֶׁר אֶעֱשֶׂה כֵּן תַּעֲשׂוּן:

יז

| | | |
|---|---|---|
| 18 | When I and all those with me blow our horns, you too, all around the camp, will blow your horns and shout, 'For GOD and for Gideon!'" | *v'-ta-ka-TEE ba-sho-FAR a-no-KHEE v'-khol a-SHER i-TEE ut-ka-TEM ba-sho-fa-ROT gam a-TEM s'-vee-VOT kol ha-ma-kha-NEH va-a-mar-TEM la-do-NAI ul-gid-ON* | וְתָקַעְתִּי בַּשּׁוֹפָר אָנֹכִי וְכָל־אֲשֶׁר אִתִּי וּתְקַעְתֶּם בַּשּׁוֹפָרוֹת גַּם־אַתֶּם סְבִיבוֹת כָּל־הַמַּחֲנֶה וַאֲמַרְתֶּם לַיהוָה וּלְגִדְעוֹן: יח |

| | | |
|---|---|---|
| 19 | Gideon and the hundred men with him arrived at the outposts of the camp, at the beginning of the middle watch, just after the sentries were posted. They sounded the horns and smashed the jars that they had with them, | *va-ya-VO gid-ON u-may-ah EESH a-sher i-TO bik-TZAY ha-ma-kha-NEH ROSH ha-ash-MO-ret ha-tee-kho-NAH AKH ha-KAYM hay-KEE-mu et ha-sho-m'-REEM va-yit-k'-U ba-sho-fa-ROT v'-na-FOTZ ha-ka-DEEM a-SHER b'-ya-DAM* | וַיָּבֹא גִדְעוֹן וּמֵאָה־אִישׁ אֲשֶׁר־אִתּוֹ בִּקְצֵה הַמַּחֲנֶה רֹאשׁ הָאַשְׁמֹרֶת הַתִּיכוֹנָה אַךְ הָקֵם הֵקִימוּ אֶת־הַשֹּׁמְרִים וַיִּתְקְעוּ בַּשּׁוֹפָרוֹת וְנָפוֹץ הַכַּדִּים אֲשֶׁר בְּיָדָם: יט |

| | | |
|---|---|---|
| 20 | and the three columns blew their horns and broke their jars. Holding the torches in their left hands and the horns for blowing in their right hands, they shouted, "A sword for GOD and for Gideon!" | *va-yit-k'-U sh'-LO-shet ha-ra-SHEEM ba-sho-fa-ROT va-yish-b'-RU ha-ka-DEEM va-ya-kha-ZEE-ku v'-yad s'-mo-LAM ba-la-pi-DEEM uv-yad y'-mee-NAM ha-sho-fa-ROT lit-KO-a va-yik-r'-U KHE-rev la-do-NAI ul-gid-ON.* | וַיִּתְקְעוּ שְׁלֹשֶׁת הָרָאשִׁים בַּשּׁוֹפָרוֹת וַיִּשְׁבְּרוּ הַכַּדִּים וַיַּחֲזִיקוּ בְיַד־שְׂמֹאולָם בַּלַּפִּדִים וּבְיַד־יְמִינָם הַשּׁוֹפָרוֹת לִתְקוֹעַ וַיִּקְרְאוּ חֶרֶב לַיהוָה וּלְגִדְעוֹן: כ |

| | | |
|---|---|---|
| 21 | They remained standing where they were, surrounding the camp; but the entire camp ran about yelling, and took to flight. | *va-ya-am-DU EESH takh-TAV sa-VEEV la-ma-kha-NEH va-YA-rotz kol ha-ma-kha-NEH va-ya-REE-u va-ya-NU-su.* | וַיַּעַמְדוּ אִישׁ תַּחְתָּיו סָבִיב לַמַּחֲנֶה וַיָּרָץ כָּל־הַמַּחֲנֶה וַיָּרִיעוּ (וַיָּנִיסוּ) [וַיָּנוּסוּ]: כא |

22

For when the three hundred horns were sounded, GOD turned every man's sword against his fellow, throughout the camp, and the entire host fled as far as Beth-shittah and on to Zererah—as far as the outskirts of Abel-meholah near Tabbath.

*va-yit-k'-U sh'-losh may-OT ha-sho-fa-ROT va-YA-sem a-do-NAI AYT KHE-rev EESH b'-ray-AYH-hu uv-khol ha-ma-kha-NEH va-YA-nos ha-ma-kha-NEH ad BAYT ha-shi-TAH tz'-ray-RA-tah AD s'-fat a-VAYL m'-kho-LAH al ta-BAT.*

וַיִּתְקְעוּ שְׁלֹשׁ־מֵאוֹת הַשּׁוֹפָרוֹת וַיָּשֶׂם יְהֹוָה אֵת חֶרֶב אִישׁ בְּרֵעֵהוּ וּבְכָל־הַמַּחֲנֶה וַיָּנָס הַמַּחֲנֶה עַד־בֵּית הַשִּׁטָּה צְרֵרָתָה עַד שְׂפַת־אָבֵל מְחוֹלָה עַל־ טַבָּת: כב

23

And now Israel's side from Naphtali and Asher and from all of Manasseh rallied for the pursuit of the Midianites.

*va-yi-tza-AYK eesh yis-ra-AYL mi-naf-ta-LEE u-min a-SHAYR, u-min kol m'-na-SHEH va-yir-d'-FU a-kha-RAY mid-YAN.*

וַיִּצָּעֵק אִישׁ־יִשְׂרָאֵל מִנַּפְתָּלִי וּמִן־אָשֵׁר וּמִן־כָּל־מְנַשֶּׁה וַיִּרְדְּפוּ אַחֲרֵי מִדְיָן: כג

24

Gideon also sent messengers all through the hill country of Ephraim with this order: "Go down ahead of the Midianites and seize their access to the water all along the Jordan down to Beth-barah." So all of Ephraim's force rallied and seized the waterside down to Beth-barah by the Jordan.

*u-mal-a-KHEEM sha-LAKH gid-ON b'-khol HAR ef-RA-yim lay-MOR r'-DU lik-RAT mid-YAN v'-likh-DU la-HEM et ha-MA-yim AD BAYT ba-RAH v'-et ha-yar-DAYN va-yi-tza-AYK kol EESH ef-RA-yim va-yil-k'-DU et ha-MA-yim AD BAYT ba-RAH v'-et ha-yar-DAYN.*

וּמַלְאָכִים שָׁלַח גִּדְעוֹן בְּכָל־הַר אֶפְרַיִם לֵאמֹר רְדוּ לִקְרַאת מִדְיָן וְלִכְדוּ לָהֶם אֶת־הַמַּיִם עַד בֵּית בָּרָה וְאֶת־ הַיַּרְדֵּן וַיִּצָּעֵק כָּל־אִישׁ־ אֶפְרַיִם וַיִּלְכְּדוּ אֶת־ הַמַּיִם עַד בֵּית בָּרָה וְאֶת־הַיַּרְדֵּן: כד

25

They pursued the Midianites and captured Midian's two generals, Oreb and Zeeb. They killed Oreb at the Rock of Oreb and they killed Zeeb at the Winepress of Zeeb; and they brought the heads of Oreb and Zeeb from the other side of the Jordan to Gideon.

*va-yil-k'-DU sh'-nay sa-RAY mid-YAN et o-RAYV v'-et z'-AYV va-ya-har-GU et o-RAYV b'-tzur o-RAYV v'-et z'-AYV ha-r'-GU v'-ye-kev z'-AYV va-yir-d'-FU el mid-YAN v'-rosh o-RAYV uz-AYV hay-VEE-U el gid-ON may-AY-ver la-yar-DAYN.*

וַיִּלְכְּדוּ שְׁנֵי־שָׂרֵי מִדְיָן
אֶת־עֹרֵב וְאֶת־זְאֵב
וַיַּהַרְגוּ אֶת־עוֹרֵב
בְּצוּר־עוֹרֵב וְאֶת־
זְאֵב הָרְגוּ בְיֶקֶב־זְאֵב
וַיִּרְדְּפוּ אֶל־מִדְיָן
וְרֹאשׁ־עֹרֵב וּזְאֵב
הֵבִיאוּ אֶל־גִּדְעוֹן
מֵעֵבֶר לַיַּרְדֵּן׃

כה

# 8

חו

1

And Ephraim's force said to him, "Why did you do that to us— not calling us when you went to fight the Midianites?" And they rebuked him severely.

*va-yo-m'-RU ay-LAV EESH ef-RA-yim, mah ha-da-VAR ha-ZEH a-SEE-ta LA-nu, l'-vil-TEE k'-ROT LA-nu, kee ha-LAKH-ta l'-hi-la-KHAYM b'-mid-YAN; vai-ree-VUN it-TO, b'-choz-KAH.*

וַיֹּאמְרוּ אֵלָיו אִישׁ אֶפְרַיִם מָה־הַדָּבָר הַזֶּה עָשִׂיתָ לָּנוּ לְבִלְתִּי קְרֹאות לָנוּ כִּי הָלַכְתָּ לְהִלָּחֵם בְּמִדְיָן וַיְרִיבוּן אִתּוֹ בְּחָזְקָה׃ א

2

But he answered them, "After all, what have I accomplished compared to you? Why, Ephraim's gleanings are better than Abiezer's vintage!

*va-yo-MER a-lay-HEM meh a-SEE-tee a-TAH ka-KHEM ha-LO TOV o-l'-LOT ef-RA-yim miv-TZEER a-vee-E-zer.*

וַיֹּאמֶר אֲלֵיהֶם מֶה־ עָשִׂיתִי עַתָּה כָּכֶם הֲלֹא טוֹב עֹלְלוֹת אֶפְרַיִם מִבְצִיר אֲבִיעֶזֶר׃ ב

3

God has delivered the Midianite generals Oreb and Zeeb into your hands, and what was I able to do compared to you?" And when he spoke in this fashion, their anger against him abated.

*b'-yed-KHEM na-TAN e-lo-HEEM et sa-RAY mid-YAN et o-RAYV v'-et z'-AYV u-mah ya-KHOL-tee a-SOT ka-KHEM AZ ra-f'-TAH ru-KHAM may-a-LAV b'-da-b'-RO ha-da-VAR ha-ZEH.*

בְּיֶדְכֶם נָתַן אֱלֹהִים אֶת־שָׂרֵי מִדְיָן אֶת־עֹרֵב וְאֶת־זְאֵב וּמַה־יָּכֹלְתִּי עֲשׂוֹת כָּכֶם אָז רָפְתָה רוּחָם מֵעָלָיו בְּדַבְּרוֹ הַדָּבָר הַזֶּה׃ ג

4

Gideon came to the Jordan and crossed it. The three hundred men with him were famished, but still in pursuit.

*va-ya-VO gid-ON ha-yar-DAY-nah o-VAYR HU ush-losh may-OT ha-EESH a-SHER i-TO a-yay-FEEM v'-ro-d'-FEEM.*

וַיָּבֹא גִדְעוֹן הַיַּרְדֵּנָה עֹבֵר הוּא וּשְׁלֹשׁ־מֵאוֹת הָאִישׁ אֲשֶׁר אִתּוֹ עֲיֵפִים וְרֹדְפִים׃ ד

5
He said to the people of Succoth, "Please give some loaves of bread to the troops who are right behind me, for they are famished, and I am pursuing Zebah and Zalmunna, the kings of Midian."

*va-YO-mer l'-an-SHAY su-KOT t'-nu NA ki-k'-ROT LE-khem la-AM a-SHER b'-rag-LAI kee a-yay-FEEM HAYM v'-a-no-KHEE ro-DAYF a-kha-RAY ZE-vakh v'-tzal-MU-na mal-KHAY mid-YAN.*

וַיֹּאמֶר לְאַנְשֵׁי סֻכּוֹת תְּנוּ־נָא כִּכְּרוֹת לֶחֶם לָעָם אֲשֶׁר בְּרַגְלָי כִּי־עֲיֵפִים הֵם וְאָנֹכִי רֹדֵף אַחֲרֵי זֶבַח וְצַלְמֻנָּע מַלְכֵי מִדְיָן: ה

6
But the officials of Succoth replied, "Are Zebah and Zalmunna already in your hands, that we should give bread to your army?"

*va-YO-mer sa-RAY su-KOT ha-KHAF ZE-vakh v'-tzal-mu-NA a-TAH b'-ya-DE-kha kee ni-TAYN litz-va-a-KHA LA-khem.*

וַיֹּאמֶר שָׂרֵי סֻכּוֹת הֲכַף זֶבַח וְצַלְמֻנָּע עַתָּה בְּיָדֶךָ כִּי־נִתֵּן לִצְבָאֲךָ לָחֶם: ו

7
"I swear," declared Gideon, "when GOD delivers Zebah and Zalmunna into my hands, I'll thresh your bodies upon desert thorns and briers!"

*va-YO-mer gid-ON la-KHAYN b'-TAYT a-do-NAI et ZE-vakh v'-et tzal-mu-NA b'-ya-DEE v'-dash-TEE et b'-sar-KHEM et ko-TZAY ha-mid-BAR v'-et ha-bar-ko-NEEM.*

וַיֹּאמֶר גִּדְעוֹן לָכֵן בְּתֵת יְהוָה אֶת־זֶבַח וְאֶת־צַלְמֻנָּע בְּיָדִי וְדַשְׁתִּי אֶת־בְּשַׂרְכֶם אֶת־קוֹצֵי הַמִּדְבָּר וְאֶת־הַבַּרְקֳנִים: ז

8
From there he went up to Penuel and made the same request of them; but the people of Penuel gave him the same reply as the people of Succoth.

*va-YA-al mi-SHAM p'-nu-AYL, vai-da-BAYR a-lay-HEM ka-ZOT; va-ya-a-NU o-TO an-SHAY f'-nu-AYL, ka-a-SHER a-NU an-SHAY su-KOT.*

וַיַּעַל מִשָּׁם פְּנוּאֵל וַיְדַבֵּר אֲלֵיהֶם כָּזֹאת וַיַּעֲנוּ אוֹתוֹ אַנְשֵׁי פְנוּאֵל כַּאֲשֶׁר עָנוּ אַנְשֵׁי סֻכּוֹת: ח

9
So he also threatened the people of Penuel: "When I come back safe, I'll tear down this tower!"

*va-YO-mer gam l'-an-SHAY f'-nu-AYL lay-MOR b'-shu-VEE v'-sha-LOM e-TOTZ et ha-mig-DAL ha-ZEH.*

וַיֹּאמֶר גַּם־לְאַנְשֵׁי פְנוּאֵל לֵאמֹר בְּשׁוּבִי בְשָׁלוֹם אֶתֹּץ אֶת־הַמִּגְדָּל הַזֶּה: ט

10 Now Zebah and Zalmunna were at Karkor with their army of about 15,000; these were all that remained of the entire host of the Kedemites, for the slain numbered 120,000 fighters.

*v'-ZE-vakh v'-tzal-mu-NA ba-kar-KOR u-ma-kha-nay-HEM i-MAM ka-kha-MAY-shet a-SAR E-lef KOL ha-no-ta-REEM mi-KOL ma-kha-NAY v'-nay KE-dem v'-ha-no-f'-LEEM may-AH v'-es-REEM E-lef EESH sho-LAYF KHA-rev.*

וְזֶבַח וְצַלְמֻנָּע בַּקַּרְקֹר וּמַחֲנֵיהֶם עִמָּם כַּחֲמֵשֶׁת עָשָׂר אֶלֶף כֹּל הַנּוֹתָרִים מִכֹּל מַחֲנֵה בְּנֵי־קֶדֶם וְהַנֹּפְלִים מֵאָה וְעֶשְׂרִים אֶלֶף אִישׁ שֹׁלֵף חָרֶב:

י

11 Gideon marched up the road of the tent dwellers, up to east of Nobah and Jogbehah, and routed the camp, which was off guard.

*va-YA-al gid-ON DE-rekh ha-sh'-khu-NAY va-o-ha-LEEM mi-KE-dem l'-NO-vakh v'-yog-b'-HAH; va-YAKH et ha-ma-kha-NEH v'-ha-ma-kha-NEH ha-YAH VE-takh.*

וַיַּעַל גִּדְעוֹן דֶּרֶךְ הַשְּׁכוּנֵי בָאֳהָלִים מִקֶּדֶם לְנֹבַח וְיָגְבֳּהָה וַיַּךְ אֶת־הַמַּחֲנֶה וְהַמַּחֲנֶה הָיָה בֶטַח:

יא

12 Zebah and Zalmunna took to flight, with Gideon in pursuit. He captured Zebah and Zalmunna, the two kings of Midian, and threw the whole army into panic.

*va-ya-NU-su ZE-vakh v'-tzal-mu-NA va-yir-DOF a-kha-ray-HEM va-yil-KOD et sh'-NAY mal-KHAY mid-YAN et ZE-vakh v'-et tzal-mu-NA v'-khol ha-ma-kha-NEH he-khe-REED.*

וַיָּנֻסוּ זֶבַח וְצַלְמֻנָּע וַיִּרְדֹּף אַחֲרֵיהֶם וַיִּלְכֹּד אֶת־שְׁנֵי מַלְכֵי מִדְיָן אֶת־זֶבַח וְאֶת־צַלְמֻנָּע וְכָל־הַמַּחֲנֶה הֶחֱרִיד:

יב

13 On his way back from the battle at the Ascent of Heres, Gideon son of Joash

*va-YA-shov gid-ON ben yo-ASH min ha-mil-kha-MAH mil-ma-a-LAY, he-KHA-res.*

וַיָּשָׁב גִּדְעוֹן בֶּן־יוֹאָשׁ מִן־הַמִּלְחָמָה מִלְמַעֲלֵה הֶחָרֶס:

יג

14 captured a young man from among the people of Succoth and interrogated him. The latter drew up for him a list of the officials and elders of Succoth, seventy-seven in number.

*va-yil-kod NA-ar may-an-SHAY su-KOT va-yish-a-LAY-hu va-yikh-TOV ay-LAV et sa-RAY su-KOT v'-et z'-kay-NE-ha shiv-EEM v'-shiv-AH EESH.*

יד וַיִּלְכָּד־נַעַר מֵאַנְשֵׁי סֻכּוֹת וַיִּשְׁאָלֵהוּ וַיִּכְתֹּב אֵלָיו אֶת־שָׂרֵי סֻכּוֹת וְאֶת־זְקֵנֶיהָ שִׁבְעִים וְשִׁבְעָה אִישׁ:

15 Then he came to the people of Succoth and said, "Here are Zebah and Zalmunna, about whom you mocked me, saying, 'Are Zebah and Zalmunna already in your hands, that we should give your famished men bread?'"

*va-ya-VO el an-SHAY su-KOT va-YO-mer hi-NAY ZE-vakh v'-tzal-mu-NA a-SHER khay-raf-TEM o-TEE lay-MOR ha-KHAF ZEV-akh v'-tzal-mu-NA a-TAH b'-ya-DE-kha KEE ni-TAYN la-a-na-SHE-kha ha-y'-ay-FEEM LA-khem.*

טו וַיָּבֹא אֶל־אַנְשֵׁי סֻכּוֹת וַיֹּאמֶר הִנֵּה זֶבַח וְצַלְמֻנָּע אֲשֶׁר חֵרַפְתֶּם אוֹתִי לֵאמֹר הֲכַף זֶבַח וְצַלְמֻנָּע עַתָּה בְּיָדֶךָ כִּי נִתֵּן לַאֲנָשֶׁיךָ הַיְּעֵפִים לָחֶם:

16 And he took the elders of the city and, [bringing] desert thorns and briers, he punished the people of Succoth with them.

*va-yi-KAKH et zik-NAY ha-EER v'-et ko-TZAY ha-mid-BAR v'-et ha-bar-ko-NEEM va-YO-da ba-HEM AYT an-SHAY su-KOT.*

טז וַיִּקַּח אֶת־זִקְנֵי הָעִיר וְאֶת־קוֹצֵי הַמִּדְבָּר וְאֶת־הַבַּרְקָנִים וַיֹּדַע בָּהֶם אֵת אַנְשֵׁי סֻכּוֹת:

17 As for Penuel, he tore down its tower and killed the townspeople.

*v'-et mig-DAL p'-nu-AYL na-TATZ; va-ya-ha-ROG et an-SHAY ha-EER.*

יז וְאֶת־מִגְדַּל פְּנוּאֵל נָתָץ וַיַּהֲרֹג אֶת־אַנְשֵׁי הָעִיר:

18 Then he asked Zebah and Zalmunna, "Those men you killed at Tabor, what were they like?" "They looked just like you," they replied, "like sons of a king."

*va-YO-mer el ZEV-akh v'-el tzal-mu-NA ay-FOH ha-a-na-SHEEM a-SHER ha-rag-TEM b'-ta-VOR; va-yo-m'-RU ka-MO-kha kh'-mo-HEM e-KHAD k'-TO-ar b'-NAY ha-ME-lekh.*

וַיֹּאמֶר אֶל־זֶבַח וְאֶל־
צַלְמֻנָּע אֵיפֹה הָאֲנָשִׁים
אֲשֶׁר הֲרַגְתֶּם בְּתָבוֹר
וַיֹּאמְרוּ כָּמוֹךָ כְמוֹהֶם
אֶחָד כְּתֹאַר בְּנֵי
הַמֶּלֶךְ: יח

19 "They were my brothers," he declared, "the sons of my mother. As GOD lives, if you had spared them, I would not kill you."

*va-YO-mer a-KHAI b'-nay i-MEE HAYM khai a-do-NAI LU ha-kha-yi-TEM o-TAM LO ha-RAG-tee et-KHEM.*

וַיֹּאמַר אַחַי בְּנֵי־
אִמִּי הֵם חַי־יְהֹוָה לוּ
הַחֲיִתֶם אוֹתָם לֹא
הָרַגְתִּי אֶתְכֶם: יט

20 And he commanded his oldest son Jether, "Go kill them!" But the boy did not draw his sword, for he was timid, being still a boy.

*va-YO-mer l'-YE-ter b'-kho-RO KUM ha-ROG o-TAM v'-LO sha-LAF ha-NA-ar khar-BO KEE ya-RAY KEE o-DE-nu NA-ar.*

וַיֹּאמֶר לְיֶתֶר בְּכוֹרוֹ
קוּם הֲרֹג אוֹתָם וְלֹא־
שָׁלַף הַנַּעַר חַרְבּוֹ כִּי
יָרֵא כִּי עוֹדֶנּוּ נָעַר: כ

21 Then Zebah and Zalmunna said, "Come, you slay us; for strength comes with manhood." So Gideon went over and killed Zebah and Zalmunna, and he took the crescents that were on the necks of their camels.

*va-YO-mer ZEV-akh v'-tzal-mu-NA KUM a-TAH uf-ga BA-nu KEE kha-EESH g'-vu-ra-TO; va-YA-kom gid-ON va-ya-ha-ROG et ZE-vakh v'-et tzal-mu-NA va-yi-KAKH et ha-sa-ha-ro-NEEM a-SHER b'-tza-v'-RAY g'-ma-lay-HEM*

וַיֹּאמֶר זֶבַח וְצַלְמֻנָּע
קוּם אַתָּה וּפְגַע־בָּנוּ כִּי
כָאִישׁ גְּבוּרָתוֹ וַיָּקָם
גִּדְעוֹן וַיַּהֲרֹג אֶת־זֶבַח
וְאֶת־צַלְמֻנָּע וַיִּקַּח
אֶת־הַשַּׂהֲרֹנִים אֲשֶׁר
בְּצַוְּארֵי גְמַלֵּיהֶם: כא

22 Then Israel's side said to Gideon, "Rule over us—you, your son, and your grandson as well; for you have saved us from the Midianites."

*va-yo-m'-RU eesh yis-ra-AYL el gid-ON m'-shol BA-nu gam a-TAH gam bin-KHA GAM ben b'-NE-kha KEE ho-sha-TA-nu mi-YAD mid-YAN.*

וַיֹּאמְרוּ אִישׁ־יִשְׂרָאֵל אֶל־גִּדְעוֹן מְשָׁל־בָּנוּ גַּם־אַתָּה גַּם־בִּנְךָ גַּם בֶּן־בְּנֶךָ כִּי הוֹשַׁעְתָּנוּ מִיַּד מִדְיָן: כב

23 But Gideon replied, "I will not rule over you myself, nor shall my son rule over you; GOD alone shall rule over you."

*va-YO-MER a-lay-HEM gid-ON lo em-SHOL a-NEE ba-KHEM v'-lo yim-SHOL b'-NEE ba-KHEM a-do-NAI yim-SHOL ba-KHEM.*

וַיֹּאמֶר אֲלֵהֶם גִּדְעוֹן לֹא־אֶמְשֹׁל אֲנִי בָּכֶם וְלֹא־יִמְשֹׁל בְּנִי בָּכֶם יְהֹוָה יִמְשֹׁל בָּכֶם: כג

24 And Gideon said to them, "I have a request to make of you: Each of you give me the earring you received as booty." (The Midianites had golden earrings, for they were Ishmaelites.)

*va-YO-MER a-lay-HEM gid-ON esh-a-LAH mi-KEM sh'-ay-LAH ut-nu LEE EESH NE-zem sh'-la-LO kee niz-MAY za-HAV la-HEM kee yish-m'-ay-LEEM HAYM.*

וַיֹּאמֶר אֲלֵהֶם גִּדְעוֹן אֶשְׁאֲלָה מִכֶּם שְׁאֵלָה וּתְנוּ־לִי אִישׁ נֶזֶם שְׁלָלוֹ כִּי־נִזְמֵי זָהָב לָהֶם כִּי יִשְׁמְעֵאלִים הֵם: כד

25 "Certainly!" they replied. And they spread out a cloth, and everyone threw onto it the earring he had received as booty.

*va-yo-m'-RU na-TON ni-TAYN va-yif-r'-SU et ha-sim-LAH va-yash-LEE-khu SHA-mah EESH NE-zem sh'-la-LO.*

וַיֹּאמְרוּ נָתוֹן נִתֵּן וַיִּפְרְשׂוּ אֶת־הַשִּׂמְלָה וַיַּשְׁלִיכוּ שָׁמָּה אִישׁ נֶזֶם שְׁלָלוֹ: כה

26 The weight of the golden earrings that he had requested came to 1,700 shekels of gold; this was in addition to the crescents and the pendants and the purple robes worn by the kings of Midian and in addition to the collars on the necks of their camels.

*vai-HEE mish-KAL niz-MAY ha-za-HAV a-SHER sha-AL E-lef ush-va may-OT za-HAV l'-VAD min ha-sa-ha-ro-NEEM v'-ha-n'-tee-FOT u-vig-DAY ha-ar-ga-MAN she-AL mal-KHAY mid-YAN ul-VAD min ha-a-na-KOT a-SHER b'-tza-v'-RAY g'-ma-lay-HEM.*

וַיְהִי מִשְׁקַל נִזְמֵי הַזָּהָב אֲשֶׁר שָׁאַל אֶלֶף וּשְׁבַע מֵאוֹת זָהָב לְבַד מִן־הַשַּׂהֲרֹנִים וְהַנְּטִיפוֹת וּבִגְדֵי הָאַרְגָּמָן שֶׁעַל מַלְכֵי מִדְיָן וּלְבַד מִן־הָעֲנָקוֹת אֲשֶׁר בְּצַוְּארֵי גְּמַלֵּיהֶם: כו

27 Gideon made an ephod of this gold and set it up in his own town of Ophrah. There all Israel went astray after it, and it became a snare to Gideon and his household.

*va-YA-as o-TO gid-ON l'-ay-FOD va-ya-TZAYG o-TO v'-ee-RO b'-of-RAH va-yiz-NU khol yis-ra-AYL a-kha-RAV SHAM vai-HEE l'-gid-ON ul-vay-TO l'-mo-KAYSH.*

וַיַּעַשׂ אוֹתוֹ גִדְעוֹן לְאֵפוֹד וַיַּצֵּג אוֹתוֹ בְעִירוֹ בְּעָפְרָה וַיִּזְנוּ כָל־יִשְׂרָאֵל אַחֲרָיו שָׁם וַיְהִי לְגִדְעוֹן וּלְבֵיתוֹ לְמוֹקֵשׁ: כז

28 Thus Midian submitted to the Israelites and did not raise its head again; and the land was tranquil for forty years in Gideon's time.

*va-yi-ka-NA mid-YAN lif-NAY b'-NAY yis-ra-AYL v'-LO ya-S'-FU la-SAYT ro-SHAM va-tish-KOT ha-A-retz ar-ba-EEM sha-NAH bee-MAY gid-ON.*

וַיִּכָּנַע מִדְיָן לִפְנֵי בְּנֵי יִשְׂרָאֵל וְלֹא יָסְפוּ לָשֵׂאת רֹאשָׁם וַתִּשְׁקֹט הָאָרֶץ אַרְבָּעִים שָׁנָה בִּימֵי גִדְעוֹן: כח

29 So Jerubbaal son of Joash retired to his own house.

*va-YAY-lekh y'-ru-BA-al ben yo-ASH va-YAY-shev b'-vay-TO.*

וַיֵּלֶךְ יְרֻבַּעַל בֶּן־יוֹאָשׁ וַיֵּשֶׁב בְּבֵיתוֹ: כט

30 Gideon had seventy sons of his own issue, for he had many wives.

*ul-gid-ON ha-YU shiv-EEM ba-NEEM, yo-tz'-AY y'-ray-KHO kee na-SHEEM ra-BOT HA-yu LO.*

וּלְגִדְעוֹן הָיוּ שִׁבְעִים בָּנִים יֹצְאֵי יְרֵכוֹ כִּי־נָשִׁים רַבּוֹת הָיוּ לוֹ: ל

| | | |
|---|---|---|
| 31 | A son was also born to him by his concubine in Shechem, and he named him Abimelech. | *u-fee-lag-SHO a-SHER bish-KHEM, ya-l'-dah LO gam HEE BAYN va-YA-sem et sh'-MO a-vee-ME-lekh.* | וּפִילַגְשׁוֹ אֲשֶׁר בִּשְׁכֶם יָלְדָה־לּוֹ גַם־הִיא בֵּן וַיָּשֶׂם אֶת־שְׁמוֹ אֲבִימֶלֶךְ: לא |
| 32 | Gideon son of Joash died at a ripe old age, and was buried in the tomb of his father Joash at Ophrah of the Abiezrites. | *va-YA-mot gid-ON ben yo-ASH b'-say-VAH to-VAH va-yi-ka-VAYR b'-KE-ver yo-ASH a-VEEV b'-of-RAH a-VEE ha-ez-REE.* | וַיָּמָת גִּדְעוֹן בֶּן־יוֹאָשׁ בְּשֵׂיבָה טוֹבָה וַיִּקָּבֵר בְּקֶבֶר יוֹאָשׁ אָבִיו בְּעָפְרָה אֲבִי הָעֶזְרִי: לב |
| 33 | After Gideon died, the Israelites again went astray after the Baalim, and they adopted Baal-berith as a god. | *vai-HEE ka-a-SHER MAYT gid-ON va-ya-SHU-vu b'-NAY yis-ra-AYL va-yiz-NU a-KHA-ray ha-b'-a-LEEM va-ya-SEE-mu la-HEM BA-al b'-REET lay-lo-HEEM.* | וַיְהִי כַּאֲשֶׁר מֵת גִּדְעוֹן וַיָּשׁוּבוּ בְּנֵי יִשְׂרָאֵל וַיִּזְנוּ אַחֲרֵי הַבְּעָלִים וַיָּשִׂימוּ לָהֶם בַּעַל בְּרִית לֵאלֹהִים: לג |
| 34 | The Israelites gave no thought to the ETERNAL their God, who saved them from all the enemies around them. | *v'-LO za-kh'-RU b'-NAY yis-ra-AYL et a-do-NAI e-lo-hay-HEM ha-ma-TZEEL o-TAM mi-YAD kol o-y'-vay-HEM mi-sa-VEEV.* | וְלֹא זָכְרוּ בְּנֵי יִשְׂרָאֵל אֶת־יְהֹוָה אֱלֹהֵיהֶם הַמַּצִּיל אוֹתָם מִיַּד כָּל־אֹיְבֵיהֶם מִסָּבִיב: לד |
| 35 | Nor did they show loyalty to the house of Jerubbaal-Gideon in return for all the good that he had done for Israel. | *v'-lo a-SU KHE-sed im BAYT y'-ru-BA-al gid-ON k'-khol ha-to-VAH a-SHER a-SAH im yis-ra-AYL.* | וְלֹא־עָשׂוּ חֶסֶד עִם־בֵּית יְרֻבַּעַל גִּדְעוֹן כְּכָל־הַטּוֹבָה אֲשֶׁר עָשָׂה עִם־יִשְׂרָאֵל: לה |

# The Leaders We Deserve

One of the Catholic practices that angered many believers and ultimately triggered the Protestant Reformation was the doctrine and practice of indulgences. The Catholic church proclaimed that sinners could buy forgiveness for their sins by paying money to the church. Even sinners who had already died and were suffering from purgatory could be immediately freed and forgiven if a living person paid for the indulgence.

Understandably, many people were repulsed by this practice, as it transformed religion into something selfish and functional. All that mattered was getting into heaven; God's larger plan for humankind was forgotten. As G.K. Chesterton wrote, "There is such a thing as a small and cramped eternity; you see it in many modern religions."

A similar phenomenon occurred among the people of Israel after the great leader Gideon died:

"After Gideon died, the Israelites again went astray after the Baalim, and they adopted Baal-berith as a god." (Judges 8:33)

What was this "Baal-berith god" that the Israelites adopted? The sages explain: "This refers to the fly-god of Baal Ekron. It teaches that everyone made a likeness of his idol and put it in his bag: whenever he thought of it he took it out of his bag and embraced and kissed it" (Talmud Shabbat 83b).

A fly-god? Why would the people of Israel abandon God for a tiny idol shaped like a fly that they could keep in their pockets?

In Jewish tradition, the fly represents the individual's evil inclination. Like a fly buzzing annoyingly around your face, the evil inclination pesters and distracts us until we lose sight of what truly matters in life, enticing us to focus on our petty desires. The fly represents smallness – those times when we focus on the trivial, selfish and insignificant while forgetting the important things and the big picture of life.

This is what happened to the people of Israel after Gideon died. They reduced God to a mini-idol that they could carry around in their pockets, transforming God and religion into something small and selfish. All they cared about were their own personal desires – a successful crop, making money, health for their family, and so on. The larger goal of the Bible – bringing God's glory down to the world – was completely forgotten.

By trivializing religion and becoming obsessed with selfish pursuits, the people paved the way for Abimelech, the evil son of Gideon, to become their leader. Like the people of his generation, Abimelech only cared about promoting himself and acquiring power. His selfishness, tragically, drove him to murder all but one of his siblings – the entire family of Gideon:

"Then he went to his father's house in Ophrah and killed his brothers, the sons of Jerubaal, seventy men on one stone." (Judges 9:5)

When a society trivializes religion and people become obsessed with their own selfish desires, it is only a matter of time before a leader with the very same qualities takes power. If our leaders are petty and selfish, it is a sign that we must reflect and look inwards. For each generation receives the leaders it deserves.

# 9

| | | |
|---|---|---|
| 1 | Abimelech son of Jerubbaal went to his mother's brothers in Shechem and spoke to them and to the whole clan of his mother's family. He said, | *va-YAY-lekh a-vee-ME-lekh ben y'-ru-BA-al sh'-KHE-mah, el a-KHAY i-MO; vai-da-BAYR a-lay-HEM v'-el kol mish-PA-hkat bayt a-VEE i-MO, lay-MOR.* |

וַיֵּלֶךְ אֲבִימֶלֶךְ בֶּן־
יְרֻבַּעַל שְׁכֶמָה אֶל־אֲחֵי
אִמּוֹ וַיְדַבֵּר אֲלֵיהֶם
וְאֶל־כָּל־מִשְׁפַּחַת בֵּית־
אֲבִי אִמּוֹ לֵאמֹר: **א**

| | | |
|---|---|---|
| 2 | "Put this question to all the citizens of Shechem: Which is better for you—to be ruled by all seventy sons of Jerubbaal, or to be ruled by one? And remember, I am your own flesh and blood." | *da-b'-ru NA b'-oz-NAY khol ba-a-LAY sh'-KHEM, mah TOV la-KHEM; ham-SHOL ba-KHEM shiv-EEM EESH, kol b'-NAY y'-ru-BA-al, im m'-SHOL ba-KHEM EESH e-KHAD, uz-khar-TEM ki atz-m'-KHEM uv-sar-KHEM A-nee.* |

דַּבְּרוּ־נָא בְּאָזְנֵי כָל־
בַּעֲלֵי שְׁכֶם מַה־טּוֹב
לָכֶם הַמְשֹׁל בָּכֶם
שִׁבְעִים אִישׁ כֹּל בְּנֵי
יְרֻבַּעַל אִם־מְשֹׁל בָּכֶם
אִישׁ אֶחָד וּזְכַרְתֶּם כִּי־
עַצְמְכֶם וּבְשַׂרְכֶם אָנִי: **ב**

| | | |
|---|---|---|
| 3 | His mother's brothers said all this in his behalf to all the citizens of Shechem, and they were won over to Abimelech; for they thought, "He is our kinsman." | *vai-da-b'-RU a-khay i-MO a-LAV b'-oz-NAY kol ba-a-LAY sh'-KHEM, AYT kol ha-d'-va-REEM ha-AY-leh, va-yayt li-BAM a-kha-RAY a-vee-ME-lekh, KEE a-m'-RU a-KHEE-nu hu.* |

וַיְדַבְּרוּ אֲחֵי־אִמּוֹ
עָלָיו בְּאָזְנֵי כָּל־בַּעֲלֵי
שְׁכֶם אֵת כָּל־הַדְּבָרִים
הָאֵלֶּה וַיֵּט לִבָּם אַחֲרֵי
אֲבִימֶלֶךְ כִּי אָמְרוּ
אָחִינוּ הוּא: **ג**

**4** They gave him seventy shekels from the temple of Baal-berith; and with this Abimelech hired some worthless and reckless men, and they followed him.

*va-yi-t'-nu LO shiv-EEM KE-sef mi-BAYT BA-al b'-REET; va-yis-KOR ba-HEM a-vee-ME-lekh, a-na-SHEEM ray-KEEM u-fo-kha-ZEEM, va-yay-l'-KHU a-kha-RAV.*

וַיִּתְּנוּ־לוֹ שִׁבְעִים כֶּסֶף מִבֵּית בַּעַל בְּרִית וַיִּשְׂכֹּר בָּהֶם אֲבִימֶלֶךְ אֲנָשִׁים רֵיקִים וּפֹחֲזִים וַיֵּלְכוּ אַחֲרָיו׃ ד

**5** Then he went to his father's house in Ophrah and killed his brothers, the sons of Jerubbaal, seventy in succession on one stone. Only Jotham, the youngest son of Jerubbaal, survived, because he went into hiding.

*va-ya-VO vayt a-VEEV of-RA-tah va-ya-ha-ROG et e-KHAV b'-NAY y'-ru-BA-al, shiv-EEM EESH al E-ven e-KHAT, va-yi-va-TAYR yo-TAM ben y'-ru-BA-al ha-ka-TON, KEE nekh-BA.*

וַיָּבֹא בֵית־אָבִיו עָפְרָתָה וַיַּהֲרֹג אֶת־אֶחָיו בְּנֵי־יְרֻבַּעַל שִׁבְעִים אִישׁ עַל־אֶבֶן אֶחָת וַיִּוָּתֵר יוֹתָם בֶּן־יְרֻבַּעַל הַקָּטֹן כִּי נֶחְבָּא׃ ה

**6** All the citizens of Shechem and all Beth-millo convened, and they proclaimed Abimelech king at the terebinth of the pillar at Shechem.

*va-yay-a-s'-FU kol ba-a-LAY sh'-KHEM v'-khol BAYT mil-LO, va-yay-l'-KHU va-yam-LEE-khu et a-vee-ME-lekh l'-ME-lekh, im ay-LON mu-TZAV a-SHER bish-KHEM.*

וַיֵּאָסְפוּ כָּל־בַּעֲלֵי שְׁכֶם וְכָל־בֵּית מִלּוֹ וַיֵּלְכוּ וַיַּמְלִיכוּ אֶת־אֲבִימֶלֶךְ לְמֶלֶךְ עִם־אֵלוֹן מֻצָּב אֲשֶׁר בִּשְׁכֶם׃ ו

**7** When Jotham was informed, he went and stood on top of Mount Gerizim and called out to them in a loud voice. "Citizens of Shechem!" he cried, "Listen to me, that God may listen to you.

*va-ya-GI-du l'-yo-TAM va-YAY-lekh va-ya-a-MOD b'-ROSH har g'-ri-ZEEM, va-yi-SA ko-LO, va-yik-RA va-YO-mer la-HEM, shim-U ay-LAI ba-a-LAY sh'-KHEM, v'-yish-MA a-lay-KHEM e-lo-HEEM.*

וַיַּגִּדוּ לְיוֹתָם וַיֵּלֶךְ וַיַּעֲמֹד בְּרֹאשׁ הַר־גְּרִזִים וַיִּשָּׂא קוֹלוֹ וַיִּקְרָא וַיֹּאמֶר לָהֶם שִׁמְעוּ אֵלַי בַּעֲלֵי שְׁכֶם וְיִשְׁמַע אֲלֵיכֶם אֱלֹהִים׃ ז

| | | | |
|---|---|---|---|
| 8 | "Once the trees went to anoint a king over themselves. They said to the olive tree, 'Reign over us.' | *ha-LOKH ha-l'-KHU ha-ay-TZEEM lim-SHO-akh a-lay-HEM ME-lekh, va-yo-m'-RU la-ZA-yit ma-l'-KHAH a-LAY-nu.* | הָלוֹךְ הָלְכוּ הָעֵצִים לִמְשֹׁחַ עֲלֵיהֶם מֶלֶךְ וַיֹּאמְרוּ לַזַּיִת (מלוכה) [מָלְכָה] עָלֵינוּ: ח |
| 9 | But the olive tree replied, 'Have I, through whom God and humans are honored, stopped yielding my rich oil, that I should go and wave above the trees?' | *va-YO-mer la-HEM ha-ZA-yit he-cho-DAL-tee et dish-NEE a-sher BEE, y'-kha-b'-DU e-lo-HEEM va-a-na-SHEEM; v'-ha-lakh-TEE la-NU-a al ha-ay-TZEEM.* | וַיֹּאמֶר לָהֶם הַזַּיִת הֶחֳדַלְתִּי אֶת־דִּשְׁנִי אֲשֶׁר־בִּי יְכַבְּדוּ אֱלֹהִים וַאֲנָשִׁים וְהָלַכְתִּי לָנוּעַ עַל־הָעֵצִים: ט |
| 10 | So the trees said to the fig tree, 'You come and reign over us.' | *va-yo-m'-RU ha-ay-TZEEM la-t'-ay-NAH, l'-khee AT mol-KHEE a-LAY-nu.* | וַיֹּאמְרוּ הָעֵצִים לַתְּאֵנָה לְכִי־אַתְּ מָלְכִי עָלֵינוּ: י |
| 11 | But the fig tree replied, 'Have I stopped yielding my sweetness, my delicious fruit, that I should go and wave above the trees?' | *va-TO-mer la-HEM ha-t'-AY-nah he-kho-DAL-tee et mot-KEE v'-et t'-nu-va-TEE ha-to-VAH, v'-ha-lakh-TEE la-NU-a al ha-ay-TZEEM.* | וַתֹּאמֶר לָהֶם הַתְּאֵנָה הֶחֳדַלְתִּי אֶת־מָתְקִי וְאֶת־תְּנוּבָתִי הַטּוֹבָה וְהָלַכְתִּי לָנוּעַ עַל־הָעֵצִים: יא |
| 12 | So the trees said to the vine, 'You come and reign over us.' | *va-yo-m'-RU ha-ay-TZEEM la-GA-fen l'-khee mol-KHEE a-LAY-nu* | וַיֹּאמְרוּ הָעֵצִים לַגֶּפֶן לְכִי־אַתְּ (מלוכי) [מָלְכִי] עָלֵינוּ: יב |

| | | |
|---|---|---|
| 13 | But the vine replied, 'Have I stopped yielding my new wine, which gladdens God and humans, that I should go and wave above the trees?' | *va-TO-mer la-HEM ha-GE-fen he-kho-DAL-tee et tee-ro-SHEE ham-sa-MAY-akh e-lo-HEEM va-a-na-SHEEM v'-ha-lakh-TEE la-NU-a al ha-ay-TZEEM* | וַתֹּאמֶר לָהֶם הַגֶּפֶן הֶחֳדַלְתִּי אֶת־תִּירוֹשִׁי הַמְשַׂמֵּחַ אֱלֹהִים וַאֲנָשִׁים וְהָלַכְתִּי לָנוּעַ עַל־הָעֵצִים: | יג |
| 14 | Then all the trees said to the thornbush, 'You come and reign over us.' | *va-yo-m'-RU khol ha-ay-TZEEM el ha-a-TAD LAYKH a-TAH m'-lokh a-LAY-ne* | וַיֹּאמְרוּ כָל־הָעֵצִים אֶל־הָאָטָד לֵךְ אַתָּה מְלָךְ־עָלֵינוּ: | יד |
| 15 | And the thornbush said to the trees, 'If you are acting honorably in anointing me king over you, come and take shelter in my shade; but if not, may fire issue from the thornbush and consume the cedars of Lebanon!' | *va-YO-mer ha-a-TAD el ha-ay-TZEEM, IM be-e-MET a-TEM mo-sh'-KHEEM o-TEE l'-ME-lekh a-lay-KHEM, BO-u kha-SU v'-tzi-LEE; v'-im A-yin TAY-tzay AYSH min ha-a-TAD, v'-to-KHAL et ar-ZAY ha-l'-va-NON.* | וַיֹּאמֶר הָאָטָד אֶל־הָעֵצִים אִם בֶּאֱמֶת אַתֶּם מֹשְׁחִים אֹתִי לְמֶלֶךְ עֲלֵיכֶם בֹּאוּ חֲסוּ בְצִלִּי וְאִם־אַיִן תֵּצֵא אֵשׁ מִן־הָאָטָד וְתֹאכַל אֶת־אַרְזֵי הַלְּבָנוֹן: | טו |
| 16 | "Now then, if you acted honorably and loyally in making Abimelech king, if you have done right by Jerubbaal and his house and have requited him according to his deserts— | *v'-a-TAH im be-e-MET uv-ta-MEEM a-see-TEM va-tam-LEE-khu et a-vee-ME-lekh v'-im to-VAH a-see-TEM im y'-ru-BA-al v'-im bay-TO v'-im kig-MUL ya-DAV a-SEE-tem LO* | וְעַתָּה אִם־בֶּאֱמֶת וּבְתָמִים עֲשִׂיתֶם וַתַּמְלִיכוּ אֶת־אֲבִימֶלֶךְ וְאִם־טוֹבָה עֲשִׂיתֶם עִם־יְרֻבַּעַל וְעִם־בֵּיתוֹ וְאִם־כִּגְמוּל יָדָיו עֲשִׂיתֶם לוֹ: | טז |

17 considering that my father fought for you and saved you from the Midianites at the risk of his life,

*a-sher nil-KHAM a-VEE a-lay-KHEM va-yash-LAYKH et naf-SHO mi-NE-ged va-ya-TZAYL et-KHEM mi-YAD mid-YAN*

אֲשֶׁר־נִלְחַם אָבִי
עֲלֵיכֶם וַיַּשְׁלֵךְ אֶת־
נַפְשׁוֹ מִנֶּגֶד וַיַּצֵּל
אֶתְכֶם מִיַּד מִדְיָן׃ יז

18 and now you have turned on my father's household, killed his sons (seventy in succession on one stone!) and set up Abimelech, the son of his handmaid, as king over the citizens of Shechem just because he is your kinsman—

*v'-a-TEM kam-TEM al BAYT a-VEE ha-YOM va-ta-har-GU et ba-NAV shiv-EEM EESH al E-ven e-KHAT va-tam-LEE-khu et a-vee-ME-lekh ben a-ma-TO al ba-a-LAY sh'-KHEM KEE a-khee-KHEM HU*

וְאַתֶּם קַמְתֶּם עַל־בֵּית
אָבִי הַיּוֹם וַתַּהַרְגוּ
אֶת־בָּנָיו שִׁבְעִים אִישׁ
עַל־אֶבֶן אֶחָת וַתַּמְלִיכוּ
אֶת־אֲבִימֶלֶךְ בֶּן־אֲמָתוֹ
עַל־בַּעֲלֵי שְׁכֶם כִּי
אֲחִיכֶם הוּא׃ יח

19 if, I say, you have this day acted honorably and loyally toward Jerubbaal and his house, have joy in Abimelech and may he likewise have joy in you.

*v'-im be-e-MET uv-ta-MEEM a-see-TEM im y'-ru-BA-al v'-im bay-TO ha-YOM ha-ZEH sim-KHU ba-a-vee-ME-lekh v'-yis-MAKH gam HU ba-KHEM*

וְאִם־בֶּאֱמֶת וּבְתָמִים
עֲשִׂיתֶם עִם־יְרֻבַּעַל
וְעִם־בֵּיתוֹ הַיּוֹם הַזֶּה
שִׂמְחוּ בַּאֲבִימֶלֶךְ
וְיִשְׂמַח גַּם־הוּא בָּכֶם׃ יט

20 But if not, may fire issue from Abimelech and consume the citizens of Shechem and Beth-millo, and may fire issue from the citizens of Shechem and Beth-millo and consume Abimelech!"

*v'-im A-yin TAY-tzay AYSH may-a-vee-ME-lekh v'-to-KHAL et ba-a-LAY sh'-KHEM v'-et BAYT mi-LO v'-tay-TZAY AYSH mi-ba-a-LAY sh'-KHEM u-mi-BAYT mi-LO v'-to-KHAL et a-vee-ME-lekh*

וְאִם־אַיִן תֵּצֵא אֵשׁ
מֵאֲבִימֶלֶךְ וְתֹאכַל
אֶת־בַּעֲלֵי שְׁכֶם וְאֶת־
בֵּית מִלּוֹא וְתֵצֵא אֵשׁ
מִבַּעֲלֵי שְׁכֶם וּמִבֵּית
מִלּוֹא וְתֹאכַל אֶת־
אֲבִימֶלֶךְ׃ כ

| | | | |
|---|---|---|---|
| 21 | With that, Jotham fled. He ran to Beer and stayed there, because of his brother Abimelech. | *va-YA-nos yo-TAM va-yiv-RAKH va-YAY-lekh b'-AY-rah va-YAY-shev SHAM mi-p'-NAY a-vee-ME-lekh a-KHEEV* | וַיָּנָס יוֹתָם וַיִּבְרַח וַיֵּלֶךְ בְּאֵרָה וַיֵּשֶׁב שָׁם מִפְּנֵי אֲבִימֶלֶךְ אָחִיו: כא |
| 22 | Abimelech held sway over Israel for three years. | *va-YA-sar a-vee-ME-lekh al yis-ra-AYL sha-LOSH sha-NEEM* | וַיָּשַׂר אֲבִימֶלֶךְ עַל־יִשְׂרָאֵל שָׁלֹשׁ שָׁנִים: כב |
| 23 | Then God sent a spirit of discord between Abimelech and the citizens of Shechem, and the citizens of Shechem broke faith with Abimelech— | *va-yish-LAKH a-lo-HEEM RU-akh ra-AH BAYN a-vee-ME-lekh u-VAYN ba-a-LAY sh'-KHEM va-yiv-g'-DU va-a-LAY sh'-KHEM ba-a-vee-ME-lekh* | וַיִּשְׁלַח אֱלֹהִים רוּחַ רָעָה בֵּין אֲבִימֶלֶךְ וּבֵין בַּעֲלֵי שְׁכֶם וַיִּבְגְּדוּ בַעֲלֵי־שְׁכֶם בַּאֲבִימֶלֶךְ: כג |
| 24 | to the end that the crime committed against the seventy sons of Jerubbaal might be avenged, and their blood recoil upon their brother Abimelech, who had slain them, and upon the citizens of Shechem, who had abetted him in the slaying of his brothers. | *la-VO kha-MAS shiv-EEM b'-nay y'-ru-BA-al v'-da-MAM la-SUM al a-vee-ME-lekh a-khee-HEM a-SHER ha-RAG o-TAM v'-AL ba-a-LAY sh'-KHEM a-sher khiz-KU et ya-DAV la-ha-ROG et e-KHAV* | לָבוֹא חֲמַס שִׁבְעִים בְּנֵי־יְרֻבָּעַל וְדָמָם לָשׂוּם עַל־אֲבִימֶלֶךְ אֲחִיהֶם אֲשֶׁר הָרַג אוֹתָם וְעַל בַּעֲלֵי שְׁכֶם אֲשֶׁר־חִזְּקוּ אֶת־יָדָיו לַהֲרֹג אֶת־אֶחָיו: כד |

| | | | |
|---|---|---|---|
| 25 | The citizens of Shechem planted ambuscades against him on the hilltops; and they robbed whoever passed by them on the road. Word of this reached Abimelech. | *va-ya-SEE-mu LO va-a-LAY sh'-KHEM m'-a-r'-VEEM AL ra-SHAY he-ha-REEM va-yig-z'-LU AYT kol a-sher ya-a-VOR a-lay-HEM ba-DA-rekh va-yu-GAD la-a-vee-ME-lekh* | וַיָּשִׂימוּ לוֹ בַעֲלֵי שְׁכֶם מְאָרְבִים עַל רָאשֵׁי הֶהָרִים וַיִּגְזְלוּ אֵת כָּל־אֲשֶׁר־יַעֲבֹר עֲלֵיהֶם בַּדָּרֶךְ וַיֻּגַּד לַאֲבִימֶלֶךְ: | כה |
| 26 | Then Gaal son of Ebed and his companions came passing through Shechem, and the citizens of Shechem gave him their confidence. | *va-ya-VO GA-al ben E-ved v'-e-KHAV va-ya-av-RU bish-KHEM va-yiv-t'-khu VO ba-a-LAY sh'-KHEM* | וַיָּבֹא גַּעַל בֶּן־עֶבֶד וְאֶחָיו וַיַּעַבְרוּ בִּשְׁכֶם וַיִּבְטְחוּ־בוֹ בַּעֲלֵי שְׁכֶם: | כו |
| 27 | They went out into the fields, gathered and trod out the vintage of their vineyards, and made a festival. They entered the temple of their god, and as they ate and drank they reviled Abimelech. | *va-yay-tz'-U ha-sa-DEH va-yiv-tz'-RU et kar-may-HEM va-yid-r'-KHU va-ya-a-SU hi-lu-LEEM va-ya-VO-u BAYT e-lo-hay-HEM va-yo-kh'-LU va-yish-TU vai-ka-l'-LU et a-vee-ME-lekh* | וַיֵּצְאוּ הַשָּׂדֶה וַיִּבְצְרוּ אֶת־כַּרְמֵיהֶם וַיִּדְרְכוּ וַיַּעֲשׂוּ הִלּוּלִים וַיָּבֹאוּ בֵּית אֱלֹהֵיהֶם וַיֹּאכְלוּ וַיִּשְׁתּוּ וַיְקַלְלוּ אֶת־אֲבִימֶלֶךְ: | כז |

| | | |
|---|---|---|
| Gaal son of Ebed said, "Who is Abimelech and who are [we] Shechemites, that we should serve him? This same son of Jerubbaal and his lieutenant Zebul once served the entourage of Hamor, the father of Shechem; so why should we serve him? | *va-YO-mer GA-al ben E-ved mee a-vee-ME-lekh u-mee sh'-KHEM KEE na-av-DE-nu ha-LO ven y'-ru-BA-al uz-VUL p'-kee-DO iv-DU et an-SHAY kha-MOR a-VEE sh'-KHEM u-ma-DU-a na-av-DE-nu a-NAKH-nu* | וַיֹּאמֶר גַּעַל בֶּן־עֶבֶד מִי־ אֲבִימֶלֶךְ וּמִי־שְׁכֶם כִּי נַעַבְדֶנּוּ הֲלֹא בֶן־יְרֻבַּעַל וּזְבֻל פְּקִידוֹ עִבְדוּ אֶת־ אַנְשֵׁי חֲמוֹר אֲבִי שְׁכֶם וּמַדּוּעַ נַעַבְדֶנּוּ אֲנָחְנוּ: כח |
| Oh, if only this people were under my command, I would get rid of Abimelech! One would challenge Abimelech, 'Fill up your ranks and come out here!'" | *u-MEE yi-TAYN et ha-AM ha-ZEH b'-ya-DEE v'-a-SEE-rah et a-vee-ME-lekh va-YO-mer la-a-vee-ME-lekh ra-BEH tz'-va-a-KHA va-TZAY-ah* | וּמִי יִתֵּן אֶת־הָעָם הַזֶּה בְּיָדִי וְאָסִירָה אֶת־אֲבִימֶלֶךְ וַיֹּאמֶר לַאֲבִימֶלֶךְ רַבֶּה צְבָאֲךָ וָצֵאָה: כט |
| When Zebul, the governor of the city, heard the words of Gaal son of Ebed, he was furious. | *va-yish-MA z'-VUL sar ha-EER et div-RAY GA-al ben A-ved va-YI-khar a-PO* | וַיִּשְׁמַע זְבֻל שַׂר־הָעִיר אֶת־דִּבְרֵי גַּעַל בֶּן־עֶבֶד וַיִּחַר אַפּוֹ: ל |
| He sent messages to Abimelech at Tormah to say, "Gaal son of Ebed and his companions have come to Shechem and they are inciting the city against you. | *va-yish-LAKH mal-a-KHEEM el a-vee-ME-lekh b'-tor-MAH lay-MOR hi-NAY GA-al ben E-ved v'-e-KHAV ba-EEM sh'-KHE-mah v'-hi-NAM tza-REEM et ha-EER a-LE-kha* | וַיִּשְׁלַח מַלְאָכִים אֶל־אֲבִימֶלֶךְ בְּתָרְמָה לֵאמֹר הִנֵּה גַעַל בֶּן־ עֶבֶד וְאֶחָיו בָּאִים שְׁכֶמָה וְהִנָּם צָרִים אֶת־הָעִיר עָלֶיךָ: לא |

| | | | |
|---|---|---|---|
| 32 | Therefore, set out at night with the forces you have with you and conceal yourself in the fields. | v'-a-TAH KUM LAI-lah a-TAH v'-ha-AM a-sher i-TAKH ve-e-ROV ba-sa-DEH | וְעַתָּה קוּם לַיְלָה אַתָּה וְהָעָם אֲשֶׁר־אִתָּךְ וֶאֱרֹב בַּשָּׂדֶה: | לב |
| 33 | Early next morning, as the sun rises, advance on the city. He and his troops will thereupon come out against you, and you will do to him whatever you find possible." | v'-ha-YAH va-BO-ker kiz-RO-akh ha-SHE-mesh tash-KEEM u-fa-shat-TA al ha-EER v'-hi-nay HU v'-ha-AM a-sher i-TO yo-tz'-EEM ay-LE-kha v'-a-SEE-ta LO ka-a-SHER tim-TZA ya-DE-kha | וְהָיָה בַבֹּקֶר כִּזְרֹחַ הַשֶּׁמֶשׁ תַּשְׁכִּים וּפָשַׁטְתָּ עַל־הָעִיר וְהִנֵּה־הוּא וְהָעָם אֲשֶׁר־אִתּוֹ יֹצְאִים אֵלֶיךָ וְעָשִׂיתָ לּוֹ כַּאֲשֶׁר תִּמְצָא יָדֶךָ: | לג |
| 34 | Abimelech and all the troops with him set out at night and disposed themselves against Shechem in four hiding places. | va-YA-kom a-vee-ME-lekh v'-khol ha-AM a-sher i-MO LAI-lah va-ye-er-VU al sh'-KHEM ar-ba-AH ra-SHEEM | וַיָּקָם אֲבִימֶלֶךְ וְכָל־הָעָם אֲשֶׁר־עִמּוֹ לָיְלָה וַיֶּאֶרְבוּ עַל־שְׁכֶם אַרְבָּעָה רָאשִׁים: | לד |
| 35 | When Gaal son of Ebed came out and stood at the entrance to the city gate, Abimelech and the troops with him emerged from concealment. | va-yay-TZAY GA-al ben E-ved va-ya-a-MOD PE-takh SHA-ar ha-EER va-YA-kom a-vee-ME-lekh v'-ha-AM a-sher i-TO min ha-ma-RAV | וַיֵּצֵא גַּעַל בֶּן־עֶבֶד וַיַּעֲמֹד פֶּתַח שַׁעַר הָעִיר וַיָּקָם אֲבִימֶלֶךְ וְהָעָם אֲשֶׁר־אִתּוֹ מִן־הַמַּאְרָב: | לה |
| 36 | Gaal saw the troops and said to Zebul, "Look, troops are coming down from the hilltops!" But Zebul said to him, "The shadows of the hills look to you like people." | va-yar GA-al et ha-AM va-YO-mer el z'-VUL hi-nay AM yo-RAYD may-ra-SHAY he-ha-REEM va-YO-mer ay-LAV z'-VUL AYT TZAYL he-ha-REEM a-TAH ro-EH ka-a-na-SHEEM | וַיַּרְא־גַּעַל אֶת־הָעָם וַיֹּאמֶר אֶל־זְבֻל הִנֵּה־עָם יוֹרֵד מֵרָאשֵׁי הֶהָרִים וַיֹּאמֶר אֵלָיו זְבֻל אֵת צֵל הֶהָרִים אַתָּה רֹאֶה כָּאֲנָשִׁים: | לו |

| | | | |
|---|---|---|---|
| 37 | Gaal spoke up again, "Look, troops are coming down from Tabbur-erez, and another column is coming from the direction of Elon-meonenim." | *va-YO-sef OD GA-al l'-da-BAYR va-YO-mer hi-nay AM yo-r'-DEEM may-IM ta-BUR ha-A-retz v'-rosh e-KHAD BA mi-DE-rekh ay-LON m'-o-n'-NEEM* | וַיֹּסֶף עוֹד גַּעַל לְדַבֵּר וַיֹּאמֶר הִנֵּה־עָם יוֹרְדִים מֵעִם טַבּוּר הָאָרֶץ וְרֹאשׁ־אֶחָד בָּא מִדֶּרֶךְ אֵלוֹן מְעוֹנְנִים: | לז |
| 38 | "Well," replied Zebul, "where is your boast, 'Who is Abimelech that we should serve him'? Are these not the troops you sneered at? Now go out and fight with them!" | *va-YO-mer ay-LAV z'-VUL a-YAY ay-FO FEE-kha a-SHER to-MAR MEE a-vee-ME-lekh KEE na-av-DE-nu ha-LO ZEH ha-AM a-SHER ma-AS-tah BO tzay NA a-TAH v'-hi-LA-khem BO* | וַיֹּאמֶר אֵלָיו זְבֻל אַיֵּה אֵפוֹא פִיךָ אֲשֶׁר תֹּאמַר מִי אֲבִימֶלֶךְ כִּי נַעַבְדֶנּוּ הֲלֹא זֶה הָעָם אֲשֶׁר מָאַסְתָּה בּוֹ צֵא־נָא עַתָּה וְהִלָּחֶם בּוֹ: | לח |
| 39 | So Gaal went out at the head of the citizens of Shechem and gave battle to Abimelech. | *va-YAY-tzay GA-al lif-NAY ba-a-LAY sh'-KHEM va-yi-LA-khem ba-a-vee-ME-lekh* | וַיֵּצֵא גַעַל לִפְנֵי בַּעֲלֵי שְׁכֶם וַיִּלָּחֶם בַּאֲבִימֶלֶךְ: | לט |
| 40 | But he had to flee before him, and Abimelech pursued him, and many fell slain, all the way to the entrance of the gate. | *va-yir-d'-FAY-hu a-vee-ME-lekh va-YA-nos mi-pa-NAV va-yi-p'-LU kha-la-LEEM ra-BEEM ad PE-takh ha-SHA-ar* | וַיִּרְדְּפֵהוּ אֲבִימֶלֶךְ וַיָּנָס מִפָּנָיו וַיִּפְּלוּ חֲלָלִים רַבִּים עַד־פֶּתַח הַשָּׁעַר: | מ |
| 41 | Then Abimelech stayed in Arumah, while Zebul expelled Gaal and his companions and kept them out of Shechem. | *va-YAY-shev a-vee-ME-lekh ba-ru-MAH vai-GA-resh z'-VUL et GA-al v'-et e-KHAV mi-SHE-vet bish-KHEM* | וַיֵּשֶׁב אֲבִימֶלֶךְ בָּארוּמָה וַיְגָרֶשׁ זְבֻל אֶת־גַּעַל וְאֶת־אֶחָיו מִשֶּׁבֶת בִּשְׁכֶם: | מא |

42 | The next day, people went out into the fields, and this was reported to Abimelech. | *vai-HEE mi-ma-kho-RAT va-yay-TZAY ha-AM ha-sa-DEH va-ya-GI-du la-a-vee-ME-lekh* | וַיְהִי מִמָּחֳרָת וַיֵּצֵא הָעָם הַשָּׂדֶה וַיַּגִּדוּ לַאֲבִימֶלֶךְ: | מב

43 | So he took his troops, divided them into three columns, and lay in ambush in the fields; and when he saw the people coming out of the city, he pounced upon them and struck them down. | *va-yi-KAKH et ha-AM va-ye-khe-TZAYM lish-lo-SHAH ra-SHEEM va-ye-e-ROV ba-sa-DEH va-YAR v'-hi-NAY ha-AM yo-TZAY min ha-EER va-YA-kom a-lay-HEM va-ya-KAYM* | וַיִּקַּח אֶת־הָעָם וַיֶּחֱצֵם לִשְׁלֹשָׁה רָאשִׁים וַיֶּאֱרֹב בַּשָּׂדֶה וַיַּרְא וְהִנֵּה הָעָם יֹצֵא מִן הָעִיר וַיָּקָם עֲלֵיהֶם וַיַּכֵּם: | מג

44 | While Abimelech and the column that followed him dashed ahead and took up a position at the entrance of the city gate, the other two columns rushed upon all that were in the open and struck them down. | *va-a-vee-ME-lekh v'-ha-ra-SHEEM a-SHER i-MO pa-sh'-TU va-ya-am-DU PE-takh SHA-ar ha-EER ush-NAY ha-ra-SHEEM pa-sh'-TU al kol a-SHER ba-sa-DEH va-ya-KUM* | וַאֲבִימֶלֶךְ וְהָרָאשִׁים אֲשֶׁר עִמּוֹ פָּשְׁטוּ וַיַּעַמְדוּ פֶּתַח שַׁעַר הָעִיר וּשְׁנֵי הָרָאשִׁים פָּשְׁטוּ עַל־כָּל־אֲשֶׁר בַּשָּׂדֶה וַיַּכּוּם: | מד

45 | Abimelech fought against the city all that day. He captured the city and massacred the people in it; he razed the town and sowed it with salt. | *va-a-vee-ME-lekh nil-KHAM ba-EER KOL ha-YOM ha-HU va-yil-KOD et ha-EER v'-et ha-AM a-sher BAH ha-RAG va-yi-TOTZ et ha-EER va-yiz-ra-E-ha ME-lakh* | וַאֲבִימֶלֶךְ נִלְחָם בָּעִיר כֹּל הַיּוֹם הַהוּא וַיִּלְכֹּד אֶת־הָעִיר וְאֶת־הָעָם אֲשֶׁר־בָּהּ הָרָג וַיִּתֹּץ אֶת־הָעִיר וַיִּזְרָעֶהָ מֶלַח: | מה

| | | |
|---|---|---|
| 46 | When all the citizens of the Tower of Shechem learned of this, they went into the tunnel of the temple of El-berith. | *va-yish-m'-U kol ba-al-LAY mig-dal sh'-KHEM va-ya-VO-u el tz'-REE-akh BAYT AYL b'-REET* | וַיִּשְׁמְעוּ כָּל־בַּעֲלֵי מִגְדַּל־שְׁכֶם וַיָּבֹאוּ אֶל־צְרִיחַ בֵּית אֵל בְּרִית: מו |
| 47 | When Abimelech was informed that all the citizens of the Tower of Shechem had gathered [there], | *va-yu-GAD la-a-vee-ME-lekh KEE hit-ka-b'-TZU kol ba-a-LAY mig-DAL sh'-KHEM* | וַיֻּגַּד לַאֲבִימֶלֶךְ כִּי הִתְקַבְּצוּ כָּל־בַּעֲלֵי מִגְדַּל־שְׁכֶם: מז |
| 48 | Abimelech and all the troops he had with him went up on Mount Zalmon. Taking an ax in his hand, Abimelech lopped off a tree limb and lifted it onto his shoulder. Then he said to the troops that accompanied him, "What you saw me do—quick, do the same!" | *va-YA-al a-vee-ME-lekh har tzal-MON HU v'-khol ha-AM a-sher i-TO va-yi-KAKH a-vee-ME-lekh et ha-kar-du-MOT b'-ya-DO va-yikh-ROT so-KHAT ay-TZEEM va-yi-sa-E-ha va-YA-sem al shikh-MO va-YO-mer el ha-AM a-sher i-MO MAH r'-ee-TEM a-SEE-tee ma-ha-RU a-SU kha-MO-nee* | וַיַּעַל אֲבִימֶלֶךְ הַר־צַלְמוֹן הוּא וְכָל־הָעָם אֲשֶׁר־אִתּוֹ וַיִּקַּח אֲבִימֶלֶךְ אֶת־הַקַּרְדֻּמּוֹת בְּיָדוֹ וַיִּכְרֹת שׂוֹכַת עֵצִים וַיִּשָּׂאֶהָ וַיָּשֶׂם עַל־שִׁכְמוֹ וַיֹּאמֶר אֶל־הָעָם אֲשֶׁר־עִמּוֹ מָה רְאִיתֶם עָשִׂיתִי מַהֲרוּ עֲשׂוּ כָמוֹנִי: מח |
| 49 | So each of the troops also lopped off a bough; then they marched behind Abimelech and laid them against the tunnel, and set fire to the tunnel over their heads. Thus all the people of the Tower of Shechem also perished, about a thousand men and women. | *va-yikh-r'-TU gam kol ha-AM EESH so-KHOH va-yay-l'-KHU a-akha-RAY a-vee-ME-lekh va-ya-SEE-mu al ha-tz'-REE-akh va-ya-TZEE-tu a-lay-HEM et ha-tz'-REE-akh ba-AYSH va-ya-MU-tu GAM kol an-SHAY mig-dal sh'-KHEM k'-E-lef EESH v'-i-SHAH* | וַיִּכְרְתוּ גַם־כָּל־הָעָם אִישׁ שׂוֹכֹה וַיֵּלְכוּ אַחֲרֵי אֲבִימֶלֶךְ וַיָּשִׂימוּ עַל־הַצְּרִיחַ וַיַּצִּיתוּ עֲלֵיהֶם אֶת־הַצְּרִיחַ בָּאֵשׁ וַיָּמֻתוּ גַּם כָּל־אַנְשֵׁי מִגְדַּל־שְׁכֶם כְּאֶלֶף אִישׁ וְאִשָּׁה: מט |

| 50 | Abimelech proceeded to Thebez; he encamped at Thebez and occupied it. | va-YAY-lekh a-vee-ME-lekh el tay-VAYTZ va-YI-khan b'-tay-VAYTZ va-yil-k'-DAH | וַיֵּלֶךְ אֲבִימֶלֶךְ אֶל־תֵּבֵץ וַיִּחַן בְּתֵבֵץ וַיִּלְכְּדָהּ: | נ |
|---|---|---|---|---|
| 51 | Within the town was a fortified tower; and men and women took refuge there, including all the citizens of the town. They shut themselves in, and went up on the roof of the tower. | u-mig-dal OZ ha-YAH v'-tokh ha-EER va-ya-NU-su SHA-mah kol ha-a-na-SHEEM v'-ha-na-SHEEM v'-KHOL ba-a-LAY ha-EER va-yis-g'-RU ba-a-DAM va-ya-a-LU al GAG ha-mig-DAL | וּמִגְדַּל־עֹז הָיָה בְתוֹךְ־הָעִיר וַיָּנֻסוּ שָׁמָּה כָּל־הָאֲנָשִׁים וְהַנָּשִׁים וְכֹל בַּעֲלֵי הָעִיר וַיִּסְגְּרוּ בַּעֲדָם וַיַּעֲלוּ עַל־גַּג הַמִּגְדָּל: | נא |
| 52 | Abimelech pressed forward to the tower and attacked it. He approached the door of the tower to set it on fire. | va-ya-VO a-vee-ME-lekh ad ha-mig-DAL va-yi-LA-khem BO va-yi-GASH ad PE-takh ha-mig-DAL l'-sor-FO va-AYSH | וַיָּבֹא אֲבִימֶלֶךְ עַד־הַמִּגְדָּל וַיִּלָּחֶם בּוֹ וַיִּגַּשׁ עַד־פֶּתַח הַמִּגְדָּל לְשָׂרְפוֹ בָאֵשׁ: | נב |
| 53 | But a woman dropped an upper millstone on Abimelech's head and cracked his skull. | va-tash-LAYKH i-SHAH a-KHAT PE-lakh RE-khev al ROSH a-vee-ME-lekh va-TA-ritz et gu-gol-TO | וַתַּשְׁלֵךְ אִשָּׁה אַחַת פֶּלַח רֶכֶב עַל־רֹאשׁ אֲבִימֶלֶךְ וַתָּרִץ אֶת־גֻּלְגָּלְתּוֹ: | נג |
| 54 | He immediately cried out to his attendant, his arms-bearer, "Draw your dagger and finish me off, that they may not say of me, 'A woman killed him!'" So his attendant stabbed him, and he died. | va-yik-RA m'-hay-RAH el ha-NA-ar no-SAY khay-LAV va-YO-mer LO sh'-LOF khar-b'-KHA u-mo-t'-TAY-nee pen YO-m'-ru LEE i-SHAH ha-ra-GAT-hu va-yid-k'-RAY-hu na-a-RO va-ya-MOT | וַיִּקְרָא מְהֵרָה אֶל־הַנַּעַר נֹשֵׂא כֵלָיו וַיֹּאמֶר לוֹ שְׁלֹף חַרְבְּךָ וּמוֹתְתֵנִי פֶּן־יֹאמְרוּ לִי אִשָּׁה הֲרָגָתְהוּ וַיִּדְקְרֵהוּ נַעֲרוֹ וַיָּמֹת: | נד |

| | | | |
|---|---|---|---|
| 55 | When those on Israel's side saw that Abimelech was dead, everyone went home. | *va-yir-U eesh yis-ra-AYL KEE MAYT a-vee-ME-lekh va-yay-l'-KHU EESH lim-ko-MO* | וַיִּרְאוּ אִישׁ־יִשְׂרָאֵל כִּי מֵת אֲבִימֶלֶךְ וַיֵּלְכוּ אִישׁ לִמְקֹמוֹ: נה |
| 56 | Thus God repaid Abimelech for the evil he had done to his father by slaying his seventy brothers; | *va-YA-shev e-lo-HEEM AYT ra-AT a-vee-ME-lekh a-SHER a-SAH l'-a-VEEV la-ha-ROG et shiv-EEM e-KHAV* | וַיָּשֶׁב אֱלֹהִים אֵת רָעַת אֲבִימֶלֶךְ אֲשֶׁר עָשָׂה לְאָבִיו לַהֲרֹג אֶת־שִׁבְעִים אֶחָיו: נו |
| 57 | and God likewise repaid the people of Shechem for all their wickedness. And so the curse of Jotham son of Jerubbaal was fulfilled upon them. | *v'-AYT kol ra-AT an-SHAY sh'-KHEM hay-SHEEV e-lo-HEEM b'-ro-SHAM va-ta-VO a-lay-HEM ki-l'-LAT yo-TAM ben y'-ru-BA-al* | וְאֵת כָּל־רָעַת אַנְשֵׁי שְׁכֶם הֵשִׁיב אֱלֹהִים בְּרֹאשָׁם וַתָּבֹא אֲלֵיהֶם קִלֲלַת יוֹתָם בֶּן־יְרֻבָּעַל: נז |

# 10   ─o⊱⊰o─   נ

| | | |
|---|---|---|
| 1 | After Abimelech, Tola son of Puah son of Dodo, of Issachar, arose to deliver Israel. He lived at Shamir in the hill country of Ephraim. | *va-YA-kom a-kha-RAY a-vee-ME-lekh l'-ho-SHEE-a et yis-ra-AYL to-LA ben pu-AH ben do-DO EESH yi-sa-KHAR v'-hu yo-SHAYV b'-sha-MEER b'-HAR ef-RA-yim* | וַיָּקָם אַחֲרֵי אֲבִימֶלֶךְ לְהוֹשִׁיעַ אֶת־יִשְׂרָאֵל תּוֹלָע בֶּן־פּוּאָה בֶּן־דּוֹדוֹ אִישׁ יִשָּׂשכָר וְהוּא־יֹשֵׁב בְּשָׁמִיר בְּהַר אֶפְרָיִם: א |
| 2 | He led Israel for twenty-three years; then he died and was buried at Shamir. | *va-yish-POT et yis-ra-AYL es-REEM v'-sha-LOSH sha-NAH va-YA-mot va-yi-ka-VAYR b'-sha-MEER* | וַיִּשְׁפֹּט אֶת־יִשְׂרָאֵל עֶשְׂרִים וְשָׁלֹשׁ שָׁנָה וַיָּמָת וַיִּקָּבֵר בְּשָׁמִיר: ב |
| 3 | After him arose Jair the Gileadite, and he led Israel for twenty-two years. | *va-ya-KOM a-kha-RAV ya-EER ha-gil-a-DEE va-yish-POT et yis-ra-AYL es-REEM ush-TA-yim sha-NAH* | וַיָּקָם אַחֲרָיו יָאִיר הַגִּלְעָדִי וַיִּשְׁפֹּט אֶת־יִשְׂרָאֵל עֶשְׂרִים וּשְׁתַּיִם שָׁנָה: ג |
| 4 | (He had thirty sons, who rode on thirty burros and owned thirty boroughs in the region of Gilead; these are called Havvoth-jair to this day.) | *vai-hee LO sh'-lo-SHEEM ba-NEEM ro-kh'-VEEM al sh'-lo-SHEEM a-ya-REEM ush-lo-SHEEM a-ya-REEM la-HEM la-HEM yik-r'-U kha-VOT ya-EER AD ha-YOM ha-ZEH a-SHER b'-E-retz ha-gil-AD* | וַיְהִי־לוֹ שְׁלֹשִׁים בָּנִים רֹכְבִים עַל־שְׁלֹשִׁים עֲיָרִים וּשְׁלֹשִׁים עֲיָרִים לָהֶם לָהֶם יִקְרְאוּ חַוֹּת יָאִיר עַד הַיּוֹם הַזֶּה אֲשֶׁר בְּאֶרֶץ הַגִּלְעָד: ד |
| 5 | Then Jair died and was buried at Kamon. | *va-YA-mot ya-EER va-yi-ka-VAYR b'-ka-MON* | וַיָּמָת יָאִיר וַיִּקָּבֵר בְּקָמוֹן: ה |

| | | |
|---|---|---|
| 6 | The Israelites again did what was offensive to GOD. They served the Baalim and the Ashtaroth, and the gods of Aram, the gods of Sidon, the gods of Moab, the gods of the Ammonites, and the gods of the Philistines; they forsook and did not serve GOD. | *va-yo-SEE-fu b'-NAY yis-ra-AYL la-a-SOT ha-RA b'-ay-NAY a-do-NAI va-ya-av-DU et ha-b'-a-LEEM v'-et ha-ash-ta-ROT v'-et e-lo-HAY a-RAM v'-et e-lo-HAY tzee-DON v'-AYT e-lo-HAY mo-AV v'-AYT e-lo-HAY v'-NAY a-MON v'-AYT e-lo-HAY f'-lish-TEEM va-ya-az-VU et a-do-NAI v'-LO a-va-DU-hu* |

וַיֹּסִיפוּ בְּנֵי יִשְׂרָאֵל
לַעֲשׂוֹת הָרַע בְּעֵינֵי
יְהוָה וַיַּעַבְדוּ אֶת־
הַבְּעָלִים וְאֶת־
הָעַשְׁתָּרוֹת וְאֶת־אֱלֹהֵי
אֲרָם וְאֶת־אֱלֹהֵי צִידוֹן
וְאֵת אֱלֹהֵי מוֹאָב וְאֵת
אֱלֹהֵי בְנֵי־עַמּוֹן וְאֵת
אֱלֹהֵי פְלִשְׁתִּים וַיַּעַזְבוּ
אֶת־יְהוָה וְלֹא עֲבָדוּהוּ: ו

| | | |
|---|---|---|
| 7 | And GOD, incensed with Israel, surrendered them to the Philistines and to the Ammonites. | *va-yi-khar AF a-do-NAI b'-yis-ra-AYL va-yim-k'-RAYM b'-yad p'-lish-TEEM uv-YAD b'-NAY a-MON* |

וַיִּחַר־אַף יְהוָה
בְּיִשְׂרָאֵל וַיִּמְכְּרֵם בְּיַד־
פְּלִשְׁתִּים וּבְיַד בְּנֵי
עַמּוֹן: ז

| | | |
|---|---|---|
| 8 | That year they battered and shattered the Israelites—for eighteen years—all the Israelites beyond the Jordan, in [what had been] the land of the Amorites in Gilead. | *va-yir-a-TZU vai-ro-tz'-TZU et b'-NAY yis-ra-AYL ba-sha-NAH ha-HEE sh'-mo-NEH es-RAY sha-NAH et kol b'-NAY yis-ra-AYL b'-AY-ver ha-yar-DAYN b'-E-retz ha-e-mor-REE a-SHER ba-gil-AD* |

וַיִּרְעֲצוּ וַיְרֹצְצוּ אֶת־בְּנֵי
יִשְׂרָאֵל בַּשָּׁנָה הַהִיא
שְׁמֹנֶה עֶשְׂרֵה שָׁנָה
אֶת־כָּל־בְּנֵי יִשְׂרָאֵל
אֲשֶׁר בְּעֵבֶר הַיַּרְדֵּן
בְּאֶרֶץ הָאֱמֹרִי אֲשֶׁר
בַּגִּלְעָד: ח

| | | |
|---|---|---|
| 9 | The Ammonites also crossed the Jordan to make war on Judah, Benjamin, and the House of Ephraim. Israel was in great distress. | *va-ya-av-RU v'-nay a-MON et ha-yar-DAYN l'-hi-la-KHAYM gam bee-hu-DAH u-vin-ya-MEEN u-v'-VAYT ef-RA-yim va-TAY-tzer l'-yis-ra-AYL m'-OD* |

וַיַּעַבְרוּ בְנֵי־עַמּוֹן
אֶת־הַיַּרְדֵּן לְהִלָּחֵם
גַּם־בִּיהוּדָה וּבְבִנְיָמִין
וּבְבֵית אֶפְרָיִם וַתֵּצֶר
לְיִשְׂרָאֵל מְאֹד: ט

| | | | |
|---|---|---|---|
| 10 | Then the Israelites cried out to GOD, "We stand guilty before You, for we have forsaken our God and served the Baalim." | *va-yiz-a-KU b'-NAY yis-ra-AYL el a-do-NAI lay-MOR kha-TA-nu LAKH v'-KHEE a-ZAV-nu et e-lo-HAY-nu va-na-a-VOD et ha-b'-a-LEEM* | וַיִּזְעֲקוּ בְּנֵי יִשְׂרָאֵל אֶל־יְהֹוָה לֵאמֹר חָטָאנוּ לָךְ וְכִי עָזַבְנוּ אֶת־אֱלֹהֵינוּ וַנַּעֲבֹד אֶת־הַבְּעָלִים׃ ‍י |
| 11 | But GOD said to the Israelites, "[I have rescued you] from the Egyptians, from the Amorites, from the Ammonites, and from the Philistines. | *va-YO-mer a-do-NAI el b'-NAY yis-ra-AYL ha-LO mi-mitz-RA-yim u-min ha-e-mor-REE u-min b'-NAY a-MON u-min p'-lish-TEEM* | וַיֹּאמֶר יְהֹוָה אֶל־בְּנֵי יִשְׂרָאֵל הֲלֹא מִמִּצְרַיִם וּמִן־הָאֱמֹרִי וּמִן־בְּנֵי עַמּוֹן וּמִן־פְּלִשְׁתִּים׃ יא |
| 12 | The Sidonians, Amalek, and Maon also oppressed you; and when you cried out to Me, I saved you from them. | *v'-tzee-do-NEEM va-a-ma-LAYK u-ma-ON la-kha-TZU et-KHEM va-titz-a-KU ay-LAI va-o-SHEE-ah et-KHEM mi-ya-DAM* | וְצִידוֹנִים וַעֲמָלֵק וּמָעוֹן לָחֲצוּ אֶתְכֶם וַתִּצְעֲקוּ אֵלַי וָאוֹשִׁיעָה אֶתְכֶם מִיָּדָם׃ יב |
| 13 | Yet you have forsaken Me and have served other gods. No, I will not deliver you again. | *v'-a-TEM a-zav-TEM o-TEE va-ta-av-DU a-lo-HEEM a-khay-REEM la-KHAYN lo o-SEEF l'-ho-SHEE-a et-KHEM* | וְאַתֶּם עֲזַבְתֶּם אוֹתִי וַתַּעַבְדוּ אֱלֹהִים אֲחֵרִים לָכֵן לֹא־אוֹסִיף לְהוֹשִׁיעַ אֶתְכֶם׃ יג |
| 14 | Go cry to the gods you have chosen; let them deliver you in your time of distress!" | *l'-KHU v'-za-a-KU el ha-e-lo-HEEM a-SHER b'-khar-TEM BAM HAY-mah yo-SHEE-u la-KHEM b'-AYT tza-rat-KHEM* | לְכוּ וְזַעֲקוּ אֶל־הָאֱלֹהִים אֲשֶׁר בְּחַרְתֶּם בָּם הֵמָּה יוֹשִׁיעוּ לָכֶם בְּעֵת צָרַתְכֶם׃ יד |

| | | | |
|---|---|---|---|
| 15 | But the Israelites implored GOD: "We stand guilty. Do to us as You see fit; only save us this day!" | *va-yo-m'-RU b'-nay yis-ra-AYL el a-do-NAI kha-TA-nu a-say a-TAH LA-nu k'-khol ha-TOV b'-ay-NE-kha AKH ha-tzee-LAY-nu NA ha-YOM ha-ZEH* | וַיֹּאמְרוּ בְנֵי־יִשְׂרָאֵל אֶל־יְהֹוָה חָטָאנוּ עֲשֵׂה־אַתָּה לָנוּ כְּכָל־הַטּוֹב בְּעֵינֶיךָ אַךְ הַצִּילֵנוּ נָא הַיּוֹם הַזֶּה: טו |
| 16 | They removed the alien gods from among them and served GOD; and [God] could not bear the miseries of Israel. | *va-ya-SEE-ru et e-lo-HAY ha-nay-KHAR mi-kir-BAM va-ya-av-DU et a-do-NAI va-tik-TZAR naf-SHO ba-a-MAL yis-ra-AYL* | וַיָּסִירוּ אֶת־אֱלֹהֵי הַנֵּכָר מִקִּרְבָּם וַיַּעַבְדוּ אֶת־יְהֹוָה וַתִּקְצַר נַפְשׁוֹ בַּעֲמַל יִשְׂרָאֵל: טז |
| 17 | The Ammonites mustered and they encamped in Gilead; and the Israelites massed and they encamped at Mizpah. | *va-yitz-a-KU b'-NAY a-MON va-ya-kha-NU ba-gil-AD va-yay-a-s'-FU b'-NAY yis-ra-AYL va-ya-kha-NU ba-mitz-PAH* | וַיִּצָּעֲקוּ בְּנֵי עַמּוֹן וַיַּחֲנוּ בַּגִּלְעָד וַיֵּאָסְפוּ בְּנֵי יִשְׂרָאֵל וַיַּחֲנוּ בַּמִּצְפָּה: יז |
| 18 | The troops—the officers of Gilead—said to one another, "Let whoever is the first to fight the Ammonites be chieftain over all the inhabitants of Gilead." | *va-yo-m'-RU ha-AM sa-RAY gil-AD EESH el ray-AY-hu MEE ha-EESH a-SHER ya-KHAYL l'-hi-la-KHAYM biv-NAY a-MON yih-YEH l'-ROSH l'-KHOL yo-sh'-VAY gil-AD* | וַיֹּאמְרוּ הָעָם שָׂרֵי גִלְעָד אִישׁ אֶל־רֵעֵהוּ מִי הָאִישׁ אֲשֶׁר יָחֵל לְהִלָּחֵם בִּבְנֵי עַמּוֹן יִהְיֶה לְרֹאשׁ לְכֹל יֹשְׁבֵי גִלְעָד: יח |

# 11

1 Jephthah the Gileadite was an able warrior, who was the son of a certain prostitute. Jephthah's father was Gilead;

*v'-yif-TAKH ha-gil-a-DEE ha-YAH gi-BOR KHA-yil v'-HU ben i-SHAH zo-NAH va-YO-led gil-AD et yif-TAKH*

וְיִפְתָּח הַגִּלְעָדִי הָיָה גִּבּוֹר חַיִל וְהוּא בֶּן־ אִשָּׁה זוֹנָה וַיּוֹלֶד גִּלְעָד אֶת־יִפְתָּח: א

2 but Gilead also had sons by his wife, and when the wife's sons grew up, they drove Jephthah out. They said to him, "You shall have no share in our father's property, for you are the son of an outsider."

*va-YAT-led ay-shet gil-AD LO ba-NEEM va-yig-d'-LU v'-NAY ha-i-SHAH vai-ga-r'-SHU et yif-TAKH va-YO-m'-ru LO lo tin-KHAL b'-vayt a-VEE-nu KEE ben i-SHAH a-KHE-ret A-tah*

וַתֵּלֶד אֵשֶׁת־גִּלְעָד לוֹ בָּנִים וַיִּגְדְּלוּ בְנֵי־ הָאִשָּׁה וַיְגָרְשׁוּ אֶת־ יִפְתָּח וַיֹּאמְרוּ לוֹ לֹא־ תִנְחַל בְּבֵית־אָבִינוּ כִּי בֶּן־אִשָּׁה אַחֶרֶת אָתָּה: ב

3 So Jephthah fled from his brothers and settled in the Tob country. Men of low character gathered about Jephthah and went out raiding with him.

*va-yiv-RAKH yif-TAKH mi-p'-NAY e-KHAV va-YAY-shev b'-E-retz TOV va-yit-la-k'-TU el yif-TAKH a-na-SHEEM ray-KEEM va-yay-tz'-U i-MO*

וַיִּבְרַח יִפְתָּח מִפְּנֵי אֶחָיו וַיֵּשֶׁב בְּאֶרֶץ טוֹב וַיִּתְלַקְּטוּ אֶל־יִפְתָּח אֲנָשִׁים רֵיקִים וַיֵּצְאוּ עִמּוֹ: ג

4 Some time later, the Ammonites went to war against Israel.

*vai-HEE mi-ya-MEEM va-yi-la-kha-MU v'-nay a-mon im yis-ra-AYL*

וַיְהִי מִיָּמִים וַיִּלָּחֲמוּ בְנֵי־עַמּוֹן עִם־יִשְׂרָאֵל: ד

| | | | |
|---|---|---|---|
| 5 | And when the Ammonites attacked Israel, the elders of Gilead went to bring Jephthah back from the Tob country. | *vai-HEE ka-a-sher nil-kha-MU v'-nay a-MON im yis-ra-AYL va-yay-l'-KHU zik-NAY gil-AD la-KA-khat et yif-TAKH may-E-retz TOV* | וַיְהִי כַּאֲשֶׁר־נִלְחֲמוּ בְנֵי־עַמּוֹן עִם־יִשְׂרָאֵל וַיֵּלְכוּ זִקְנֵי גִלְעָד לָקַחַת אֶת־יִפְתָּח מֵאֶרֶץ טוֹב׃ ה |
| 6 | They said to Jephthah, "Come be our chief, so that we can fight the Ammonites." | *va-yo-m'-RU l'-yif-TAKH l'-KHAH v'-ha-YEE-tah LA-nu l'-ka-TZEEN v'-nil-kha-MAH biv-NAY a-MON* | וַיֹּאמְרוּ לְיִפְתָּח לְכָה וְהָיִיתָה לָּנוּ לְקָצִין וְנִלָּחֲמָה בִּבְנֵי עַמּוֹן׃ ו |
| 7 | Jephthah replied to the elders of Gilead, "You are the very people who rejected me and drove me out of my father's house. How can you come to me now when you are in trouble?" | *va-YO-mer yif-TAKH l'-zik-NAY gil-AD ha-LO a-TEM s'-nay-TEM o-TEE va-t'-ga-r'-SHU-nee mi-BAYT a-VEE u-ma-DU-a ba-TEM ay-LAI A-tah ka-a-SHER TZAR la-KHEM* | וַיֹּאמֶר יִפְתָּח לְזִקְנֵי גִלְעָד הֲלֹא אַתֶּם שְׂנֵאתֶם אוֹתִי וַתְּגָרְשׁוּנִי מִבֵּית אָבִי וּמַדּוּעַ בָּאתֶם אֵלַי עַתָּה כַּאֲשֶׁר צַר לָכֶם׃ ז |
| 8 | The elders of Gilead said to Jephthah, "Honestly, we have now turned back to you. If you come with us and fight the Ammonites, you shall be our commander over all the inhabitants of Gilead." | *va-yo-m'-RU zik-NAY gil-AD el yif-TAKH la-KHAYN a-TAH SHAV-nu ay-LE-kha v'-ha-lakh-TA i-MA-nu v'-nil-kham-TA biv-NAY a-MON v'-ha-YEE-ta LA-nu l'-ROSH l'-KHOL yo-sh'-VAY gil-AD* | וַיֹּאמְרוּ זִקְנֵי גִלְעָד אֶל־יִפְתָּח לָכֵן עַתָּה שַׁבְנוּ אֵלֶיךָ וְהָלַכְתָּ עִמָּנוּ וְנִלְחַמְתָּ בִּבְנֵי עַמּוֹן וְהָיִיתָ לָּנוּ לְרֹאשׁ לְכֹל יֹשְׁבֵי גִלְעָד׃ ח |

| | | | |
|---|---|---|---|
| 9 | Jephthah said to the elders of Gilead, "[Very well,] if you bring me back to fight the Ammonites and GOD delivers them to me, I am to be your commander." | *va-YO-mer yif-TAKH el zik-NAY gil-AD im m'-shee-VEEM a-TEM o-TEE l'-hi-la-KHAYM biv-NAY a-MON v'-na-TAN a-do-NAI o-TAM li-fa-NAI a-no-KHEE eh-YEH la-KHEM l'-ROSH* | וַיֹּאמֶר יִפְתָּח אֶל־זִקְנֵי גִלְעָד אִם־מְשִׁיבִים אַתֶּם אוֹתִי לְהִלָּחֵם בִּבְנֵי עַמּוֹן וְנָתַן יְהוָה אוֹתָם לְפָנָי אָנֹכִי אֶהְיֶה לָכֶם לְרֹאשׁ׃ | ט |
| 10 | And the elders of Gilead answered Jephthah, "GOD shall be witness between us: we will do just as you have said." | *va-yo-m'-RU zik-NAY gil-AD el yif-TAKH a-do-NAI yih-YEH sho-MAY-a bay-no-TAY-nu im LO khid-va-r'-KHA KAYN na-a-SEH* | וַיֹּאמְרוּ זִקְנֵי־גִלְעָד אֶל־יִפְתָּח יְהוָה יִהְיֶה שֹׁמֵעַ בֵּינוֹתֵינוּ אִם־לֹא כִדְבָרְךָ כֵּן נַעֲשֶׂה׃ | י |
| 11 | Jephthah went with the elders of Gilead, and the people made him their commander and chief. And Jephthah repeated all these terms before GOD at Mizpah. | *va-YAY-lekh yif-TAKH im zik-NAY gil-AD va-ya-SEE-mu ha-AM o-TO a-lay-HEM l'-ROSH ul-ka-TZEEN vai-da-BAYR yif-TAKH et kol d'-va-RAV lif-NAY a-do-NAI ba-mitz-PAH* | וַיֵּלֶךְ יִפְתָּח עִם־זִקְנֵי גִלְעָד וַיָּשִׂימוּ הָעָם אוֹתוֹ עֲלֵיהֶם לְרֹאשׁ וּלְקָצִין וַיְדַבֵּר יִפְתָּח אֶת־כָּל־דְּבָרָיו לִפְנֵי יְהוָה בַּמִּצְפָּה׃ | יא |
| 12 | Jephthah then sent messengers to the king of the Ammonites, saying, "What have you against me that you have come to make war on my country?" | *va-yish-LAKH yif-TAKH mal-a-KHEEM el ME-lekh b'-nay a-MON lay-MOR mah LEE v'-LAKH kee VA-ta ay-LAI l'-hi-la-KHAYM b'-ar-TZEE* | וַיִּשְׁלַח יִפְתָּח מַלְאָכִים אֶל־מֶלֶךְ בְּנֵי־עַמּוֹן לֵאמֹר מַה־לִּי וָלָךְ כִּי־בָאתָ אֵלַי לְהִלָּחֵם בְּאַרְצִי׃ | יב |

13 The king of the
Ammonites replied
to Jephthah's
messengers, "When
Israel came from
Egypt, they seized
the land that is mine,
from the Arnon to
the Jabbok as far as
the Jordan. Now,
then, restore it
peaceably."

*va-YO-mer ME-lekh
b'-nay a-MON el mal-
a-KHAY yif-TAKH kee
la-KAKH yis-ra-AYL
et ar-TZEE ba-a-lo-TO
mi-mitz-RA-yim may-ar-
NON v'-ad ha-ya-BOK
v'-ad ha-yar-DAYN
v'-a-TAH ha-SHEE-vah
et-HEN b'-sha-LOM*

יג וַיֹּאמֶר מֶלֶךְ בְּנֵי־עַמּוֹן
אֶל־מַלְאֲכֵי יִפְתָּח כִּי־
לָקַח יִשְׂרָאֵל אֶת־אַרְצִי
בַּעֲלוֹתוֹ מִמִּצְרַיִם
מֵאַרְנוֹן וְעַד־הַיַּבֹּק
וְעַד־הַיַּרְדֵּן וְעַתָּה
הָשִׁיבָה אֶתְהֶן בְּשָׁלוֹם:

14 Jephthah again
sent messengers
to the king of the
Ammonites.

*va-YO-sef OD yif-TAKH
va-yish-LAKH mal-a-
KHEEM el ME-lekh
b'-NAY a-MON*

יד וַיּוֹסֶף עוֹד יִפְתָּח
וַיִּשְׁלַח מַלְאָכִים אֶל־
מֶלֶךְ בְּנֵי עַמּוֹן:

15 He said to him,
"Thus said Jephthah:
Israel did not seize
the land of Moab
or the land of the
Ammonites.

*va-YO-mer LO KOH
a-MAR yif-TAKH lo
la-KAKH yis-ra-AYL et
E-retz mo-AV v'-et E-retz
b'-NAY a-MON*

טו וַיֹּאמֶר לוֹ כֹּה אָמַר
יִפְתָּח לֹא־לָקַח יִשְׂרָאֵל
אֶת־אֶרֶץ מוֹאָב וְאֶת־
אֶרֶץ בְּנֵי עַמּוֹן:

16 When they left
Egypt, Israel
traveled through the
wilderness to the Sea
of Reeds and went on
to Kadesh.

*KEE ba-a-lo-TAM mi-
mitz-RA-yim va-YAY-lekh
yis-ra-AYL ba-mid-BAR
ad yam SUF va-ya-VO
ka-DAY-shah*

טז כִּי בַּעֲלוֹתָם מִמִּצְרַיִם
וַיֵּלֶךְ יִשְׂרָאֵל בַּמִּדְבָּר
עַד־יַם־סוּף וַיָּבֹא
קָדֵשָׁה:

| | | | |
|---|---|---|---|
| 17 | Israel then sent messengers to the king of Edom, saying, 'Allow us to cross your country.' But the king of Edom would not consent. They also sent a mission to the king of Moab, and he refused. So Israel, after staying at Kadesh, | va-yish-LAKH yis-ra-AYL mal-a-KHEEM el ME-lekh e-DOM lay-MOR e-b'-rah NA v'-ar-TZE-kha v'-LO sha-MA ME-lekh e-DOM v'-GAM el ME-lekh mo-AV sha-LAKH v'-LO a-VAH va-yay-SHEV yis-ra-AYL b'-ka-DAYSH | וַיִּשְׁלַח יִשְׂרָאֵל מַלְאָכִים אֶל־מֶלֶךְ אֱדוֹם לֵאמֹר אֶעְבְּרָה־נָּא בְאַרְצֶךָ וְלֹא שָׁמַע מֶלֶךְ אֱדוֹם וְגַם אֶל־מֶלֶךְ מוֹאָב שָׁלַח וְלֹא אָבָה וַיֵּשֶׁב יִשְׂרָאֵל בְּקָדֵשׁ: יז |
| 18 | traveled on through the wilderness, skirting the land of Edom and the land of Moab. They kept to the east of the land of Moab until they encamped on the other side of the Arnon; and, since Moab ends at the Arnon, they never entered Moabite territory. | va-YAY-lekh ba-mid-BAR va-YA-sov et E-retz e-DOM v'-et E-retz mo-AV va-ya-VO mi-miz-rakh SHE-mesh l'-E-retz mo-AV va-ya-kha-NUN b'-AY-ver ar-NON v'-lo VA-u big-VUL mo-AV KEE ar-NON g-VUL mo-AV | וַיֵּלֶךְ בַּמִּדְבָּר וַיָּסָב אֶת־אֶרֶץ אֱדוֹם וְאֶת־אֶרֶץ מוֹאָב וַיָּבֹא מִמִּזְרַח־שֶׁמֶשׁ לְאֶרֶץ מוֹאָב וַיַּחֲנוּן בְּעֵבֶר אַרְנוֹן וְלֹא־בָאוּ בִּגְבוּל מוֹאָב כִּי אַרְנוֹן גְּבוּל מוֹאָב: יח |
| 19 | "Then Israel sent messengers to Sihon king of the Amorites, the king of Heshbon. Israel said to him, 'Allow us to cross through your country to our homeland.' | va-yish-LAKH yis-ra-AYL mal-a-KHEEM el see-KHON me-lekh ha-e-mo-REE ME-lekh khesh-BON va-YO-mer LO yis-ra-AYL na-b'-rah NA v'-ar-tz'-KHA ad m'-ko-MEE | וַיִּשְׁלַח יִשְׂרָאֵל מַלְאָכִים אֶל־סִיחוֹן מֶלֶךְ־הָאֱמֹרִי מֶלֶךְ חֶשְׁבּוֹן וַיֹּאמֶר לוֹ יִשְׂרָאֵל נַעְבְּרָה־נָּא בְאַרְצֶךָ עַד־מְקוֹמִי: יט |

| | | | |
|---|---|---|---|
| 20 | But Sihon would not trust Israel to pass through his territory. Sihon mustered all his troops, and they encamped at Jahaz; he engaged Israel in battle. | *v'-lo he-e-MEEN see-KHON et yis-ra-AYL a-VOR big-vu-LO va-ye-e-SOF see-KHON et kol a-MO va-ya-kha-NU b'-yah-TZAH va-yi-LA-khem im yis-ra-AYL* | וְלֹא־הֶאֱמִין סִיחוֹן אֶת־יִשְׂרָאֵל עֲבֹר בִּגְבֻלוֹ וַיֶּאֱסֹף סִיחוֹן אֶת־כָּל־עַמּוֹ וַיַּחֲנוּ בְּיָהְצָה וַיִּלָּחֶם עִם־יִשְׂרָאֵל: | כ |

| | | | |
|---|---|---|---|
| 21 | But the ETERNAL, the God of Israel, delivered Sihon and all his troops into Israel's hands, and they defeated them; and Israel took possession of all the land of the Amorites, the inhabitants of that land. | *va-yi-TAYN a-do-NAI e-lo-HAY yis-ra-AYL et see-KHON v'-et kol a-MO b'-YAD yis-ra-AYL va-ya-KUM va-YEE-rash yis-ra-AYL AYT kol E-retz ha-e-mo-REE yo-SHAYV ha-A-retz ha-HEE* | וַיִּתֵּן יְהוָה אֱלֹהֵי־יִשְׂרָאֵל אֶת־סִיחוֹן וְאֶת־כָּל־עַמּוֹ בְּיַד יִשְׂרָאֵל וַיַּכּוּם וַיִּירַשׁ יִשְׂרָאֵל אֵת כָּל־אֶרֶץ הָאֱמֹרִי יוֹשֵׁב הָאָרֶץ הַהִיא: | כא |

| | | | |
|---|---|---|---|
| 22 | Thus they possessed all the territory of the Amorites from the Arnon to the Jabbok and from the wilderness to the Jordan. | *va-YEE-r'-SHU AYT kol g'-VUL ha-e-mo-REE may-ar-NON v'-ad ha-ya-BOK u-min ha-mid-BAR v'-ad ha-yar-DAYN* | וַיִּירְשׁוּ אֵת כָּל־גְּבוּל הָאֱמֹרִי מֵאַרְנוֹן וְעַד־הַיַּבֹּק וּמִן־הַמִּדְבָּר וְעַד־הַיַּרְדֵּן: | כב |

| | | | |
|---|---|---|---|
| 23 | "Now, then, the ETERNAL, the God of Israel, dispossessed the Amorites before this covenanted people Israel; and should you possess their land? | *v'-a-TAH a-do-NAI e-lo-HAY yis-ra-AYL ho-REESH et ha-e-mo-REE mi-p'-NAY a-MO yis-ra-AYL v'-a-TAH tee-ra-SHE-nu* | וְעַתָּה יְהוָה אֱלֹהֵי יִשְׂרָאֵל הוֹרִישׁ אֶת־הָאֱמֹרִי מִפְּנֵי עַמּוֹ יִשְׂרָאֵל וְאַתָּה תִּירָשֶׁנּוּ: | כג |

| | | | |
|---|---|---|---|
| 24 | Do you not hold what Chemosh your god gives you to possess? So we will hold on to everything that the ETERNAL our God has given us to possess. | *ha-LO AYT a-SHER yo-ree-sh'-KHA k'-MOSH e-lo-HE-kha o-TO tee-RASH v'-AYT kol a-SHER ho-REESH a-do-NAI e-lo-HAY-nu mi-pa-NAY-nu o-TO nee-RASH* | הֲלֹא אֵת אֲשֶׁר יוֹרִישְׁךָ כְּמוֹשׁ אֱלֹהֶיךָ אוֹתוֹ תִירָשׁ וְאֵת כָּל־אֲשֶׁר הוֹרִישׁ יְהֹוָה אֱלֹהֵינוּ מִפָּנֵינוּ אוֹתוֹ נִירָשׁ: כד |
| 25 | "Besides, are you any better than Balak son of Zippor, king of Moab? Did he start a quarrel with Israel or go to war with them? | *v'-a-TAH ha-TOV TOV a-TAH mi-ba-LAK ben tzi-POR ME-lekh mo-AV ha-ROV RAV im yis-ra-AYL im nil-KHOM nil-KHAM BAM* | וְעַתָּה הֲטוֹב טוֹב אַתָּה מִבָּלָק בֶּן־צִפּוֹר מֶלֶךְ מוֹאָב הֲרוֹב רָב עִם־יִשְׂרָאֵל אִם־נִלְחֹם נִלְחַם בָּם: כה |
| 26 | "While Israel has been inhabiting Heshbon and its dependencies, and Aroer and its dependencies, and all the towns along the Arnon for three hundred years, why have you not tried to recover them all this time? | *b'-SHE-vet yis-ra-AYL b'-khesh-BON u-viv-no-TE-ha uv-ar-OR u-viv-no-TE-ha uv-khol he-a-REEM a-SHER al y'-DAY ar-NON sh'-LOSH may-OT sha-NAH u-ma-DU-a lo hi-tzal-TEM ba-AYT ha-HEE* | בְּשֶׁבֶת יִשְׂרָאֵל בְּחֶשְׁבּוֹן וּבִבְנוֹתֶיהָ וּבְעַרְעוֹר וּבִבְנוֹתֶיהָ וּבְכָל־הֶעָרִים אֲשֶׁר עַל־יְדֵי אַרְנוֹן שְׁלֹשׁ מֵאוֹת שָׁנָה וּמַדּוּעַ לֹא־הִצַּלְתֶּם בָּעֵת הַהִיא: כו |
| 27 | I have done you no wrong; yet you are doing me harm and making war on me. May GOD, who judges, decide today between the Israelites and the Ammonites!" | *v'-a-no-KHEE lo kha-TA-tee LAKH v'-a-TAH o-SEH i-TEE ra-AH l'-hi-LA-khem BEE yish-POT a-do-NAI ha-sho-FAYT ha-YOM BAYN b'-NAY yis-ra-AYL u-VAYN b'-NAY a-MON* | וְאָנֹכִי לֹא־חָטָאתִי לָךְ וְאַתָּה עֹשֶׂה אִתִּי רָעָה לְהִלָּחֶם בִּי יִשְׁפֹּט יְהֹוָה הַשֹּׁפֵט הַיּוֹם בֵּין בְּנֵי יִשְׂרָאֵל וּבֵין בְּנֵי עַמּוֹן: כז |

| |  |  |  |
|---|---|---|---|
| 28 | But the king of the Ammonites paid no heed to the message that Jephthah sent him. | v'-LO sha-MA ME-lekh b'-NAY a-MON el div-RAY yif-TAKH a-SHER sha-LAKH ay-LAV | וְלֹא שָׁמַע מֶלֶךְ בְּנֵי עַמּוֹן אֶל־דִּבְרֵי יִפְתָּח אֲשֶׁר שָׁלַח אֵלָיו: | כח |
| 29 | Then the spirit of GOD came upon Jephthah. He marched through Gilead and Manasseh, passing Mizpeh of Gilead; and from Mizpeh of Gilead he crossed over [to] the Ammonites. | va-t'-HEE al yif-TAKH RU-akh a-do-NAI va-ya-a-VOR et ha-gil-AD v'-et m'-na-SHEH va-ya-a-VOR et mitz-PAY gil-AD u-mi-mitz-PAY gil-AD a-VAR b'-NAY a-MON | וַתְּהִי עַל־יִפְתָּח רוּחַ יְהֹוָה וַיַּעֲבֹר אֶת־הַגִּלְעָד וְאֶת־מְנַשֶּׁה וַיַּעֲבֹר אֶת־מִצְפֵּה גִלְעָד וּמִמִּצְפֵּה גִלְעָד עָבַר בְּנֵי עַמּוֹן: | כט |
| 30 | And Jephthah made the following vow to GOD: "If you deliver the Ammonites into my hands, | va-yi-DAR yif-TAKH NE-der la-do-NAI va-yo-MAR im na-TON ti-TAYN et b'-NAY a-MON b'-ya-DEE | וַיִּדַּר יִפְתָּח נֶדֶר לַיהֹוָה וַיֹּאמַר אִם־נָתוֹן תִּתֵּן אֶת־בְּנֵי עַמּוֹן בְּיָדִי: | ל |
| 31 | then whatever comes out of the door of my house to meet me on my safe return from the Ammonites shall be GOD's and shall be offered by me as a burnt offering." | v'-ha-YAH ha-yo-TZAY a-SHER yay-TZAY mi-dal-TAY vay-TEE lik-ra-TEE b'-shu-VEE v'-sha-LOM mi-b'-NAY a-MON v'-ha-YAH la-do-NAI v'-ha-a-lee-TEE-hu o-LAH | וְהָיָה הַיּוֹצֵא אֲשֶׁר יֵצֵא מִדַּלְתֵי בֵיתִי לִקְרָאתִי בְּשׁוּבִי בְשָׁלוֹם מִבְּנֵי עַמּוֹן וְהָיָה לַיהֹוָה וְהַעֲלִיתִיהוּ עֹלָה: | לא |
| 32 | Jephthah crossed over to the Ammonites and attacked them, and GOD delivered them into his hands. | va-ya-a-VOR yif-TAKH el b'-NAY a-MON l'-hi-la-KHAYM BAM va-yi-t'-NAYM a-do-NAI b'-ya-DO | וַיַּעֲבֹר יִפְתָּח אֶל־בְּנֵי עַמּוֹן לְהִלָּחֶם בָּם וַיִּתְּנֵם יְהֹוָה בְּיָדוֹ: | לב |

33 He utterly routed them—from Aroer as far as Minnith, twenty towns—all the way to Abel-cheramim. So the Ammonites submitted to the Israelites.

va-ya-KAYM may-a-ro-AYR v'-ad bo-a-KHA mi-NEET es-REEM EER v'-AD a-VAYL k'-ra-MEEM ma-KAH g'-do-LAH m'-OD va-yi-ka-n'-U b'-NAY a-MON mi-p'-NAY b'-NAY yis-ra-AYL

וַיַּכֵּם מֵעֲרוֹעֵר וְעַד־בּוֹאֲךָ מִנִּית עֶשְׂרִים עִיר וְעַד אָבֵל כְּרָמִים מַכָּה גְּדוֹלָה מְאֹד וַיִּכָּנְעוּ בְּנֵי עַמּוֹן מִפְּנֵי בְּנֵי יִשְׂרָאֵל: לג

34 When Jephthah arrived at his home in Mizpah, there was his daughter coming out to meet him, with hand-drum and dance! She was an only child; he had no other son or daughter.

va-ya-VO yif-TAKH ha-mitz-PAH el bay-TO v'-hi-NAY vi-TO yo-TZAYT lik-ra-TO b'-tu-PEEM u-vim-kho-LOT v'-RAK HEE y'-khee-DAH ayn LO mi-ME-nu BAYN or VAT

וַיָּבֹא יִפְתָּח הַמִּצְפָּה אֶל־בֵּיתוֹ וְהִנֵּה בִתּוֹ יֹצֵאת לִקְרָאתוֹ בְּתֻפִּים וּבִמְחֹלוֹת וְרַק הִיא יְחִידָה אֵין־לוֹ מִמֶּנּוּ בֵּן אוֹ־בַת: לד

35 On seeing her, he rent his clothes and said, "Alas, daughter! You have brought me low; you have become my troubler! For I have uttered a vow to GOD and I cannot retract."

vai-HEE khir-o-TO o-TAH va-yik-RA et b'-ga-DAV va-YO-mer a-HAH bi-TEE hakh-RAY-a hikh-ra-TI-nee v'-AT ha-YEET b'-o-kh'-RAI v'-a-no-KHEE pa-TZEE-tee FEE el a-do-NAI v'-LO u-KHAL la-SHUV

וַיְהִי כִרְאוֹתוֹ אוֹתָהּ וַיִּקְרַע אֶת־בְּגָדָיו וַיֹּאמֶר אֲהָהּ בִּתִּי הַכְרֵעַ הִכְרַעְתִּנִי וְאַתְּ הָיִיתְ בְּעֹכְרָי וְאָנֹכִי פָּצִיתִי פִי אֶל־יְהֹוָה וְלֹא אוּכַל לָשׁוּב: לה

36 "Father," she said, "you have uttered a vow to GOD; do to me as you have vowed, seeing that GOD has vindicated you against your enemies, the Ammonites."

va-TO-mer ay-LAV a-VEE pa-TZEE-tah et PEE-kha el a-do-NAI a-SAY LEE ka-a-SHER ya-TZA mi-PEE-kha a-kha-RAY a-SHER a-SAH l'-KHA a-do-NAI n'-ka-MOT may-o-y'-VE-kha mi-b'-NAY a-MON

וַתֹּאמֶר אֵלָיו אָבִי פָּצִיתָה אֶת־פִּיךָ אֶל־יְהֹוָה עֲשֵׂה לִי כַּאֲשֶׁר יָצָא מִפִּיךָ אַחֲרֵי אֲשֶׁר עָשָׂה לְךָ יְהֹוָה נְקָמוֹת מֵאֹיְבֶיךָ מִבְּנֵי עַמּוֹן: לו

37 She further said to her father, "Let this be done for me: let me be for two months, and I will go with my companions and lament upon the hills and there bewail my maidenhood."

*va-TO-mer el a-VEE-ha yay-A-seh LEE ha-da-VAR ha-ZEH har-PAY mi-ME-nee sh'-NA-yim kho-da-SHEEM v'-ay-l'-KHA v'-ya-rad-TEE al he-ha-REEM v'-ev-KEH al b'-tu-LAI a-no-KHEE v'-ray-o-TAI*

וַתֹּאמֶר אֶל־אָבִיהָ יֵעָשֶׂה לִּי הַדָּבָר הַזֶּה הַרְפֵּה מִמֶּנִּי שְׁנַיִם חֳדָשִׁים וְאֵלְכָה וְיָרַדְתִּי עַל־הֶהָרִים וְאֶבְכֶּה עַל־בְּתוּלַי אָנֹכִי (ורעיתי) [וְרֵעוֹתָי]: לז

38 "Go," he replied. He let her go for two months, and she and her companions went and bewailed her maidenhood upon the hills.

*va-YO-mer LAY-khee va-yish-LAKH o-TAH sh'-NAY kho-da-SHEEM va-TAY-lekh HEE v'-ray-o-TE-ha va-TAYVK al b'-tu-lo-TE-he al he-ha-REEM*

וַיֹּאמֶר לֵכִי וַיִּשְׁלַח אוֹתָהּ שְׁנֵי חֳדָשִׁים וַתֵּלֶךְ הִיא וְרֵעוֹתֶיהָ וַתֵּבְךְּ עַל־בְּתוּלֶיהָ עַל־הֶהָרִים: לח

39 After two months' time, she returned to her father, and he did to her as he had vowed. She had never known a man. So it became a custom in Israel

*vai-HEE mi-KAYTZ sh'-NA-yim kho-da-SHEEM va-TA-shov el a-VEE-ha va-YA-as LAH et nid-RO a-SHER na-DAR v'-HEE lo ya-d'-AH EESH va-t'-hee KHOK b'-yis-ra-AYL*

וַיְהִי מִקֵּץ שְׁנַיִם חֳדָשִׁים וַתָּשָׁב אֶל־אָבִיהָ וַיַּעַשׂ לָהּ אֶת־נִדְרוֹ אֲשֶׁר נָדָר וְהִיא לֹא־יָדְעָה אִישׁ וַתְּהִי־חֹק בְּיִשְׂרָאֵל: לט

40 for the maidens of Israel to go every year, for four days in the year, and chant dirges for the daughter of Jephthah the Gileadite.

*mi-ya-MEEM ya-MEE-mah tay-LAKH-nah b'-NOT yis-ra-AYL l'-ta-NOT l'-vat yif-TAKH ha-gil-a-DEE ar-BA-at ya-MEEM ba-sha-NAH*

מִיָּמִים יָמִימָה תֵּלַכְנָה בְּנוֹת יִשְׂרָאֵל לְתַנּוֹת לְבַת־יִפְתָּח הַגִּלְעָדִי אַרְבַּעַת יָמִים בַּשָּׁנָה: מ

# Mysterious Ways

Whatever else might be said about America's last two Presidents, Joe Biden and Donald Trump, one thing is indisputably clear: the moral image of the American presidency has seen better days. Joe Biden regularly lies about his past, and it seems certain that he and his corrupt son profited from shady dealings in Ukraine and China. Meanwhile, Donald Trump regularly insults his rivals and shuns humility of any sort.

How can God allow people who reject fundamental truths of the Bible to become the leaders of the most powerful nation on earth? Does their success imply that God has rejected or given up on us?

The Bible answers this question with a resounding "No!"

When the Bible introduces Jephthah, the future judge and leader of Israel, it does so with great honesty:

"Jephthah the Gileadite was an able warrior, who was the son of a prostitute... So Jephthah fled from his brothers and settled in the Tob country. Men of low character gathered about Jephthah and went out raiding with him." (Judges 11:1-3)

The son of a prostitute, Jephthah spent his days with men of low character, leading them on raids of innocent travelers. His sole redeeming quality was that he was an "able warrior." And this man became the leader of all of Israel!

Despite his flaws, the Sages explain that Jephthah must be respected:

"Scripture also says, "And Samuel said to the people, It is the Lord that made Moses and Aaron" (I Samuel 12:6) and it says [in the same passage], "And the Lord sent Jerubbaal [Gideon] and Bedan [Samson] and Jephthah and Samuel" (I Samuel 16:11). [We see therefore that] the Scripture places three of the most questionable characters on the same level as three of the most estimable characters, to show that Gideon in his generation is like Moses in his generation, Samson in his generation is like Aaron in his generation, Jephthah in his generation is like Samuel in his generation, to teach you that the most worthless man, once he has been appointed a leader of the community, is to be accounted like the mightiest of the mighty." (Talmud Rosh Hashana 25a)

In this passage, the Sages are making an extraordinary point. God is the Master of this world, and nothing happens on earth without His involvement. In some generations, God chooses to bless the nation of Israel with great and holy leaders like Moses, Aaron and Samuel. But in other generations, God gives the people of Israel flawed leaders like Jephthah and Samson. But regardless of the quality of our leaders, one thing remains the same: God is in charge!

Despite their moral flaws, men like Jephthah and Samson served as God's messengers on earth. They led God's chosen people, the nation of Israel, to great and miraculous military victories. Similarly, in modern times, leaders like David Ben Gurion, an avowed atheist (though also a great admirer of the Bible), merited to lead the people of Israel back to the Holy Land and establish the State of Israel.

Why does God choose to bring salvation through flawed and immoral people? This is a great mystery, a mystery that reminds us that God's ways and understanding are infinitely deeper than our own. But one thing is clear – regardless of who our leaders may be, God never abandons us to chance. The events of this world are all a part of God's plan, the wisdom of which we will one day merit to see!

# Understanding the Past to Fight for the Future

Initially scorned by his brothers, Jephthah was appointed as the leader of Israel at a moment of crisis. When the evil Ammonites invaded the land of Gilead, Jephthah's brothers begged him to return home to lead them in battle against the enemy. Jephthah agreed to serve as general of the men of Gilead, and immediately took action:

"Jephthah then sent messengers to the king of the Ammonites, saying, 'What have you against me that you have come to make war on my country?'" (Judges 11:12)

The King of Ammon responds by accusing the people of Israel of stealing Ammonite land on the eastern shore of the Jordan River over 300 years earlier, when the Israelites first left Egypt and entered the land of Israel. The king then threatens Jephthah, demanding that Israel cede the land back to Ammon – or prepare for an invasion.

That should have ended the conversation. But for the next thirteen verses, Jephthah continues to argue with the king of Ammon, carefully explaining why the land in dispute did, indeed, belong to the people of Israel and not to Ammon. He explained that Sihon the Amorite had originally conquered the disputed land from the Ammonites, and the people of Israel then took the land from Sihon. The people of Israel had never attacked the Ammonites, and so the land belonged to Israel, fair and square!

"Now, then, the ETERNAL, the God of Israel, dispossessed the Amorites before this covenanted people Israel; and should you possess their land?... While Israel has been inhabiting... all the towns along the Arnon for three hundred years, why have you not tried to recover them all this time?" (Judges 11:23, 26)

Unsurprisingly, the king of Ammon was not persuaded by Jephthah's argument and proceeded to invade the nation of Israel. His accusations against the people of Israel were merely a pretext for the invasion, and so he brushed aside Jephthah's arguments and declared war.

Jephthah certainly understood that the king of Ammon intended to attack and that his arguments would not dissuade him. Why, then, did Jephthah engage the king of Ammon in a public argument to convince Ammon of Israel's legal right to the land? What did he hope to accomplish with this exchange?

Although Jephthah was addressing the king of Ammon, I believe his true audience was the nation of Israel itself. He knew that the Ammonites would not listen to his arguments, but he made them anyway in order to remind his own people of their history and their right to the land.

Jephthah understood that he could only defeat the Ammonites in battle if the people of Israel were conscious of their own history and their God-given right to the land of Israel. When a nation loses its self-confidence and begins to sympathize with its enemies' points of view, it is only a matter of time before the nation is doomed to defeat. And so Jephthah recounted the history of the people of Israel and their conquering of the land to ensure that every last Israelite soldier would be confident in his people's righteousness and their God-given rights to the land of Israel.

Jephthah's insight is critically important for our own time, when many nations, from the Palestinians to the European Union, are challenging the right of the Jewish people to the land of Israel. The corrupt and antisemitic United Nations General Assembly frequently issues resolutions condemning Israel's "prolonged occupation, settlement and annexation of Palestinian territory." In the face of these spurious attacks, the Jewish people must respond with clear and strong arguments that demonstrate to all that God Himself gave the land of Israel to the Jewish people. Although the corrupt and antisemitic nations that dominate the United Nations are unlikely to accept these arguments, Israel must continue to make them, so that the Jewish people themselves understand that the Holy Land belongs to them!

As Jephthah made his arguments to remind his own people of their history and their right to the land, we must also clearly state our own arguments to ensure the Jewish people understand that Judea and Samaria, Israel's biblical heartland, belong to them.

In this mission, Israel's non-Jewish friends can play a critically important role. In the final days of the Trump administration, former Secretary of State Mike Pompeo visited the Psagot Winery in Samaria, located in Israel's Biblical heartland. While there, he emphatically stated that Judea and Samaria are the "rightful homeland for the people of Israel." Later, on the One Decision podcast, he elaborated: "[Israel] is not an occupying nation. As an evangelical Christian, I am convinced by my reading of the Bible that 3,000 years on now, in spite of the denial of so many, [this land] is the rightful homeland of the Jewish people."

Though Pompeo's Biblical arguments are unlikely to change the minds of Israel's enemies, they were critically important for the Jewish people themselves, giving them the clarity and strength to stand up to Israel's many enemies. Similarly, when Christian groups from abroad visit Judea and Samaria and declare their support to the brave Jews who live there, they remind the people of Israel of their God-given mission to resettle the Holy Land and bring it back to life.

We pray for the success of Israel's defense forces in their fight against Arab terrorists who deny Israel's right to the land of Israel. But just as important as the military battle is the battle for the hearts and minds of the Jewish people themselves. For only by understanding the past will we have the strength to fight for the future.

# 12

יב

| | | |
|---|---|---|
| 1 | Ephraim's force mustered and crossed [the Jordan] to Zaphon. They said to Jephthah, "Why did you march to fight the Ammonites without calling us to go with you? We'll burn your house down over you!" | *va-yi-tza-AYK EESH ef-RA-yim va-ya-a-VOR tza-FO-nah va-yo-m'-RU l'-yif-TAKH ma-DU-a a-VAR-ta l'-hi-la-KAHYM biv-nay a-MON v'-LA-nu LO ka-RA-ta la-LE-khet i-MAKH bay-t'-KHA nis-ROF a-LE-kha ba-AYSH* |

וַיִּצָּעֵק אִישׁ אֶפְרַיִם<br>
וַיַּעֲבֹר צָפוֹנָה וַיֹּאמְרוּ<br>
לְיִפְתָּח מַדּוּעַ עָבַרְתָּ<br>
לְהִלָּחֵם בִּבְנֵי־עַמּוֹן<br>
וְלָנוּ לֹא קָרָאתָ לָלֶכֶת<br>
עִמָּךְ בֵּיתְךָ נִשְׂרֹף עָלֶיךָ<br>
בָּאֵשׁ: א

| | | |
|---|---|---|
| 2 | Jephthah answered them, "I and my people were involved in a bitter conflict with the Ammonites; and I summoned you, but you did not save me from them. | *va-YO-mer yif-TAKH a-lay-HEM EESH REEV ha-YEEY-tee a-NEE v'-a-MEE uv-nay a-MON m'-OD va-ez-AK et-KHEM v'-lo ho-sha-TEM o-TEE mi-ya-DAM* |

וַיֹּאמֶר יִפְתָּח אֲלֵיהֶם<br>
אִישׁ רִיב הָיִיתִי אֲנִי<br>
וְעַמִּי וּבְנֵי־עַמּוֹן מְאֹד<br>
וָאֶזְעַק אֶתְכֶם וְלֹא־<br>
הוֹשַׁעְתֶּם אוֹתִי מִיָּדָם: ב

| | | |
|---|---|---|
| 3 | When I saw that you were no saviors, I risked my life and advanced against the Ammonites; and GOD delivered them into my hands. Why have you come here now to fight against me?" | *va-er-EH kee ay-n'-KHA mo-SHEE-a va-a-SEE-mah naf-SHEE v'-kha-PEE va-e-b'-RAH el b'-NAY a-MON va-yi-t'-NAYM a-do-NAI b'-ya-DEE v'-la-MAH a-lee-TEM ay-LAI ha-YOM ha-ZEH l'-hi-LA-khem BEE* |

וָאֶרְאֶה כִּי־אֵינְךָ<br>
מוֹשִׁיעַ וָאָשִׂימָה נַפְשִׁי<br>
בְכַפִּי וָאֶעְבְּרָה אֶל־בְּנֵי<br>
עַמּוֹן וַיִּתְּנֵם יְהוָה בְּיָדִי<br>
וְלָמָה עֲלִיתֶם אֵלַי<br>
הַיּוֹם הַזֶּה לְהִלָּחֶם בִּי: ג

| | | |
|---|---|---|
| 4 | And Jephthah gathered all the Gileadites and fought Ephraim. The Gileadites defeated Ephraim; for they had said, "You, Gilead, are nothing but fugitives from Ephraim—being in Manasseh is like being in Ephraim." | *va-yik-BOTZ yif-TAKH et kol an-SHAY gil-AD va-yi-LA-khem et af-RA-yim KEE a-m'-RU p'-lee-TAY ef-RA-yim a-TEM gil-AD b'-TOKH ef-RA-yim b'-TOKH m'-na-SHEH* |

וַיִּקְבֹּץ יִפְתָּח אֶת־כָּל־
אַנְשֵׁי גִלְעָד וַיִּלָּחֶם
אֶת־אֶפְרָיִם וַיַּכּוּ אַנְשֵׁי
גִלְעָד אֶת־אֶפְרַיִם כִּי
אָמְרוּ פְּלִיטֵי אֶפְרַיִם
אַתֶּם גִּלְעָד בְּתוֹךְ
אֶפְרַיִם בְּתוֹךְ מְנַשֶּׁה: ד

| | | |
|---|---|---|
| 5 | Gilead held the fords of the Jordan against Ephraim. And when any fugitive from Ephraim said, "Let me cross," the Gileadites would ask him, "Are you an Ephraimite?"; if he said "No," | *va-yil-KOD gil-AD et ma-b'-ROT ha-yar-DAYN l'-ef-RA-yim v'-ha-YAH KEE yo-m'-RU p'-lee-TAY ef-RA-yim e-e-VO-rah va-yo-m'-RU LO an-shay gil-AD ha-ef-ra-TEE A-tah va-YO-mer LO* |

וַיִּלְכֹּד גִּלְעָד אֶת־
מַעְבְּרוֹת הַיַּרְדֵּן
לְאֶפְרָיִם וְהָיָה כִּי
יֹאמְרוּ פְּלִיטֵי אֶפְרַיִם
אֶעֱבֹרָה וַיֹּאמְרוּ לוֹ
אַנְשֵׁי־גִלְעָד הַאֶפְרָתִי
אַתָּה וַיֹּאמֶר לֹא: ה

| | | |
|---|---|---|
| 6 | they would say to him, "Then say shibboleth"; but he would say "sibboleth," not being able to pronounce it correctly. Thereupon they would seize him and slay him by the fords of the Jordan. Forty-two thousand from Ephraim fell at that time. | *va-YO-m'-ru LO e-mor NA shi-BO-let va-YO-mer si-BO-let v'-LO ya-KHEEN l'-da-BAYR KAYN va-yo-kha-ZU o-TO va-yish-kha-TU-hu el ma-b'-ROT ha-yar-DAYN va-yi-POL ba-AYT ha-HEE may-ef-RA-yim ar-ba-EEM ush-NA-yim A-lef* |

וַיֹּאמְרוּ לוֹ אֱמָר־
נָא שִׁבֹּלֶת וַיֹּאמֶר
סִבֹּלֶת וְלֹא יָכִין
לְדַבֵּר כֵּן וַיֹּאחֲזוּ
אוֹתוֹ וַיִּשְׁחָטוּהוּ אֶל־
מַעְבְּרוֹת הַיַּרְדֵּן וַיִּפֹּל
בָּעֵת הַהִיא מֵאֶפְרַיִם
אַרְבָּעִים וּשְׁנַיִם אָלֶף: ו

| | | | |
|---|---|---|---|
| 7 | Jephthah led Israel six years. Then Jephthah the Gileadite died and he was buried in one of the towns of Gilead. | *va-yish-POT yif-TAKH et yis-ra-AYL SHAYSH sha-NEEM va-YA-mot yif-TAKH ha-gil-a-DEE va-yi-ka-VAYR b'-a-RAY gil-AD* | וַיִּשְׁפֹּט יִפְתָּח אֶת־יִשְׂרָאֵל שֵׁשׁ שָׁנִים וַיָּמָת יִפְתָּח הַגִּלְעָדִי וַיִּקָּבֵר בְּעָרֵי גִלְעָד: | ז |
| 8 | After him, Ibzan of Bethlehem led Israel. | *va-yish-POT a-kha-RAV et yis-ra-AYL iv-TZAN mi-BAYT LA-khem* | וַיִּשְׁפֹּט אַחֲרָיו אֶת־יִשְׂרָאֵל אִבְצָן מִבֵּית לָחֶם: | ח |
| 9 | He had thirty sons, and he married off thirty daughters outside the clan and likewise brought in thirty from outside the clan for his sons. He led Israel seven years. | *vai-hee LO sh'-lo-SHEEM ba-NEEM ush-lo-SHEEM ba-NOT shi-LAKH ha-KHU-tzah ush'-lo-SHEEM ba-NOT hay-VEE l'-va-NAV min ha-KHUTZ va-yish-POT et yis-ra-AYL SHE-va sha-NEEM* | וַיְהִי־לוֹ שְׁלֹשִׁים בָּנִים וּשְׁלֹשִׁים בָּנוֹת שִׁלַּח הַחוּצָה וּשְׁלֹשִׁים בָּנוֹת הֵבִיא לְבָנָיו מִן־הַחוּץ וַיִּשְׁפֹּט אֶת־יִשְׂרָאֵל שֶׁבַע שָׁנִים: | ט |
| 10 | Then Ibzan died and was buried in Bethlehem. | *va-YA-mot iv-TZAN va-yi-ka-VAYR b'-VAYT LA-khem* | וַיָּמָת אִבְצָן וַיִּקָּבֵר בְּבֵית לָחֶם: | י |
| 11 | After him, Elon the Zebulunite led Israel; he led Israel for ten years. | *va-yish-POT a-kha-RAV et yis-ra-AYL ay-LON ha-z'-vu-lo-NEE va-yish-POT et yis-ra-AYL E-ser sha-NEEM* | וַיִּשְׁפֹּט אַחֲרָיו אֶת־יִשְׂרָאֵל אֵילוֹן הַזְּבוּלֹנִי וַיִּשְׁפֹּט אֶת־יִשְׂרָאֵל עֶשֶׂר שָׁנִים: | יא |
| 12 | Then Elon the Zebulunite died and was buried in Aijalon, in the territory of Zebulun. | *va-YA-mot ay-LON ha-z'-vu-lo-NEE va-yi-ka-VAYR b'-a-ya-LON b'-E-retz z'-vu-LUN* | וַיָּמָת אֵילוֹן הַזְּבוּלֹנִי וַיִּקָּבֵר בְּאַיָּלוֹן בְּאֶרֶץ זְבוּלֻן: | יב |

| | | | |
|---|---|---|---|
| 13 | After him, Abdon son of Hillel the Pirathonite led Israel. | va-yish-POT a-kha-RAV et yis-ra-AYL av-DON ben hi-LAYL ha-pir-a-to-NEE | וַיִּשְׁפֹּט אַחֲרָיו אֶת־יִשְׂרָאֵל עַבְדּוֹן בֶּן־הִלֵּל הַפִּרְעָתוֹנִי: |
| 14 | He had forty sons and thirty grandsons, who rode on seventy jackasses. He led Israel for eight years. | vai-hee LO ar-ba-EEM ba-NEE ush-lo-SHEEM b'-NAY va-NEEM ro-kh'-VEEM al shiv-EEM a-ya-RIM va-yish-POT et yis-ra-AYL sh'-mo-NEH sha-NEEM | וַיְהִי־לוֹ אַרְבָּעִים בָּנִים וּשְׁלֹשִׁים בְּנֵי בָנִים רֹכְבִים עַל־שִׁבְעִים עֲיָרִם וַיִּשְׁפֹּט אֶת־יִשְׂרָאֵל שְׁמֹנֶה שָׁנִים: |
| 15 | Then Abdon son of Hillel the Pirathonite died. He was buried in Pirathon, in the territory of Ephraim, on the hill of the Amalekites. | va-YA-mot av-DON ben hi-LAYL ha-pir-a-to-NEE va-yi-ka-VAYR bi-fir-a-TON b'-E-retz ef-RA-yim b'-HAR ha-a-ma-lay-KEE | וַיָּמָת עַבְדּוֹן בֶּן־הִלֵּל הַפִּרְעָתוֹנִי וַיִּקָּבֵר בְּפִרְעָתוֹן בְּאֶרֶץ אֶפְרַיִם בְּהַר הָעֲמָלֵקִי: |

# 13

| | | | |
|---|---|---|---|
| 1 | The Israelites again did what was offensive to GOD, and GOD delivered them into the hands of the Philistines for forty years. | *va-yo-SEE-fu b'-NAY yis-ra-AYL la-a-SOT ha-RA b'-ay-NAY a-do-NAI va-yi-t'-NAYM a-do-NAI b'-yad p'-lish-TEEM ar-ba-EEM sha-NAH* | וַיֹּסִפוּ בְּנֵי יִשְׂרָאֵל לַעֲשׂוֹת הָרַע בְּעֵינֵי יְהוָה וַיִּתְּנֵם יְהוָה בְּיַד־פְּלִשְׁתִּים אַרְבָּעִים שָׁנָה: |
| 2 | There was a certain man from Zorah, of the stock of Dan, whose name was Manoah. His wife was infertile and had borne no children. | *vai-HEE EESH e-KAHD mi-tzor-AH mi-mish-PA-khat ha-da-NEE ush-MO ma-NO-akh v'-ish-TO a-ka-RAH v'-LO ya-LA-dah* | וַיְהִי אִישׁ אֶחָד מִצָּרְעָה מִמִּשְׁפַּחַת הַדָּנִי וּשְׁמוֹ מָנוֹחַ וְאִשְׁתּוֹ עֲקָרָה וְלֹא יָלָדָה: |
| 3 | An angel of GOD appeared to the woman and said to her, "You are infertile and have borne no children; but you shall conceive and bear a son. | *va-yay-RA mal-akh a-do-NAI el ha-i-SHAH va-YO-mer ay-LE-ha hi-nay NA at a-ka-RAH v'-LO ya-LADT v'-ha-REET v'-ya-LADT BAYN* | וַיֵּרָא מַלְאַךְ־יְהוָה אֶל־הָאִשָּׁה וַיֹּאמֶר אֵלֶיהָ הִנֵּה־נָא אַתְּ־עֲקָרָה וְלֹא יָלַדְתְּ וְהָרִית וְיָלַדְתְּ בֵּן: |
| 4 | Now be careful not to drink wine or other intoxicant, or to eat anything impure. | *v'-a-TAH hi-SHA-m'-ree NA v'-al tish-TEE YA-yin v'-shay-KHAR v'-al to-kh'-LEE kol ta-MAY* | וְעַתָּה הִשָּׁמְרִי נָא וְאַל־תִּשְׁתִּי יַיִן וְשֵׁכָר וְאַל־תֹּאכְלִי כָּל־טָמֵא: |

5

For you are going to
conceive and bear
a son; let no razor
touch his head, for
the boy is to be a
nazirite to God from
the womb on. He
shall be the first to
deliver Israel from
the Philistines."

*KEE hi-NAKH ha-RAH
v'-ya-LADT BAYN
u-mo-RAH lo ya-a-LEH
al ro-SHO kee n'-ZEER
e-lo-HEEM yih-YEH
ha-NA-ar min ha-BA-ten
v'-HU ya-KHAYL l'-ho-
SHEE-a et yis-ra-AYL
mi-YAD p'-lish-TEEM*

כִּי הִנָּךְ הָרָה וְיֹלַדְתְּ בֵּן
וּמוֹרָה לֹא־יַעֲלֶה עַל־
רֹאשׁוֹ כִּי־נְזִיר אֱלֹהִים
יִהְיֶה הַנַּעַר מִן־הַבָּטֶן
וְהוּא יָחֵל לְהוֹשִׁיעַ
אֶת־יִשְׂרָאֵל מִיַּד
פְּלִשְׁתִּים:

ה

6

The woman went and
told her husband,
"An agent of God
came to me; he
looked like an
angel of God, very
frightening. I did not
ask him where he was
from, nor did he tell
me his name.

*va-ta-VO ha-i-SHAH
va-TO-mer l'-i-SHAH
lay-MOR EESH ha-e-
lo-HEEM BA ay-LAI
u-mar-AY-hu k'-mar-AY
mal-AKH ha-e-lo-HEEM
no-RA m'-OD v'-LO
sh'-il-TEE-hu ay mi-
ZEH HU v'-et sh'-MO lo
hi-GEED LEE*

וַתָּבֹא הָאִשָּׁה וַתֹּאמֶר
לְאִישָׁהּ לֵאמֹר אִישׁ
הָאֱלֹהִים בָּא אֵלַי
וּמַרְאֵהוּ כְּמַרְאֵה
מַלְאַךְ הָאֱלֹהִים נוֹרָא
מְאֹד וְלֹא שְׁאִלְתִּיהוּ
אֵי־מִזֶּה הוּא וְאֶת־שְׁמוֹ
לֹא־הִגִּיד לִי:

ו

7

He said to me, 'You
are going to conceive
and bear a son. Drink
no wine or other
intoxicant, and eat
nothing impure, for
the boy is to be a
nazirite to God from
the womb to the day
of his death!'"

*va-YO-mer LEE hi-
NAKH ha-RAH v'-ya-
LADT BAYN v'-a-TAH
al tish-TEE YA-yin
v'-shay-KHAR v'-al
to-kh'-LEE kol tum-AH
kee n'-ZEER e-lo-HEEM
yih-YEH ha-NA-ar min
ha-BE-ten ad YOM mo-
TO*

וַיֹּאמֶר לִי הִנָּךְ הָרָה
וְיֹלַדְתְּ בֵּן וְעַתָּה
אַל־תִּשְׁתִּי יַיִן וְשֵׁכָר
וְאַל־תֹּאכְלִי כָּל־טֻמְאָה
כִּי־נְזִיר אֱלֹהִים יִהְיֶה
הַנַּעַר מִן־הַבָּטֶן עַד־יוֹם
מוֹתוֹ:

ז

8

Manoah pleaded with GOD. "Oh, my Sovereign!" he said, "please let the agent of God that You sent come to us again, and let him instruct us how to act with the child that is to be born."

*va-ye-TAR ma-NO-akh el a-do-NAI va-YO-mer BEE a-do-NEE EESH ha-e-lo-HEEM a-SHER sha-LAKH-ta ya-vo NA OD ay-LAY-nu v'-yo-RAY-nu mah na-a-SEH la-NA-ar ha-yu-LAD*

וַיֶּעְתַּר מָנוֹחַ אֶל־יְהֹוָה וַיֹּאמַר בִּי אֲדוֹנָי אִישׁ הָאֱלֹהִים אֲשֶׁר שָׁלַחְתָּ יָבוֹא־נָא עוֹד אֵלֵינוּ וְיוֹרֵנוּ מַה־נַּעֲשֶׂה לַנַּעַר הַיּוּלָּד: ח

9

God heeded Manoah's plea, and the angel of God came to the woman again. She was sitting in the field and her husband Manoah was not with her.

*va-yish-MA ha-e-lo-HEEM b'-KOL ma-NO-akh va-ya-VO mal-AKH ha-e-lo-HEEM OD el ha-i-SHAH v'-HEE yo-SHE-vet ba-sa-DEH u-ma-NO-akh ee-SHAH AYN i-MAH*

וַיִּשְׁמַע הָאֱלֹהִים בְּקוֹל מָנוֹחַ וַיָּבֹא מַלְאַךְ הָאֱלֹהִים עוֹד אֶל־ הָאִשָּׁה וְהִיא יוֹשֶׁבֶת בַּשָּׂדֶה וּמָנוֹחַ אִישָׁהּ אֵין עִמָּהּ: ט

10

The woman ran in haste to tell her husband. She said to him, "The man who came to me before has just appeared to me."

*va-t'-ma-HAYR ha-i-SHAH va-TA-ratz va-ta-GAYD l'-ee-SHAH va-TO-mer ay-LAV hi-NAY nir-AH ay-LAI ha-EESH a-sher BA va-YOM ay-LAI*

וַתְּמַהֵר הָאִשָּׁה וַתָּרָץ וַתַּגֵּד לְאִישָׁהּ וַתֹּאמֶר אֵלָיו הִנֵּה נִרְאָה אֵלַי הָאִישׁ אֲשֶׁר־בָּא בַיּוֹם אֵלָי: י

11

Manoah promptly followed his wife. He came to that figure and asked him: "Are you the one who spoke to my wife?" "Yes," he answered.

*va-YA-kom va-YAY-lekh ma-NO-akh a-kha-RAY ish-TO va-ya-VO el ha-EESH va-YO-mer LO ha-a-TAH ha-EESH a-sher di-bar-TA el ha-i-SHAH va-YO-mer A-nee*

וַיָּקָם וַיֵּלֶךְ מָנוֹחַ אַחֲרֵי אִשְׁתּוֹ וַיָּבֹא אֶל־הָאִישׁ וַיֹּאמֶר לוֹ הַאַתָּה הָאִישׁ אֲשֶׁר־דִּבַּרְתָּ אֶל־ הָאִשָּׁה וַיֹּאמֶר אָנִי: יא

| | | | |
|---|---|---|---|
| 12 | Then Manoah said, "May your words soon come true! What rules shall be observed for the boy?" | *va-YO-mer ma-NO-akh a-TAH ya-VO d'-va-RE-kha mah yih-YEH mish-PAT ha-NA-ar u-ma-a-SAY-hu* | וַיֹּאמֶר מָנוֹחַ עַתָּה יָבֹא דְבָרֶיךָ מַה־יִּהְיֶה מִשְׁפַּט־הַנַּעַר וּמַעֲשֵׂהוּ: יב |
| 13 | The angel of GOD said to Manoah, "The woman must abstain from all the things against which I warned her. | *va-YO-mer mal-AKH a-do-NAI el ma-NO-akh mi-KOL a-sher a-MAR-tee el ha-i-SHAH ti-sha-MAYR* | וַיֹּאמֶר מַלְאַךְ יְהוָה אֶל־מָנוֹחַ מִכֹּל אֲשֶׁר־אָמַרְתִּי אֶל־הָאִשָּׁה תִּשָּׁמֵר: יג |
| 14 | She must not eat anything that comes from the grapevine, or drink wine or other intoxicant, or eat anything impure. She must observe all that I commanded her." | *mi-KOL a-sher yay-TZAY mi-GE-fen ha-YA-yin LO to-KHAL v'-YA-yin v'-shay-KHAR al TAYSHT v'-khol tum-AH al to-KHAL KOL a-sher tzi-vee-TEE-ha tish-MOR* | מִכֹּל אֲשֶׁר־יֵצֵא מִגֶּפֶן הַיַּיִן לֹא תֹאכַל וְיַיִן וְשֵׁכָר אַל־תֵּשְׁתְּ וְכָל־טֻמְאָה אַל־תֹּאכַל כֹּל אֲשֶׁר־צִוִּיתִיהָ תִּשְׁמֹר: יד |
| 15 | Manoah said to the angel of GOD, "Let us detain you and prepare a kid for you." | *va-YO-mer ma-NO-akh el mal-AKH a-do-NAI na-tz'-rah NA o-TAKH v'-na-a-SEH l'-fa-NE-kha g'-DEE i-ZEEM* | וַיֹּאמֶר מָנוֹחַ אֶל־מַלְאַךְ יְהוָה נַעְצְרָה־נָּא אוֹתָךְ וְנַעֲשֶׂה לְפָנֶיךָ גְּדִי עִזִּים: טו |
| 16 | But the angel of GOD said to Manoah, "If you detain me, I shall not eat your food; and if you present a burnt offering, offer it to GOD."—For Manoah did not know that he was an angel of GOD. | *va-YO-mer mal-AKH a-do-NAI el ma-NO-akh im tza-tz'-RAY-nee lo o-KHAL b'-lakh-ME-kha v'-im ta-a-SEH o-LAH la-do-NAI ta-a-LE-nah KEE lo ya-DA ma-NO-akh kee mal-AKH a-do-NAI HU* | וַיֹּאמֶר מַלְאַךְ יְהוָה אֶל־מָנוֹחַ אִם־תַּעְצְרֵנִי לֹא־אֹכַל בְּלַחְמֶךָ וְאִם־תַּעֲשֶׂה עֹלָה לַיהוָה תַּעֲלֶנָּה כִּי לֹא־יָדַע מָנוֹחַ כִּי־מַלְאַךְ יְהוָה הוּא: טז |

17 So Manoah said to the angel of GOD, "What is your name? We should like to honor you when your words come true."

*va-YO-mer ma-NO-akh el mal-AKH a-do-NAI MEE sh'-ME-kha kee ya-VO d'-va-r'-KHA v'-khi-bad-NU-kha*

וַיֹּאמֶר מָנוֹחַ אֶל־מַלְאַךְ יְהֹוָה מִי שְׁמֶךָ כִּי־יָבֹא (דבריך) [דְבָרְךָ] וְכִבַּדְנוּךָ׃ יז

18 The angel said to him, "You must not ask for my name; it is unknowable!"

*va-YO-mer LO mal-AKH a-do-NAI LA-mah ZEH tish-AL lish-MEE v'-hu FE-lee*

וַיֹּאמֶר לוֹ מַלְאַךְ יְהֹוָה לָמָּה זֶּה תִּשְׁאַל לִשְׁמִי וְהוּא־פֶלִאי׃ יח

19 Manoah took the kid and the grain offering and offered them up on the rock to GOD; and a marvelous thing happened while Manoah and his wife looked on.

*va-yi-KAKH ma-NO-akh et g'-DEE ha-i-ZEEM v'-et ha-min-KHAH va-YA-al al ha-TZUR la-do-NAI u-maf-LI la-a-SOT u-ma-NO-ash v'-ish-TO ro-EEM*

וַיִּקַּח מָנוֹחַ אֶת־גְּדִי הָעִזִּים וְאֶת־הַמִּנְחָה וַיַּעַל עַל־הַצּוּר לַיהֹוָה וּמַפְלִא לַעֲשׂוֹת וּמָנוֹחַ וְאִשְׁתּוֹ רֹאִים׃ יט

20 As the flames leaped up from the altar toward the sky, the angel of GOD ascended in the flames of the altar, while Manoah and his wife looked on; and they flung themselves on their faces to the ground.—

*vai-HEE va-a-LOT ha-LA-hav may-AL ha-miz-BAY-akh ha-sha-MAI-mah va-YA-al mal-AKH a-do-NAI b'-LA-hav ha-miz-BAY-akh u-ma-NO-akh v'-ish-TO ro-EEM va-yi-p'-LU al p'-nay-HEM AR-tzah*

וַיְהִי בַעֲלוֹת הַלַּהַב מֵעַל הַמִּזְבֵּחַ הַשָּׁמַיְמָה וַיַּעַל מַלְאַךְ־יְהֹוָה בְּלַהַב הַמִּזְבֵּחַ וּמָנוֹחַ וְאִשְׁתּוֹ רֹאִים וַיִּפְּלוּ עַל־פְּנֵיהֶם אָרְצָה׃ כ

21 The angel of GOD never appeared again to Manoah and his wife.—Manoah then realized that it had been an angel of GOD.

*v'-lo YA-saf OD mal-AKH a-do-NAI l'-hay-ra-OT el ma-NO-akh v'-el ish-TO AZ ya-DA ma-NO-akh kee mal-AKH a-do-NAI HU*

וְלֹא־יָסַף עוֹד מַלְאַךְ יְהֹוָה לְהֵרָאֹה אֶל־מָנוֹחַ וְאֶל־אִשְׁתּוֹ אָז יָדַע מָנוֹחַ כִּי־מַלְאַךְ יְהֹוָה הוּא׃ כא

| |  |  |  |
|---|---|---|---|
| 22 | And Manoah said to his wife, "We will surely die, for we have seen a divine being." | va-YO-mer ma-NO-akh el ish-TO MOT na-MUT KEE e-lo-HEEM ra-EE-nu | וַיֹּאמֶר מָנוֹחַ אֶל־אִשְׁתּוֹ מוֹת נָמוּת כִּי אֱלֹהִים רָאִינוּ: כב |
| 23 | But his wife said to him, "Had GOD meant to take our lives, our burnt offering and grain offering would not have been accepted, nor would we have been shown all these things—and [God] would not have made such an announcement to us." | va-TO-mer LO ish-TO LU kha-FAYTZ a-do-NAI la-ha-mee-TAY-nu lo la-KAKH mi-ya-DAY-nu o-LAH u-min-KHAH v'-LO her-A-nu et kol AY-leh v'-kha-AYT LO hish-mee-A-nu ka-ZOT | וַתֹּאמֶר לוֹ אִשְׁתּוֹ לוּ חָפֵץ יְהֹוָה לַהֲמִיתֵנוּ לֹא־לָקַח מִיָּדֵנוּ עֹלָה וּמִנְחָה וְלֹא הֶרְאָנוּ אֶת־כָּל־אֵלֶּה וְכָעֵת לֹא הִשְׁמִיעָנוּ כָּזֹאת: כג |
| 24 | The woman bore a son, and she named him Samson. The boy grew up, and GOD blessed him. | va-TAY-led ha-i-SHAH BAYN va-tik-RA et sh'-MO shim-SHON va-yig-DAL ha-NA-ar vai-va-r'-KHAY-hu a-do-NAI | וַתֵּלֶד הָאִשָּׁה בֵּן וַתִּקְרָא אֶת־שְׁמוֹ שִׁמְשׁוֹן וַיִּגְדַּל הַנַּעַר וַיְבָרְכֵהוּ יְהֹוָה: כד |
| 25 | The spirit of GOD first moved him in the encampment of Dan, between Zorah and Eshtaol. | va-TA-khel RU-akh a-do-NAI l'-fa-a-MO b'-ma-kha-nay DAN BAYN tzor-AH u-VAYN esh-ta-OL | וַתָּחֶל רוּחַ יְהֹוָה לְפַעֲמוֹ בְּמַחֲנֵה־דָן בֵּין צָרְעָה וּבֵין אֶשְׁתָּאֹל: כה |

# Palestinians
# and Philistines

Since Jews began returning to the land of Israel in the late 19th century, they have faced no shortage of enemies. Surrounded by nations such as Syria, Egypt and Iran, Israel has overcome many powerful and frightening foes with armies far larger than the Jewish State could ever muster.

Somehow, Israel has managed to more than hold its own against these enemies. But the one enemy that Israel has not yet found a way to overcome is perhaps the least likely of all: the so-called Palestinians. "Palestinians," the name adopted by Israel's Arab inhabitants, is misleading, for the modern-day Palestinians do not descend from, and bear no relation to, the ancient Philistines who dwelled along Israel's coast in Biblical times. It was only on May 28, 1964, the date on which the PLO was established, that the name "Palestinian" began being used.

Nevertheless, today's "Palestinians" share something in common with the Philistines of old. The Philistines of the Biblical era were also the Jewish people's most persistent and difficult adversary. Beginning with the era of Samson (Judges 13:1) and continuing through the generations of Samuel, Saul and David, the Philistines were consistently the most dangerous foe of the twelve tribes of Israel.

Why have both modern Palestinians and ancient Philistines been such difficult enemies of the people of Israel?

After the destruction of the Egyptian army at the Red Sea, Moses and the people of Israel sang in thanks to God:

"The peoples hear, they tremble; agony grips the dwellers in Philistia. Now are the clans of Edom dismayed; the tribes of Moab—trembling grips them; all the dwellers in Canaan are aghast" (Exodus 15:14-15).

In this prophetic song, three enemies of Israel are mentioned: Edom (the descendants of Esau), Moab (the descendants of Lot), and the Philistines. Rabbi Elijah of Vilna (1720-1797) explains that these three nations represent three distinct types of enemies that the people of Israel were destined to confront throughout their history.

Edom represents those enemies, like the evil Nazis, who seek to physically harm the Jewish people as much as possible. Moab, by contrast, attacks the people of Israel spiritually, seeking to pollute them with impurity, as they did when their daughters seduced the men of Israel (Numbers 25:1).

And what about the Philistines?

"The Philistines caused Israel great suffering and did not allow them to be sovereign in their own land" (Rabbi Elijah of Vilna, Commentary to Habakuk).

Throughout Jewish history, the vast majority of Israel's enemies either sought to physically destroy the Jewish people or to force them to assimilate into the broader culture and lose their unique identity. The Philistines, however, were unique. Though they certainly murdered many Jews, their primary goal was not to seduce or annihilate the Jewish people but rather to prevent the Jewish people from ruling their own land!

A close look at the Biblical verses describing Philistine society reveals that the Philistines – unlike the Jews – left no positive legacy for the world. A pagan people who never developed an advanced legal system or culture, the Philistine identity was shaped almost entirely by its goal of subduing the people of Israel.

In our own time, the Palestinian people have continued the tradition of the Biblical Philistines. Over the last 75 years, as Israel has grown to become a spiritual and economic light unto the nations, the Palestinians have accomplished nothing. The Palestinian identity is shaped by one thing, and one thing alone: hatred of Israel and their battle with the Jewish people for sovereignty over the Holy Land.

Day after day, year after year, the Palestinians do everything in their power to torture the Jewish people. They will stop at nothing – including the murder of innocent men, women and children – in their quest to prevent the Jewish people from achieving their destiny: sovereignty over the Land of Israel. But just as King David ultimately defeated and destroyed the Philistine enemy, we know that one day, hopefully soon, God will deliver the Palestinian enemy into the hands of David's heir, the Messiah that we pray and long for. May he soon come!

# 14

יד

**1**

Once Samson went down to Timnah; and while in Timnah, he noticed a certain young Philistine woman.

*va-YAY-red shim-SHON tim-NA-tah va-YAR i-SHAH b'-tim-NA-tah mi-b'-NOT p'-lish-TEEM*

וַיֵּרֶד שִׁמְשׁוֹן תִּמְנָתָה וַיַּרְא אִשָּׁה בְּתִמְנָתָה מִבְּנוֹת פְּלִשְׁתִּים: א

**2**

On his return, he told his father and mother, "I noticed one of the Philistine women in Timnah; please get her for me as a wife."

*va-YA-al va-ya-GAYD l'-a-VEEV ul-i-MO va-YO-mer i-SHAH ra-EE-tee v'-tim-NA-tah mi-b'-NOT p'-lish-TEEM v'-a-TAH k'-khu o-TAH LEE l'-i-SHAH*

וַיַּעַל וַיַּגֵּד לְאָבִיו וּלְאִמּוֹ וַיֹּאמֶר אִשָּׁה רָאִיתִי בְתִמְנָתָה מִבְּנוֹת פְּלִשְׁתִּים וְעַתָּה קְחוּ־אוֹתָהּ לִי לְאִשָּׁה: ב

**3**

His father and mother said to him, "Is there no one among the daughters of your own kindred and among all our people, that you must go and take a wife from the uncircumcised Philistines?" But Samson answered his father, "Get me that one, for she is the one that pleases me."

*va-YO-mer LO a-VEEV v'-i-MO ha-AYN biv-NOT a-KHE-kha uv-khol a-MEE i-SHAH kee a-TAH ho-LAYKH la-KA-khat i-SHAH mi-p'-lish-TEEM ha-a-ray-LEEM v-YO-mer shim-SHON el a-VEEV o-TAH kakh LEE kee HEE yash-RAH v'-ay-NAI*

וַיֹּאמֶר לוֹ אָבִיו וְאִמּוֹ הַאֵין בִּבְנוֹת אַחֶיךָ וּבְכָל־עַמִּי אִשָּׁה כִּי־אַתָּה הוֹלֵךְ לָקַחַת אִשָּׁה מִפְּלִשְׁתִּים הָעֲרֵלִים וַיֹּאמֶר שִׁמְשׁוֹן אֶל־אָבִיו אוֹתָהּ קַח־לִי כִּי־הִיא יָשְׁרָה בְעֵינָי: ג

| | | | |
|---|---|---|---|
| 4 | His father and mother did not realize that his request was from GOD, who was seeking a pretext against the Philistines, for the Philistines were ruling over Israel at that time. | *v'-a-VEEV v'-i-MO LO ya-d'-U KEE may-a-do-NAI HEE kee to-a-NAH hu m'-va-KAYSH mi-p'-lish-TEEM u-va-AYT ha-HEE p'-lish-TEEM mo-sh'-LEEM b'-yis-ra-AYL* | וְאָבִיו וְאִמּוֹ לֹא יָדְעוּ כִּי מֵיְהֹוָה הִיא כִּי־תֹאֲנָה הוּא־מְבַקֵּשׁ מִפְּלִשְׁתִּים וּבָעֵת הַהִיא פְּלִשְׁתִּים מֹשְׁלִים בְּיִשְׂרָאֵל: ד |
| 5 | So Samson and his father and mother went down to Timnah. When he came to the vineyards of Timnah [for the first time], a full-grown lion came roaring at him. | *va-YAY-red shim-SHON v'-a-VEEV v'-i-MO tim-NA-tah va-ya-VO-u ad kar-MAY tim-na-TAH v'-hi-NAY k'-FEER a-ra-YOT sho-AYG lik-ra-TO* | וַיֵּרֶד שִׁמְשׁוֹן וְאָבִיו וְאִמּוֹ תִּמְנָתָה וַיָּבֹאוּ עַד־כַּרְמֵי תִמְנָתָה וְהִנֵּה כְּפִיר אֲרָיוֹת שֹׁאֵג לִקְרָאתוֹ: ה |
| 6 | The spirit of GOD gripped him, and he tore him asunder with his bare hands as one might tear a kid asunder; but he did not tell his father and mother what he had done. | *va-titz-LAKH a-LAV RU-akh a-do-NAI vai-sha-s'-AY-hu k'-sha-SA ha-g'-DEE um-U-mah AYN b'-ya-DO v'-LO hi-GEED l'-a-VEEV ul-i-MO AYT a-SHER a-SAH* | וַתִּצְלַח עָלָיו רוּחַ יְהֹוָה וַיְשַׁסְּעֵהוּ כְּשַׁסַּע הַגְּדִי וּמְאוּמָה אֵין בְּיָדוֹ וְלֹא הִגִּיד לְאָבִיו וּלְאִמּוֹ אֵת אֲשֶׁר עָשָׂה: ו |
| 7 | Then he went down and spoke to the woman, and she pleased Samson. | *va-YAY-red vai-da-BAYR la-i-SHAH va-tee-SHAR b'-ay-NAY shim-SHON* | וַיֵּרֶד וַיְדַבֵּר לָאִשָּׁה וַתִּישַׁר בְּעֵינֵי שִׁמְשׁוֹן: ז |

8

Returning the following year to marry her, he turned aside to look at the remains of the lion; and in the lion's skeleton he found a swarm of bees, and honey.

*va-YA-shov mi-ya-MEEM l'-kakh-TAH va-YA-sar lir-OT AYT ma-PE-let ha-ar-YAY v'-hi-NAY a-DAT d'-vo-REEM big-vi-YAT ha-ar-YAY ud-VASH*

וַיָּשָׁב מִיָּמִים לְקַחְתָּהּ וַיָּסַר לִרְאוֹת אֵת מַפֶּלֶת הָאַרְיֵה וְהִנֵּה עֲדַת דְּבוֹרִים בִּגְוִיַּת הָאַרְיֵה וּדְבָשׁ: ח

9

He scooped it into his palms and ate it as he went along. When he rejoined his father and mother, he gave them some and they ate it; but he did not tell them that he had scooped the honey out of a lion's skeleton.

*va-yir-DAY-hu el ka-PAV va-YAY-lekh ha-LOKH v'-a-KHOL va-YAY-lekh el a-VEEV v-el i-MO va-yi-TAYN la-HEM va-yo-KHAY-lu v'-lo hi-GEED la-HEM KEE mi-g'-vi-YAT ha-ar-YAY ra-DAH ha-d'-VASH*

וַיִּרְדֵּהוּ אֶל־כַּפָּיו וַיֵּלֶךְ הָלוֹךְ וְאָכֹל וַיֵּלֶךְ אֶל־אָבִיו וְאֶל־אִמּוֹ וַיִּתֵּן לָהֶם וַיֹּאכֵלוּ וְלֹא־הִגִּיד לָהֶם כִּי מִגְּוִיַּת הָאַרְיֵה רָדָה הַדְּבָשׁ: ט

10

So his father came down to the woman, and Samson made a feast there, as young men used to do.

*va-YAY-red a-VEE-hu el ha-i-SHAH va-YA-as SHAM shim-SHON mish-TEH KEE KAYN ya-a-SU ha-ba-khu-REEM*

וַיֵּרֶד אָבִיהוּ אֶל־הָאִשָּׁה וַיַּעַשׂ שָׁם שִׁמְשׁוֹן מִשְׁתֶּה כִּי כֵּן יַעֲשׂוּ הַבַּחוּרִים: י

11

When the people of Timnah saw him, they designated thirty companions to be with him.

*vai-HEE kir-o-TEM o-TO va-yik-KHU sh'-lo-SHEEM may-ray-EEM va-yih-YU i-TO*

וַיְהִי כִּרְאוֹתָם אוֹתוֹ וַיִּקְחוּ שְׁלֹשִׁים מֵרֵעִים וַיִּהְיוּ אִתּוֹ: יא

12 Then Samson said to them, "Let me propound a riddle to you. If you can give me the right answer during the seven days of the feast, I shall give you thirty linen tunics and thirty sets of clothing;

*va-YO-mer la-HEM shim-SHON a-khu-dah NA la-KHEM khee-DAH im ha-GAYD ta-GEE-du LEE shiv-AT y'-MAY ha-mish-TEH um-tza-TEM v'-na-ta-TEE la-KHEM sh'-lo-SHEEM s'-dee-NEEM ush-lo-SHEEM kha-li-FOT b'-ga-DEEM*

וַיֹּאמֶר לָהֶם שִׁמְשׁוֹן אָחוּדָה־נָּא לָכֶם חִידָה אִם־הַגֵּד תַּגִּידוּ אוֹתָהּ לִי שִׁבְעַת יְמֵי הַמִּשְׁתֶּה וּמְצָאתֶם וְנָתַתִּי לָכֶם שְׁלֹשִׁים סְדִינִים וּשְׁלֹשִׁים חֲלִפֹת בְּגָדִים: יב

13 but if you are not able to tell it to me, you must give me thirty linen tunics and thirty sets of clothing." And they said to him, "Ask your riddle and we will listen."

*v'-im LO tu-kh'-LU l'-ha-GEED LEE un-ta-TEM a-TEM LEE sh'-lo-SHEEM s'-dee-NEEM ush-lo-SHEEM kha-lee-FOT b'-ga-DEEM va-YO-m'-ru LO KHU-dah khee-da-t'-KHA v'-nish-ma-E-nah*

וְאִם־לֹא תוּכְלוּ לְהַגִּיד לִי וּנְתַתֶּם אַתֶּם לִי שְׁלֹשִׁים סְדִינִים וּשְׁלֹשִׁים חֲלִיפוֹת בְּגָדִים וַיֹּאמְרוּ לוֹ חוּדָה חִידָתְךָ וְנִשְׁמָעֶנָּה: יג

14 So he said to them:"Out of the eater came something to eat, Out of the strong came something sweet." For three days they could not answer the riddle.

*va-YO-mer la-HEM may-ha-o-KHAYL ya-TZA ma-a-KHAL u-may-AZ ya-TZA ma-TOK v'-LO ya-kh'-LU l'-ha-GEED ha-khee-DAH sh'-LO-shet ya-MEEM*

וַיֹּאמֶר לָהֶם מֵהָאֹכֵל יָצָא מַאֲכָל וּמֵעַז יָצָא מָתוֹק וְלֹא יָכְלוּ לְהַגִּיד הַחִידָה שְׁלֹשֶׁת יָמִים: יד

15

On the seventh day, they said to Samson's wife, "Coax your husband to provide us with the answer to the riddle; else we shall put you and your father's household to the fire; have you invited us here in order to impoverish us?"

*vai-HEE ba-YOM ha-sh'-vee-EE va-yo-m'-RU l'-AY-shet shim-SHON pa-TEE et i-SHAYKH v'-ya-ged LA-nu et ha-khee-DAH pen nis-ROF o-TAKH v'-et BAYT a-VEEKH ba-AYSH hal-yor-SHAY-nu k'-ra-TEM LA-nu ha-LO*

וַיְהִי בַּיּוֹם הַשְּׁבִיעִי
וַיֹּאמְרוּ לְאֵשֶׁת־שִׁמְשׁוֹן
פַּתִּי אֶת־אִישֵׁךְ וְיַגֶּד־
לָנוּ אֶת־הַחִידָה פֶּן־
נִשְׂרֹף אוֹתָךְ וְאֶת־בֵּית
אָבִיךְ בָּאֵשׁ הַלְיָרְשֵׁנוּ
קְרָאתֶם לָנוּ הֲלֹא: טו

16

Then Samson's wife harassed him with tears, and she said, "You really hate me, you don't love me. You asked my people a riddle, and you didn't tell me the answer." He replied, "I haven't even told my father and mother; shall I tell you?"

*va-TAYVK AY-shet shim-SHON a-LAV va-TO-mer rak s'-nay-TA-nee v'-LO a-hav-TA-nee ha-khee-DAH KHAD-ta liv-NAY a-MEE v'-LEE LO hi-GAD-tah va-YO-mer LAH hi-NAY l'-a-VEE ul-i-MEE LO hi-GAD-tee v'-LAKH a-GEED*

וַתֵּבְךְּ אֵשֶׁת שִׁמְשׁוֹן
עָלָיו וַתֹּאמֶר רַק־
שְׂנֵאתַנִי וְלֹא אֲהַבְתָּנִי
הַחִידָה חַדְתָּ לִבְנֵי עַמִּי
וְלִי לֹא הִגַּדְתָּה וַיֹּאמֶר
לָהּ הִנֵּה לְאָבִי וּלְאִמִּי
לֹא הִגַּדְתִּי וְלָךְ אַגִּיד: טז

17

During the rest of the seven days of the feast she continued to harass him with her tears, and on the seventh day he told her, because she nagged him so. And she explained the riddle to her people.

*va-TAYVK a-LAV shiv-AT ha-ya-MEEM a-sher ha-YAH la-HEM ha-mish-TEH vai-HEE ba-YOM ha-sh'-vee-EE va-ya-ged LAH KEE he-tzee-KAT-hu va-ta-GAYD ha-khee-DAH liv-NAY a-MAH*

וַתֵּבְךְּ עָלָיו שִׁבְעַת
הַיָּמִים אֲשֶׁר־הָיָה
לָהֶם הַמִּשְׁתֶּה וַיְהִי
בַּיּוֹם הַשְּׁבִיעִי וַיַּגֶּד־לָהּ
כִּי הֱצִיקַתְהוּ וַתַּגֵּד
הַחִידָה לִבְנֵי עַמָּהּ: יז

18

On the seventh day, before the sunset, the townspeople said to him: "What is sweeter than honey, And what is stronger than a lion?" He responded: "Had you not plowed with my heifer, You would not have guessed my riddle!"

*va-YO'-m'-ru LO an-SHAY ha-EER ba-YOM ha-sh'-vee-EE b'-TE-rem ya-VO ha-KHAR-sah mah ma-TOK mid-VASH u-MEH AZ may-a-REE va-YO-mer la-HEM lu-LAY kha-rash-TEM b'-eg-la-TEE LO m'-tza-TEM khee-da-TEE*

וַיֹּאמְרוּ לוֹ אַנְשֵׁי
הָעִיר בַּיּוֹם הַשְּׁבִיעִי
בְּטֶרֶם יָבֹא הַחַרְסָה
מַה־מָּתוֹק מִדְּבַשׁ
וּמֶה עַז מֵאֲרִי וַיֹּאמֶר
לָהֶם לוּלֵא חֲרַשְׁתֶּם
בְּעֶגְלָתִי לֹא מְצָאתֶם
חִידָתִי:

יח

19

The spirit of GOD gripped him. He went down to Ashkelon and killed thirty of its men. He stripped them and gave the sets of clothing to those who had answered the riddle. And he left in a rage for his father's house.

*va-titz-LAKH a-LAV RU-akh a-do-NAI va-YAY-red ash-k'-LON va-YAKH may-HEM sh'-lo-SHEEM EESH va-yi-KAKH et kha-LEE-tzo-TAM va-yi-TAYN ha-kha-lee-FOT l'-ma-gee-DAY ha-khee-DAH va-yi-KHAR a-PO va-YA-al BAYT a-VEE-hu*

וַתִּצְלַח עָלָיו רוּחַ
יְהוָה וַיֵּרֶד אַשְׁקְלוֹן
וַיַּךְ מֵהֶם שְׁלֹשִׁים אִישׁ
וַיִּקַּח אֶת־חֲלִיצוֹתָם
וַיִּתֵּן הַחֲלִיפוֹת לְמַגִּידֵי
הַחִידָה וַיִּחַר אַפּוֹ וַיַּעַל
בֵּית אָבִיהוּ:

יט

20

Samson's wife then got married to one of those who had been his wedding companions.

*va-t'-HEE AY-shet shim-SHON l'-may-ray-AY-hu a-SHER ray-AH LO*

וַתְּהִי אֵשֶׁת שִׁמְשׁוֹן
לְמֵרֵעֵהוּ אֲשֶׁר רֵעָה
לוֹ:

כ

# Should We Be Ashamed of Samson?

Powerful warriors don't fare very well in the Bible, to put it kindly.

When Og, the giant warrior King of Bashan, attacked the people of Israel in the wilderness, Moses made quick work of him:

"King Og of Bashan, with all his people, came out to Edrei to engage them in battle. But Hashem said to Moses, "Do not fear him, for I give him and all his people and his land into your hand... They defeated him and his sons and all his people, until no remnant was left him" (Numbers 21:33-35).

Goliath, the terrifying Philistine warrior, fared no better against young David:

"A champion of the Philistine forces stepped forward; his name was Goliath of Gath, and he was six cubits [ten feet] tall... David put his hand into the bag; he took out a stone and slung it. It struck the Philistine in the forehead; the stone sank into his forehead, and he fell face down on the ground" (I Samuel, 17:4,49)

This, it would seem, is no mere coincidence. While the pagan nations of antiquity placed their trust in their own physical strength, the people of Israel were called upon to trust in God:

"They [call] on chariots, they [call] on horses, but we call on the name of the LORD our God" (Psalms 20:8).

With the passing of time, physical strength became even more suspect in Jewish tradition. When the Second Temple was destroyed and the Jewish people were sent into exile, they constantly found themselves in a position of physical weakness. In the dynamic of Jewish exile, warriors, by and large, were antisemites, while Jews were scholars and businessmen. Over time, some Jews even took pride in their powerlessness, feeling that it conferred upon them the moral high ground.

Given this history, what are we to make of Samson, the most powerful Israelite warrior in the Bible?

Samson's defining characteristic was his superhuman strength, which first emerges in a one-on-one battle with a lion:

"When he came to the vineyards of Timnah [for the first time], a full-grown lion came roaring at him. The spirit of GOD gripped him, and he tore him asunder with his bare hands as one might tear a kid asunder..." (Judges 14:5-6)

But Samson's unbelievable strength is most apparent when he single-handedly takes on the entire Philistine army – and emerges victorious!

"He came upon a fresh jawbone of an ass and he picked it up; and with it he killed a thousand men" (Judges 15:14).

Though Samson's physical strength and fierceness as a warrior make many people uncomfortable, Rabbi Abraham Isaac Kook, one of the greatest Jewish thinkers of modern times, had a very different perspective on Samson and his physical strength:

"Samson, who was praised for his great physical strength, was holy to God, judged the people before their Father in Heaven and is even associated with the name of God itself... In the end of days, the people of Israel will require great physical strength in service of holiness... And the holiness the people will muster is drawn from the original and holy Nazirite of God – Samson" (Letters, Volume 4, 89).

Rabbi Kook believed that not only shouldn't we be ashamed of Samson, but that the Jewish people of today must turn to Samson for inspiration! To bring the final redemption, the Jewish people must partner with God in resettling the land of Israel. 120 years ago, when the Jewish people began returning to the land, Israel was a desolate land of mosquito-infested swamps and barren hills. To brave the elements and bring the land back to life, the Jewish people would need brute, physical strength. Incredibly, with God's help and decades of intense labor, the pioneers succeeded in making the land flower once again.

Physical strength is also needed to protect the nation of Israel from the enemies that surround it. Though many in the Western world reflexively support the Palestinians "because Israel is so powerful," this is foolish thinking. If the Israeli army was weak, Israel's enemies would inflict another Holocaust upon the Jewish people, God forbid. There is no shame in being strong; it is essential to God's plan for the people of Israel!

At the same time, the people of Israel must never make the mistake of the pagans. Ultimately, no matter how physically strong we might be, we must always remember that our success is due to God. As David so beautifully said to Goliath:

"You come against me with sword and spear and javelin; but I come against you in the name of the Lord of Hosts, the God of the ranks of Israel" (I Samuel, 17:45).

Not only must we remember that our strength comes from God, but Samson reminds us that physical strength, like any other gift or ability, must be used for the sake of heaven. We are called upon to serve God with all our might, using our strength and talents to make the world a better place and to protect our people from harm. Samson's strength, then, becomes a symbol not only of physical prowess but of the potential for the great good that lies within each and every one of us. Let us strive to use our strength and abilities in service of holiness, following in the footsteps of Samson.

# 15  טֽו

| | | |
|---|---|---|
| 1 | Some time later, in the season of the wheat harvest, Samson came to visit his wife, bringing a kid as a gift. He said, "Let me go into the chamber to my wife." But her father would not let him go in. | vai-HEE mi-ya-MEEM bee-MAY k'-tzeer khi-TEEM va-yif-KOD shim-SHON et ish-TO big-DEE i-ZEEM va-YO-mer a-VO-ah el ish-TEE he-KHAD-rah v'-lo n'-ta-NO a-VEE-ha la-VO | וַיְהִי מִיָּמִים בִּימֵי קְצִיר־חִטִּים וַיִּפְקֹד שִׁמְשׁוֹן אֶת־אִשְׁתּוֹ בִּגְדִי עִזִּים וַיֹּאמֶר אָבֹאָה אֶל־אִשְׁתִּי הֶחָדְרָה וְלֹא־נְתָנוֹ אָבִיהָ לָבוֹא: |
| 2 | "I was sure," said her father, "that you had taken a dislike to her, so I gave her to your wedding companion. But her younger sister is more beautiful than she; let her become your wife instead." | va-YO-mer a-VEE-ha a-MOR a-MAR-tee kee sa-NO s'-nay-TAH va-e-t'-NE-nah l'-may-ray-E-kha ha-LO a-kho-TAH ha-k'-ta-NAH to-VAH mi-ME-nah t'-hee NA l'-KHA takh-TE-ha | וַיֹּאמֶר אָבִיהָ אָמֹר אָמַרְתִּי כִּי־שָׂנֹא שְׂנֵאתָהּ וָאֶתְּנֶנָּה לְמֵרֵעֶךָ הֲלֹא אֲחֹתָהּ הַקְּטַנָּה טוֹבָה מִמֶּנָּה תְּהִי־נָא לְךָ תַּחְתֶּיהָ: |
| 3 | Thereupon Samson declared, "Now the Philistines can have no claim against me for the harm I shall do them." | va-YO-mer la-HEM shim-SHON ni-KAY-tee ha-PA-am mi-p'-lish-TEEM kee o-SEH a-NEE i-MAM ra-AH | וַיֹּאמֶר לָהֶם שִׁמְשׁוֹן נִקֵּיתִי הַפַּעַם מִפְּלִשְׁתִּים כִּי־עֹשֶׂה אֲנִי עִמָּם רָעָה: |

| | | | |
|---|---|---|---|
| 4 | Samson went and caught three hundred foxes. He took torches and, turning [the foxes] tail to tail, he placed a torch between each pair of tails. | *va-YAY-lekh shim-SHON va-yil-KOD sh'-losh may-OT shu-a-LEEM va-yi-KAKH la-pi-DEEM va-YE-fen za-NAV el za-NAV va-YA-sem la-PEED e-KHAD bayn sh'-NAY ha-z'-na-VOT ba-TA-vekh* | וַיֵּלֶךְ שִׁמְשׁוֹן וַיִּלְכֹּד שְׁלֹשׁ־מֵאוֹת שׁוּעָלִים וַיִּקַּח לַפִּדִים וַיֶּפֶן זָנָב אֶל־זָנָב וַיָּשֶׂם לַפִּיד אֶחָד בֵּין־שְׁנֵי הַזְּנָבוֹת בַּתָּוֶךְ: ד |
| 5 | He lit the torches and turned [the foxes] loose among the standing grain of the Philistines, setting fire to stacked grain, standing grain, vineyards, [and] olive trees. | *va-yav-er AYSH ba-la-pee-DEEM vai-sha-LAKH b'-ka-MOT p'-lish-TEEM va-yav-AYR mi-ga-DEESH v'-ad ka-MAH v'-ad KE-rem ZA-yit* | וַיַּבְעֶר־אֵשׁ בַּלַּפִּידִים וַיְשַׁלַּח בְּקָמוֹת פְּלִשְׁתִּים וַיַּבְעֵר מִגָּדִישׁ וְעַד־קָמָה וְעַד־כֶּרֶם זָיִת: ה |
| 6 | The Philistines asked, "Who did this?" And they were told, "It was Samson, the son-in-law of the Timnite, who took Samson's wife and gave her to his wedding companion." Thereupon the Philistines came up and put her and her father to the fire. | *va-yo-m'-RU f'-lish-TEEM MEE A-sah ZOT va-yo-m'-RU shim-SHON kha-TAN ha-tim-NEE KEE la-KAKH et ish-TO va-yi-t'-NAH l'-may-ray-AY-hu va-ya-a-LU f'-lish-TEEM va-yis-r'-FU o-TAH v'-et a-VEE-ha ba-AYSH* | וַיֹּאמְרוּ פְלִשְׁתִּים מִי עָשָׂה זֹאת וַיֹּאמְרוּ שִׁמְשׁוֹן חֲתַן הַתִּמְנִי כִּי לָקַח אֶת־אִשְׁתּוֹ וַיִּתְּנָהּ לְמֵרֵעֵהוּ וַיַּעֲלוּ פְלִשְׁתִּים וַיִּשְׂרְפוּ אוֹתָהּ וְאֶת־אָבִיהָ בָּאֵשׁ: ו |
| 7 | Samson said to them, "If that is how you act, I will not rest until I have taken revenge on you." | *va-YO-mer la-HEM shim-SHON im ta-a-SUN ka-ZOT KEE im ni-KAM-tee va-KHEM v'-a-KHAR ekh-DAL* | וַיֹּאמֶר לָהֶם שִׁמְשׁוֹן אִם־תַּעֲשׂוּן כָּזֹאת כִּי אִם־נִקַּמְתִּי בָכֶם וְאַחַר אֶחְדָּל: ז |

| |  |  |  | |
|---|---|---|---|---|
| 8 | He gave them a sound and thorough thrashing. Then he went down and stayed in the cave of the rock of Etam. | va-YAKH o-TAM SHOK al ya-RAYKH ma-KAH g'-do-LAH va-YAY-red va-YAY-shev bis-EEF SE-la ay-TAM | וַיַּךְ אוֹתָם שׁוֹק עַל־יָרֵךְ מַכָּה גְדוֹלָה וַיֵּרֶד וַיֵּשֶׁב בִּסְעִיף סֶלַע עֵיטָם: | ח |
| 9 | The Philistines came up, pitched camp in Judah and spread out over Lehi. | va-ya-a-LU f'-lish-TEEM va-ya-kha-NU bee-hu-DAH va-yi-na-t'-SHU ba-LE-khee | וַיַּעֲלוּ פְלִשְׁתִּים וַיַּחֲנוּ בִּיהוּדָה וַיִּנָּטְשׁוּ בַּלֶּחִי: | ט |
| 10 | Judah's side asked, "Why have you come up against us?" They answered, "We have come to take Samson prisoner, and to do to him as he did to us." | va-yo-m'-RU EESH y'-hu-DAH la-MAH a-lee-TEM a-LAY-nu va-yo-m'-RU le-e-SOR et shim-SHON a-LEE-nu la-a-SOT LO ka-a-SHER A-sah LA-nu | וַיֹּאמְרוּ אִישׁ יְהוּדָה לָמָה עֲלִיתֶם עָלֵינוּ וַיֹּאמְרוּ לֶאֱסוֹר אֶת־שִׁמְשׁוֹן עָלִינוּ לַעֲשׂוֹת לוֹ כַּאֲשֶׁר עָשָׂה לָנוּ: | י |
| 11 | Thereupon three thousand Judahites went down to the cave of the rock of Etam, and they said to Samson, "You knew that the Philistines rule over us; why have you done this to us?" He replied, "As they did to me, so I did to them." | va-yay-r'-DU sh'-LO-shet a-la-FEEM EESH mee-hu-DAH el s'-EEF SE-la ay-TAM va-yo-m'-RU l'-shim-SHON ha-LO ya-DA-ta kee mo-sh'-LEEM BA-nu p'-lish-TEEM u-mah ZOT a-SEE-ta LA-nu va-YO-mer la-HEM ka-a-SHER A-su LEE KAYN a-SEE-tee la-HEM | וַיֵּרְדוּ שְׁלֹשֶׁת אֲלָפִים אִישׁ מִיהוּדָה אֶל־סְעִיף סֶלַע עֵיטָם וַיֹּאמְרוּ לְשִׁמְשׁוֹן הֲלֹא יָדַעְתָּ כִּי־מֹשְׁלִים בָּנוּ פְּלִשְׁתִּים וּמַה־זֹּאת עָשִׂיתָ לָּנוּ וַיֹּאמֶר לָהֶם כַּאֲשֶׁר עָשׂוּ לִי כֵּן עָשִׂיתִי לָהֶם: | יא |

| | | |
|---|---|---|
| 12 | "We have come down," they told him, "to take you prisoner and to hand you over to the Philistines." "But swear to me," said Samson to them, "that you yourselves will not attack me." | *va-YO-m'-ru LO le-e-sor-KHA ya-RAD-nu l'-ti-t'-KHA b'-yad p'-lish-TEEM va-YO-mer la-HEM shim-SHON hi-sha-v'-U LEE pen tif-g'-UN BEE a-TEM* | וַיֹּאמְרוּ לוֹ לֶאֱסָרְךָ יָרַדְנוּ לְתִתְּךָ בְּיַד־פְּלִשְׁתִּים וַיֹּאמֶר לָהֶם שִׁמְשׁוֹן הִשָּׁבְעוּ לִי פֶּן־תִּפְגְּעוּן בִּי אַתֶּם: | יב |
| 13 | "We won't," they replied. "We will only take you prisoner and hand you over to them; we will not slay you." So they bound him with two new ropes and brought him up from the rock. | *va-YO-m'-ru LO lay-MOR LO kee a-SOR ne-e-sor-KHA un-ta-NU-kha v'-ya-DAM v'-ha-MAYT LO n'-mee-TE-kha va-ya-as-RU-hu bish-NA-yim a-vo-TEEM kha-da-SHEEM va-ya-a-LU-hu min ha-SA-la* | וַיֹּאמְרוּ לוֹ לֵאמֹר לֹא כִּי־אָסֹר נֶאֱסָרְךָ וּנְתַנּוּךָ בְיָדָם וְהָמֵת לֹא נְמִיתֶךָ וַיַּאַסְרֻהוּ בִּשְׁנַיִם עֲבֹתִים חֲדָשִׁים וַיַּעֲלוּהוּ מִן־הַסָּלַע: | יג |
| 14 | When he reached Lehi, the Philistines came shouting to meet him. Thereupon the spirit of GOD gripped him, and the ropes on his arms became like flax that catches fire; the bonds melted off his hands. | *hu VA ad LE-khee uf-lish-TEEM hay-REE-u lik-ra-TO va-titz-LAKH a-LAV RU-akh a-do-NAI va-tih-YE-nah ha-a-vo-TEEM a-SHER al z'-ro-o-TAV ka-pish-TEEM a-SHER ba-a-RU va-AYSH va-yi-MA-su e-su-RAV may-AL ya-DAV* | הוּא־בָא עַד־לֶחִי וּפְלִשְׁתִּים הֵרִיעוּ לִקְרָאתוֹ וַתִּצְלַח עָלָיו רוּחַ יְהֹוָה וַתִּהְיֶינָה הָעֲבֹתִים אֲשֶׁר עַל־זְרוֹעוֹתָיו כַּפִּשְׁתִּים אֲשֶׁר בָּעֲרוּ בָאֵשׁ וַיִּמַּסּוּ אֱסוּרָיו מֵעַל יָדָיו: | יד |
| 15 | He came upon a fresh jawbone of a donkey and he picked it up; and with it he killed a thousand men. | *va-yim-TZA l'-khee kha-MOR t'-ri-YAH va-yish-LAKH ya-DO va-yi-ka-KHE-ha va-yakh BAH E-lef EESH* | וַיִּמְצָא לְחִי־חֲמוֹר טְרִיָּה וַיִּשְׁלַח יָדוֹ וַיִּקָּחֶהָ וַיַּךְ־בָּהּ אֶלֶף אִישׁ: | טו |

155

| | | | |
|---|---|---|---|
| 16 | "Then Samson said: "With the jaw of an ass, Mass upon mass! With the jaw of an ass I have slain a thousand men." | *va-YO-mer shim-SHON bil-KHEE ha-kha-MOR kha-MOR kha-mo-ra-TA-yim bil-KHEE ha-kha-MOR hi-KAY-tee E-lef EESH* | וַיֹּאמֶר שִׁמְשׁוֹן בִּלְחִי הַחֲמוֹר חֲמוֹר חֲמֹרָתָיִם בִּלְחִי הַחֲמוֹר הִכֵּיתִי אֶלֶף אִישׁ: | טז |
| 17 | As he finished speaking, he threw the jawbone away; hence that place was called Ramath-lehi. | *vai-HEE kikh-LOT l'-da-BAYR va-yash-LAYKH ha-l'-KHEE mi-ya-DO va-yik-RA la-ma-KOM ha-HU RA-mat LE-khee* | וַיְהִי כְּכַלֹּתוֹ לְדַבֵּר וַיַּשְׁלֵךְ הַלְּחִי מִיָּדוֹ וַיִּקְרָא לַמָּקוֹם הַהוּא רָמַת לֶחִי: | יז |
| 18 | He was very thirsty and he called to GOD, "You Yourself have granted this great victory through Your servant; and must I now die of thirst and fall into the hands of the uncircumcised?" | *va-yitz-MA m'-OD va-yik-RA el a-do-NAI va-YO-mer a-TAH na-TA-tah v'-yad av-d'-KHA et ha-t'-shu-AH ha-g'-do-LAH ha-ZOT v'-a-TAH a-MUT ba-tza-MA v'-na-fal-TEE b'-YAD ha-a-ray-LEEM* | וַיִּצְמָא מְאֹד וַיִּקְרָא אֶל־יְהוָה וַיֹּאמַר אַתָּה נָתַתָּ בְיַד־עַבְדְּךָ אֶת־הַתְּשׁוּעָה הַגְּדֹלָה הַזֹּאת וְעַתָּה אָמוּת בַּצָּמָא וְנָפַלְתִּי בְּיַד הָעֲרֵלִים: | יח |
| 19 | So God split open the hollow that is at Lehi, and the water gushed out of it; he drank, regained his strength, and revived. That is why it is called to this day "En-hakkore of Lehi." | *va-yiv-KA e-lo-HEEM et ha-makh-TAYSH a-sher ba-LE-khee va-yay-tz'-U mi-ME-nu MA-yim va-yaysht va-TA-shov ru-KHO va-YE-khee al KAYN ka-RA sh'-MAH AYN ha-ko-RAY a-SHER ba-LE-khee AD ha-YOM ha-ZEH* | וַיִּבְקַע אֱלֹהִים אֶת־הַמַּכְתֵּשׁ אֲשֶׁר־בַּלֶּחִי וַיֵּצְאוּ מִמֶּנּוּ מַיִם וַיֵּשְׁתְּ וַתָּשָׁב רוּחוֹ וַיֶּחִי עַל־כֵּן קָרָא שְׁמָהּ עֵין הַקּוֹרֵא אֲשֶׁר בַּלֶּחִי עַד הַיּוֹם הַזֶּה: | יט |
| 20 | He led Israel in the days of the Philistines for twenty years. | *va-yish-POT et yis-ra-AYL bee-MAY f'-lish-TEEM es-REEM sha-NAH* | וַיִּשְׁפֹּט אֶת־יִשְׂרָאֵל בִּימֵי פְלִשְׁתִּים עֶשְׂרִים שָׁנָה: | כ |

# Who is Truly Strong?

It was one of the very worst moments in modern Jewish history.

On May 14, 1948, Israel was reborn. Five Arab nations immediately invaded the new state of Israel, which was forced to fight for its life with a limited supply of guns and ammunition. To help remedy the situation, the Irgun, the underground Jewish fighting force led by future Prime Minister Menachem Begin, sent a ship, the Altalena, loaded with volunteers and ammunition, from Europe to Israel. Meanwhile, the Irgun reached an agreement with Israel's newly established army, with plans for the army to absorb the Irgun and its fighters into its ranks.

Despite the agreement, the new Israeli government, led by David Ben Gurion, viewed the arrival of the Altalena as a threat to its power. Ben Gurion ordered his new army to confiscate the ship and its cargo, and to use force if necessary. Though Menachem Begin hoped to reach a peaceful agreement with the new government, events soon spun out of control. On June 20, as the ship sat off the coast of Tel Aviv, Ben Gurion ordered the shelling of the Altalena. One of the shells struck the Altalena, and the crew was afraid the resulting fire would spread to the holds which contained large amounts of ammunition and explosives. Hundreds of people jumped into the water, swimming to shore, where they were confronted by the army. Sixteen Irgun volunteers were killed.

Just as Israel was born, it was about to be torn in two; civil war seemed inevitable, even as the new country was fighting for its life on all fronts against external foes. Members of the Irgun, furious at the government for its unprovoked attack, were ready to declare war on their fellow Jews. But that night, after the Altalena was destroyed, Menachem Begin spoke over the radio about the ship and those who had died. He wept over the tragedy and gave honor to those who had needlessly died. And then he made the most fateful decision of his life: he ordered his men not to fight back. Instead, he called for them to assemble in Jerusalem and continue the battle for the Old City. "And so it came to pass that there was no fratricidal war in Israel to destroy the Jewish State before it was properly born. In spite of everything – there was no civil war!" (Menachem Begin, The Revolt). It was, as Begin himself said, the greatest accomplishment of his life.

But it was not the first time in Israel's history that a leader's greatest accomplishment was defined by awesome self-restraint. For that, we must turn to the Bible.

The entire people of Israel were terrified of their Philistine oppressors, with one exception: Samson. Samson fearlessly sabotaged Philistine warriors and destroyed their crops, the only Israelite willing to stand up to their oppressors. In response, the Philistine army threatened to attack the men of Judah. Terrified, the men of Judah captured Samson and resolved to hand him over to the Philistines, in hopes of appeasing the Philistines and saving their own skins:

"Thereupon three thousand men of Judah... said to Samson, "You knew that the Philistines rule over us; why have you done this to us?" He replied, "As they did to me, so I did to them." "We have come down," they told him, "to take you prisoner and to hand you over to the Philistines." "But swear to me," said Samson to them, "that you yourselves will not attack me." "We won't," they replied. "We will only take you prisoner and hand you over to them; we will not slay you." So they bound him with two new ropes and brought him up from the rock" (Judges 15:11-13).

The people of Israel finally had a leader brave enough to fight the Philistines. But instead of embracing him, the terrified and defeatist people handed Samson over to the enemy!

Samson had every right to be furious. In Jewish tradition, handing over a fellow Jew to the enemy is a terrible sin, for it is a violation of Jewish unity and the obligation that citizens of the nation owe to one another. But not only did Samson not lash out at his own people, he goes to great lengths to ensure that his battle with the Philistines would not involve his frightened countrymen. He allows the men of Judah to hand him over to the Philistines, proving their "loyalty" to the hated oppressors!

Though Samson is most famous for his incredible physical strength, which he used to kill thousands of Israel's enemies, I believe that this was his greatest accomplishment. Like Menachem Begin, he refused to fight his fellow Jews, even when they showed no love or loyalty to him.

"Who is strong? One who overpowers his inclinations." (Ethics of the Fathers, 4:1)

# 16

| | | | |
|---|---|---|---|
| 1 | Once Samson went to Gaza; there he met a prostitute and slept with her. | va-YAY-lekh shim-SHON a-ZA-tah va-yar SHAM i-SHAH zo-NAH va-ya-VO ay-LE-ha | וַיֵּלֶךְ שִׁמְשׁוֹן עַזָּתָה וַיַּרְא־שָׁם אִשָּׁה זוֹנָה וַיָּבֹא אֵלֶיהָ: א |
| 2 | The Gazites [learned] that Samson had come there, so they gathered and lay in ambush for him in the town gate the whole night; and all night long they kept whispering to each other, "When daylight comes, we'll kill him." | la-a-za-TEEM lay-MOR BA shim-SHON HAY-nah va-ya-SO-bu va-ye-er-vu LO khol ha-LAI-lah b'-SHA-ar ha-EER va-yit-kha-r'-SHU khol ha-LAI-lah lay-MOR ad OR ha-BO-ker va-ha-rag-NU-hu | לַעַזָּתִים לֵאמֹר בָּא שִׁמְשׁוֹן הֵנָּה וַיָּסֹבּוּ וַיֶּאֶרְבוּ־לוֹ כָל־הַלַּיְלָה בְּשַׁעַר הָעִיר וַיִּתְחָרְשׁוּ כָל־הַלַּיְלָה לֵאמֹר עַד־אוֹר הַבֹּקֶר וַהֲרַגְנֻהוּ: ב |
| 3 | But Samson lay in bed only till midnight. At midnight he got up, grasped the doors of the town gate together with the two gateposts, and pulled them out along with the bar. He placed them on his shoulders and carried them off to the top of the hill that is near Hebron. | va-yish-KAV shim-SHON ad kha-TZEE ha-LAI-lah va-YA-kom ba-kha-TZEE ha-LAI-lah va-ye-e-KHOZ b'-dal-TOT sha-ar ha-EER u-vish-TAY ha-m'-zu-ZOT va-yi-sa-AYM im ha-b'-REE-akh va-YA-sem al k'-tay-FAV va-ya-a-LAYM el ROSH ha-HAR a-SHER al p'-NAY khev-RON | וַיִּשְׁכַּב שִׁמְשׁוֹן עַד־חֲצִי הַלַּיְלָה וַיָּקָם בַּחֲצִי הַלַּיְלָה וַיֶּאֱחֹז בְּדַלְתוֹת שַׁעַר־הָעִיר וּבִשְׁתֵּי הַמְּזוּזוֹת וַיִּסָּעֵם עִם־הַבְּרִיחַ וַיָּשֶׂם עַל־כְּתֵפָיו וַיַּעֲלֵם אֶל־רֹאשׁ הָהָר אֲשֶׁר עַל־פְּנֵי חֶבְרוֹן: ג |

4  After that, he fell in love with a woman in the Wadi Sorek, named Delilah.

*vai-HEE a-kha-ray KHAYN va-ye-e-HAV i-SHAH b'-NA-khal so-RAYK ush-MAH d'-lee-LAH*

וַיְהִי אַחֲרֵי־כֵן וַיֶּאֱהַב אִשָּׁה בְּנַחַל שֹׂרֵק וּשְׁמָהּ דְּלִילָה:  ד

5  The lords of the Philistines went up to her and said, "Coax him and find out what makes him so strong, and how we can overpower him, tie him up, and make him helpless; and we'll each give you eleven hundred shekels of silver."

*va-ya-a-LU ay-LE-ha sar-NAY f'-lish-TEEM va-YO-m'-ru LAH pa-TEE o-TO ur-EE ba-MEH ko-KHO ga-DOL u-va-MEH NU-khal LO va-a-sar-NU-hu l'-a-no-TO va-a-NAKH-nu ni-tan LAKH EESH E-lef u-may-AH KA-sef*

וַיַּעֲלוּ אֵלֶיהָ סַרְנֵי פְלִשְׁתִּים וַיֹּאמְרוּ לָהּ פַּתִּי אוֹתוֹ וּרְאִי בַּמֶּה כֹּחוֹ גָדוֹל וּבַמֶּה נוּכַל לוֹ וַאֲסַרְנוּהוּ לְעַנּוֹתוֹ וַאֲנַחְנוּ נִתַּן־לָךְ אִישׁ אֶלֶף וּמֵאָה כָּסֶף:  ה

6  So Delilah said to Samson, "Tell me, what makes you so strong? And how could you be tied up and made helpless?"

*va-TO-mer d'-lee-LAH el shim-SHON ha-gee-dah NA LEE ba-MEH ko-kha-KHA ga-DOL u-va-MEH tay-a-SAYR l'-a-no-TE-kha*

וַתֹּאמֶר דְּלִילָה אֶל־שִׁמְשׁוֹן הַגִּידָה־נָּא לִי בַּמֶּה כֹּחֲךָ גָדוֹל וּבַמֶּה תֵאָסֵר לְעַנּוֹתֶךָ:  ו

7  Samson replied, "If I were to be tied with seven fresh tendons that had not been dried, I should become as weak as an ordinary man."

*va-YO-mer ay-LE-ha shim-SHON im ya-as-RU-nee b'-shiv-AH y'-ta-REEM la-KHEEM a-SHER lo kho-RA-vu v'-kha-LEE-tee v'-ha-YEE-tee k'-a-KHAD ha-a-DAM*

וַיֹּאמֶר אֵלֶיהָ שִׁמְשׁוֹן אִם־יַאַסְרֻנִי בְּשִׁבְעָה יְתָרִים לַחִים אֲשֶׁר לֹא־חֹרָבוּ וְחָלִיתִי וְהָיִיתִי כְּאַחַד הָאָדָם:  ז

8  So the lords of the Philistines brought up to her seven fresh tendons that had not been dried. She bound him with them,

*va-ya-a-lu LAH sar-NAY f'-lish-TEEM shiv-AH y'-ta-REEM la-KHEEM a-SHER lo kho-RA-vu va-ta-as-RAY-hu ba-HEM*

וַיַּעֲלוּ־לָהּ סַרְנֵי פְלִשְׁתִּים שִׁבְעָה יְתָרִים לַחִים אֲשֶׁר לֹא־חֹרָבוּ וַתַּאַסְרֵהוּ בָּהֶם:  ח

9    while an ambush was
waiting in her room.
Then she called out
to him, "Samson, the
Philistines are upon
you!" Whereupon he
pulled the tendons
apart, as a strand
of tow comes apart
at the touch of fire.
So the secret of his
strength remained
unknown.

*v'-ha-o-RAYV yo-SHAYV
LAH ba-KHE-der
v'-TO-mer ay-LAV p'-
lish-TEEM a-LE-kha
shim-SHON vai-na-
TAYK et hai-ta-REEM
ka-a-SHER yi-na-TAYK
p'-teel han'-O-ret ba-ha-
ree-KHO AYSH v'-LO
no-DA ko-KHO*

וְהָאֹרֵב יֹשֵׁב לָהּ בַּחֶדֶר
וַתֹּאמֶר אֵלָיו פְּלִשְׁתִּים
עָלֶיךָ שִׁמְשׁוֹן וַיְנַתֵּק
אֶת-הַיְתָרִים כַּאֲשֶׁר
יִנָּתֵק פְּתִיל-הַנְּעֹרֶת
בַּהֲרִיחוֹ אֵשׁ וְלֹא נוֹדַע
כֹּחוֹ:

ט

10   Then Delilah said to
Samson, "Oh, you
deceived me; you lied
to me! Do tell me
now how you could
be tied up."

*va-TO-mer d'-lee-LAH
el shim-SHON hi-NAY
hay-TAL-ta BEE va-
ti-da-BAYR ay-LAI
k'-za-VEEM a-TAH ha-
gee-dah LEE ba-MEH
tay-a-SAYR*

וַתֹּאמֶר דְּלִילָה אֶל-
שִׁמְשׁוֹן הִנֵּה הֵתַלְתָּ
בִּי וַתְּדַבֵּר אֵלַי כְּזָבִים
עַתָּה הַגִּידָה-נָּא לִי
בַּמֶּה תֵּאָסֵר:

י

11   He said, "If I were to
be bound with new
ropes that had never
been used, I would
become as weak as an
ordinary man."

*va-YO-mer ay-LE-ha
im a-SOR ya-as-RU-nee
ba-a-vo-TEEM kha-
da-SHEEM a-SHER
lo na-a-SAH va-HEM
m'-la-KHAH v'-kha-
LEE-tee v'-ha-YEE-tee
k'-a-KHAD ha-a-DAM*

וַיֹּאמֶר אֵלֶיהָ אִם-
אָסוֹר יַאַסְרוּנִי
בַּעֲבֹתִים חֲדָשִׁים
אֲשֶׁר לֹא-נַעֲשָׂה בָהֶם
מְלָאכָה וְחָלִיתִי
וְהָיִיתִי כְּאַחַד הָאָדָם:

יא

12   So Delilah took new
ropes and bound him
with them, while an
ambush was waiting
in a room. And she
cried, "Samson, the
Philistines are upon
you!" But he tore
them off his arms like
a thread.

*va-ti-KAKH d'-lee-LAH
a-vo-TEEM kha-da-
SHEEM va-ta-as-RAY-hu
va-HEM va-TO-mer
ay-LAV p'-lish-TEEM
a-LE-kha shim-SHON
v'-ha-o-RAYV yo-SHAYV
be-KHA-der vai-na-t'-
KAYM may-AL z'-ro-o-
TAV ka-KHUT*

וַתִּקַּח דְּלִילָה עֲבֹתִים
חֲדָשִׁים וַתַּאַסְרֵהוּ
בָהֶם וַתֹּאמֶר אֵלָיו
פְּלִשְׁתִּים עָלֶיךָ שִׁמְשׁוֹן
וְהָאֹרֵב יֹשֵׁב בֶּחָדֶר
וַיְנַתְּקֵם מֵעַל זְרֹעֹתָיו
כַּחוּט:

יב

| | | |
|---|---|---|
| 13 | Then Delilah said to Samson, "You have been deceiving me all along; you have been lying to me! Tell me, how could you be tied up?" He answered her, "If you weave seven locks of my head into the web." | *va-TO-mer d'-lee-LAH el shim-SHON ad HAY-nah hay-TAL-ta BEE va-t'-da-BAYR ay-LAI k'-za-VEEM ha-GEE-dah LEE ba-MEH tay-a-SAYR va-YO-mer ay-LE-ha im ta-ar-GEE et SHE-va makh-l'-FOT ro-SHEE im ha-ma-SA-khet* | וַתֹּאמֶר דְּלִילָה אֶל־שִׁמְשׁוֹן עַד־הֵנָּה הֵתַלְתָּ בִּי וַתְּדַבֵּר אֵלַי כְּזָבִים הַגִּידָה לִּי בַּמֶּה תֵּאָסֵר וַיֹּאמֶר אֵלֶיהָ אִם־תַּאַרְגִי אֶת־שֶׁבַע מַחְלְפוֹת רֹאשִׁי עִם־הַמַּסָּכֶת: |
| 14 | And she pinned it with a peg and cried to him, "Samson, the Philistines are upon you!" Awaking from his sleep, he pulled out the peg, the loom, and the web. | *va-tit-KA ba-ya-TAYD va-TO-mer ay-LAV p'-lish-TEEM a-LE-kha shim-SHON va-YEE-katz mish-na-TO va-yi-SA et hai-TAD ha-E-reg v'-et ha-ma-SA-khet* | וַתִּתְקַע בַּיָּתֵד וַתֹּאמֶר אֵלָיו פְּלִשְׁתִּים עָלֶיךָ שִׁמְשׁוֹן וַיִּיקַץ מִשְּׁנָתוֹ וַיִּסַּע אֶת־הַיְתַד הָאֶרֶג וְאֶת־הַמַּסָּכֶת: |
| 15 | Then she said to him, "How can you say you love me, when you don't confide in me? This makes three times that you've deceived me and haven't told me what makes you so strong." | *va-TO-mer ay-LAV AYKH to-MAR a-hav-TEEKH v'-li-b'-KHA AYN i-TEE ZEH sha-LOSH p'-a-MEEM hay-TAL-ta BEE v'-lo hi-GAD-ta LEE ba-MEH ko-kha-KHA ga-DOL* | וַתֹּאמֶר אֵלָיו אֵיךְ תֹּאמַר אֲהַבְתִּיךְ וְלִבְּךָ אֵין אִתִּי זֶה שָׁלֹשׁ פְּעָמִים הֵתַלְתָּ בִּי וְלֹא־הִגַּדְתָּ לִּי בַּמֶּה כֹּחֲךָ גָדוֹל: |
| 16 | Finally, after she had nagged him and pressed him constantly, he was wearied to death | *vai-HEE kee hay-TZEE-kah LO vid-va-RE-ha kol ha-ya-MEEM va-t'-al-TZAY-hu va-tik-TZAR naf-SHO la-MUT* | וַיְהִי כִּי־הֵצִיקָה לּוֹ בִדְבָרֶיהָ כָּל־הַיָּמִים וַתְּאַלְצֵהוּ וַתִּקְצַר נַפְשׁוֹ לָמוּת: |

| | | | |
|---|---|---|---|
| 17 | and he confided everything to her. He said to her, "No razor has ever touched my head, for I have been a nazirite to God since I was in my mother's womb. If my hair were cut, my strength would leave me and I should become as weak as an ordinary man." | *va-ya-ged LAH et kol li-BO va-YO-mer LAH mo-RAH lo a-LAH al ro-SHEE kee n'-ZEER e-lo-HEEM a-NEE mi-BE-ten i-MEE im gu-LAKH-tee v'-SAR mi-ME-nee kho-KHEE v'-kha-LEE-tee v'-ha-YEE-tee k'-khol ha-a-DAM* | וַיַּגֶּד־לָהּ אֶת־כָּל־לִבּוֹ וַיֹּאמֶר לָהּ מוֹרָה לֹא־עָלָה עַל־רֹאשִׁי כִּי־נְזִיר אֱלֹהִים אֲנִי מִבֶּטֶן אִמִּי אִם־גֻּלַּחְתִּי וְסָר מִמֶּנִּי כֹחִי וְחָלִיתִי וְהָיִיתִי כְּכָל־הָאָדָם׃ יז |
| 18 | Sensing that he had confided everything to her, Delilah sent for the lords of the Philistines, with this message: "Come up once more, for he has confided everything to me." And the lords of the Philistines came up and brought the money with them. | *va-TAY-re d'-lee-LAH kee hi-GEED LAH et kol li-BO va-tish-LAKH va-tik-RA l'-sar-NAY f'-lish-TEEM lay-MOR a-LU ha-PA-am kee hi-GEED LEE et kol li-BO v'-a-LU ay-LE-ha sar-NAY f'-lish-TEEM va-ya-LU ha-KE-sef b'-ya-DAM* | וַתֵּרֶא דְּלִילָה כִּי־הִגִּיד לָהּ אֶת־כָּל־לִבּוֹ וַתִּשְׁלַח וַתִּקְרָא לְסַרְנֵי פְלִשְׁתִּים לֵאמֹר עֲלוּ הַפַּעַם כִּי־הִגִּיד (לה) [לִי] אֶת־כָּל־לִבּוֹ וְעָלוּ אֵלֶיהָ סַרְנֵי פְלִשְׁתִּים וַיַּעֲלוּ הַכֶּסֶף בְּיָדָם׃ יח |
| 19 | She lulled him to sleep on her lap. Then she called in someone else, and she had him cut off the seven locks of his head; thus she weakened him and made him helpless: his strength slipped away from him. | *va-t'-yash-NAY-hu al bir-KE-ha va-tik-RA la-EESH va-ti-ga-LAKH et SHE-va makh-l'-FOT ro-SHOR va-TA-khel l'-a-no-TO va-YA-sar ko-KHO may-a-LAV* | וַתְּיַשְּׁנֵהוּ עַל־בִּרְכֶּיהָ וַתִּקְרָא לָאִישׁ וַתְּגַלַּח אֶת־שֶׁבַע מַחְלְפוֹת רֹאשׁוֹ וַתָּחֶל לְעַנּוֹתוֹ וַיָּסַר כֹּחוֹ מֵעָלָיו׃ יט |

20 She cried, "Samson, the Philistines are upon you!" And he awoke from his sleep, thinking he would break loose and shake himself free as he had the other times. For he did not know that GOD had departed from him.

*va-TO-mer p'-lish-TEEM a-LE-kha shim-SHON va-yi-KATZ mi-sh'-na-TO va-YO-mer ay-TZAY k'-FA-am b'-FA-am v'-i-na-AYR v'-HU LO ya-DA KEE a-do-NAI SAR may-a-LAV*

וַתֹּאמֶר פְּלִשְׁתִּים עָלֶיךָ שִׁמְשׁוֹן וַיִּקַץ מִשְּׁנָתוֹ וַיֹּאמֶר אֵצֵא כְּפַעַם בְּפַעַם וְאִנָּעֵר וְהוּא לֹא יָדַע כִּי יְהוָה סָר מֵעָלָיו: כ

21 The Philistines seized him and gouged out his eyes. They brought him down to Gaza and shackled him in bronze fetters, and he became a mill slave in the prison.

*va-yo-kha-ZU-hu f'-lish-TEEM vai-na-k'-RU et ay-NAV va-yo-REE-du o-TO a-ZA-tah va-ya-as-RU-hu ban-khush-TA-yim vai-HEE to-KHAYN b'-VAYT ha-a-su-REEM*

וַיֹּאחֲזוּהוּ פְלִשְׁתִּים וַיְנַקְּרוּ אֶת־עֵינָיו וַיּוֹרִידוּ אוֹתוֹ עַזָּתָה וַיַּאַסְרוּהוּ בַּנְחֻשְׁתַּיִם וַיְהִי טוֹחֵן בְּבֵית (האסירים) [הָאֲסוּרִים]: כא

22 After his hair was cut off, it began to grow back.

*va-YA-khel s'-ar ro-SHO l'-tza-MAY-akh ka-a-SHER gu-LAKH*

וַיָּחֶל שְׂעַר־רֹאשׁוֹ לְצַמֵּחַ כַּאֲשֶׁר גֻּלָּח: כב

23 "Now the lords of the Philistines gathered to offer a great sacrifice to their god Dagon and to make merry. They chanted, "Our god has delivered into our hands Our enemy Samson."

*v'-sar-NAY f'-lish-TEEM ne-es-FU liz-BO-akh ze-vakh ga-DOL l'-da-GON e-lo-hay-HEM ul-sim-KHAH va-yo-m'-RU na-TAN e-lo-HAY-nu b'-ya-DAY-nu AYT shim-SHON o-y'-VAY-nu*

וְסַרְנֵי פְלִשְׁתִּים נֶאֶסְפוּ לִזְבֹּחַ זֶבַח־גָּדוֹל לְדָגוֹן אֱלֹהֵיהֶם וּלְשִׂמְחָה וַיֹּאמְרוּ נָתַן אֱלֹהֵינוּ בְּיָדֵנוּ אֵת שִׁמְשׁוֹן אוֹיְבֵנוּ: כג

24
"When the people saw him, they sang praises to their god, chanting, "Our god has delivered into our hands The enemy who devastated our land, And who slew so many of us."

*va-yir-U o-TO ha-AM vai-ha-l'-LU et e-lo-hay-HEM KEE a-m'-RU na-TAN e-lo-HAY-nu v'-ya-DAY-nu et o-y'-VAY-nu v'-AYT ma-kha-REEV ar-TZAY-nu va-a-SHER hir-BAH et kha-la-LAY-nu*

וַיִּרְאוּ אֹתוֹ הָעָם וַיְהַלְלוּ אֶת־אֱלֹהֵיהֶם כִּי אָמְרוּ נָתַן אֱלֹהֵינוּ בְּיָדֵנוּ אֶת־אוֹיְבֵנוּ וְאֵת מַחֲרִיב אַרְצֵנוּ וַאֲשֶׁר הִרְבָּה אֶת־חֲלָלֵינוּ: כד

25
As their spirits rose, they said, "Call Samson here and let him dance for us." Samson was fetched from the prison, and he danced for them. Then they put him between the pillars.

*vai-HEE k'-TOV li-BAM va-yo-m'-RU kir-U l-shim-SHON vee-sa-khek LA-nu va-yik-r'-U l'-shim-SHON mi-BAYT ha-a-su-REEM vai-tza-KHAYK lif-nay-HEM va-ya-a-MEE-du o-TO BAYN ha-a-mu-DEEM*

וַיְהִי (כי טוב) [כְּטוֹב] לִבָּם וַיֹּאמְרוּ קִרְאוּ לְשִׁמְשׁוֹן וִישַׂחֶק־לָנוּ וַיִּקְרְאוּ לְשִׁמְשׁוֹן מִבֵּית (הָאסירים) [הָאֲסוּרִים] וַיְצַחֵק לִפְנֵיהֶם וַיַּעֲמִידוּ אוֹתוֹ בֵּין הָעַמּוּדִים: כה

26
And Samson said to the boy who was leading him by the hand, "Let go of me and let me feel the pillars that the temple rests upon, that I may lean on them."

*va-YO-mer shim-SHON el ha-NA-ar ha-ma-kha-ZEEK b'-ya-DO ha-NEE-khah o-TEE va-ha-mee-SHAY-nee et ha-a-mu-DEEM a-SHER ha-BA-yit na-KHON a-lay-HEM v'-e-sha-AYN a-lay-HEM*

וַיֹּאמֶר שִׁמְשׁוֹן אֶל־הַנַּעַר הַמַּחֲזִיק בְּיָדוֹ הַנִּיחָה אוֹתִי (והימשני) [וַהֲמִשֵׁנִי] אֶת־הָעַמֻּדִים אֲשֶׁר הַבַּיִת נָכוֹן עֲלֵיהֶם וְאֶשָּׁעֵן עֲלֵיהֶם: כו

27
Now the temple was full of men and women; all the lords of the Philistines were there, and there were some three thousand men and women on the roof watching Samson dance.

*v'-ha-BA-yit ma-LAY ha-a-na-SHEEM v'-ha-na-SHEEM v'-SHA-mah KOL sar-NAY f'-lish-TEEM v'-al ha-GAG kish-LO-shet a-la-FEEM EESH v'-i-SHAH ha-ro-EEM bis-KHOK shim-SHON*

וְהַבַּיִת מָלֵא הָאֲנָשִׁים וְהַנָּשִׁים וְשָׁמָּה כֹּל סַרְנֵי פְלִשְׁתִּים וְעַל־הַגָּג כִּשְׁלֹשֶׁת אֲלָפִים אִישׁ וְאִשָּׁה הָרֹאִים בִּשְׂחוֹק שִׁמְשׁוֹן: כז

| | | | |
|---|---|---|---|
| 28 | Then Samson called to GOD, "O Sovereign GOD ! Please remember me, and give me strength just this once, O God, to take revenge of the Philistines, if only for one of my two eyes." | va-yik-RA shim-SHON el a-do-NAI va-yo-MAR a-do-NAI e-lo-HEEM zokh-RAY-nee NA v'-kha-z'-KAY-nee NA AKH ha-PA-am ha-ZEH h-e-lo-HEEM v'-i-na-k'-MAH n'-kam a-KHAT mi-sh'-TAY ay-NAI mi-p'-lish-TEEM | וַיִּקְרָא שִׁמְשׁוֹן אֶל־יְהוָה וַיֹּאמַר אֲדֹנָי יֱהֹוִה זָכְרֵנִי נָא וְחַזְּקֵנִי נָא אַךְ הַפַּעַם הַזֶּה הָאֱלֹהִים וְאִנָּקְמָה נְקַם־אַחַת מִשְּׁתֵי עֵינַי מִפְּלִשְׁתִּים: |
| | | | כח |
| 29 | He embraced the two middle pillars that the temple rested upon, one with his right arm and one with his left, and leaned against them; | va-yil-POT shim-SHON et sh'-NAY a-mu-DAY ha-TA-vekh a-SHER ha-BA-yit na-KHON a-lay-HEM va-yi-sa-MAYKH a-lay-HEM e-KHAD bee-mee-NO v'-e-KHAD bis-mo-LO | וַיִּלְפֹּת שִׁמְשׁוֹן אֶת־שְׁנֵי עַמּוּדֵי הַתָּוֶךְ אֲשֶׁר הַבַּיִת נָכוֹן עֲלֵיהֶם וַיִּסָּמֵךְ עֲלֵיהֶם אֶחָד בִּימִינוֹ וְאֶחָד בִּשְׂמֹאלוֹ: |
| | | | כט |
| 30 | Samson cried, "Let me die with the Philistines!" and he pulled with all his might. The temple came crashing down on the lords and on all the people in it. Those who were slain by him as he died outnumbered those who had been slain by him when he lived. | va-YO-mer shim-SHON ta-MOT naf-SHEE im p'-lish-TEEM va-YAYT b'-KHO-akh va-yi-POL ha-BA-yit al ha-s'-ra-NEEM v'-al kol ha-AM a-sher BO va-yih-YU ha-may-TEEM a-SHER hay-MEET b'-mo-TO ra-BEEM may-a-SHER hay-MEET b'-kha-YAV | וַיֹּאמֶר שִׁמְשׁוֹן תָּמוֹת נַפְשִׁי עִם־פְּלִשְׁתִּים וַיֵּט בְּכֹחַ וַיִּפֹּל הַבַּיִת עַל־הַסְּרָנִים וְעַל־כָּל־הָעָם אֲשֶׁר־בּוֹ וַיִּהְיוּ הַמֵּתִים אֲשֶׁר הֵמִית בְּמוֹתוֹ רַבִּים מֵאֲשֶׁר הֵמִית בְּחַיָּיו: |
| | | | ל |

31 His brothers and all his father's household came down and carried him up and buried him in the tomb of his father Manoah, between Zorah and Eshtaol. He had led Israel for twenty years.

*va-yay-r'-DU e-KHAV v'-khol BAYT a-VEE-hu va-yis-U o-TO va-ya-a-LU va-yik-b'-RU o-TO BAYN tzor-AH u-VAYN esh-ta-OL b'-KE-ver ma-NO-akh a-VEEV v'-HU sha-FAT et yis-ra-AYL es-REEM sha-NAH*

וַיֵּרְדוּ אֶחָיו וְכָל־
בֵּית אָבִיהוּ וַיִּשְׂאוּ
אֹתוֹ וַיַּעֲלוּ וַיִּקְבְּרוּ
אוֹתוֹ בֵּין צָרְעָה וּבֵין
אֶשְׁתָּאֹל בְּקֶבֶר מָנוֹחַ
אָבִיו וְהוּא שָׁפַט אֶת־
יִשְׂרָאֵל עֶשְׂרִים שָׁנָה:

לא

# Planting Seeds

A wounded veteran of the US Army who fought in World War II, my grandfather, Julius Mischel, was overjoyed to get married and start a family. But when he moved to Queens, New York, he was disturbed by the local Jewish community's attitude towards religion. The great majority only rarely attended synagogue services, and only a small percentage of Jewish families provided their children with any sort of Jewish education. How would the American Jewish community survive?

Upset by what he saw, he wrote a short manifesto entitled "Back to the Synagogue," calling his friends and neighbors to join him and rededicate themselves to Jewish life. Though he himself was not given a Jewish education, my grandfather understood that he had to "up his religious game" if he wanted his own children to grow up to become proud Jews who believed in God and the Bible. And so he brought his sons to the synagogue every week on the Sabbath and ensured that they attended Hebrew school several times each week.

Tragically, my grandfather died suddenly of a heart attack at the very young age of 42. Since his children were still young, he died without knowing the religious path they would one day choose. I can only imagine the anxiety and doubt he must have experienced in his final hours, as he realized he would not be there to guide them. As he left this world, he did not know if he had succeeded in leading his children down a holy path.

My grandfather couldn't have known that 54 years after his death he would have dozens of great-grandchildren living according to the teachings of the Bible in the Holy Land. He couldn't have known that two of his grandsons would become Orthodox rabbis, and that his granddaughters would become courageous settlers in Judea and Samaria. He saw none of this come to fruition – but he was the one who planted the seeds.

This, I believe, is also the legacy of Samson.

Samson was a leader unlike any ever seen before or since. He possessed superhuman strength and extraordinary potential, but also boundless desires. He single-handedly tortured and took righteous vengeance upon the evil Philistines who oppressed the people of Israel, killing many of their soldiers. But despite his awesome strength, he was overcome by his temptations, betrayed by Delilah and captured by the Philistines, who gouged out his eyes and made him a slave:

"The Philistines seized him and gouged out his eyes. They brought him down to Gaza and shackled him in bronze fetters, and he became a mill slave in the prison... Now the lords of the Philistines gathered to offer a great sacrifice to their god Dagon and to make merry. They chanted, 'Our god has delivered into our hands our enemy Samson.'" (Judges 16:21, 23)

A life that began so promisingly seemed destined to end in sadness and humiliation. Blind and humbled, Samson cried out to God:

"'Let me die with the Philistines!'" and he pulled with all his might. The temple came crashing down on the lords and on all the people in it. Those who were slain by him as he died outnumbered those who had been slain by him when he lived." (Judges 16:30)

Samson's final prayer to God was answered, and he succeeded in killing many of the hated Philistine leaders as he pulled the temple down upon himself in his heroic last stand. But despite all of this, what had Samson truly accomplished? After his death, the Philistines continued to rule over and oppress the people of Israel, just as they had done in Samson's lifetime. And so it's fair to ask: was Samson's life ultimately a failure?

Though Samson could not have known it at the time of his death, his life's struggle to free the people of Israel from the yoke of the Philistines was not for naught. As the angel of God prophesied, "He shall begin to deliver Israel from the Philistines" (Judges 13:5). Before Samson, the people of Israel had completely given up hope. The Philistines were strong and powerful, possessing powerful weapons, while the Israelites were weak and divided. They never even contemplated rebelling against the mighty Philistines!

But Samson changed the dynamic. Samson was the first Israelite to dare to fight back against the Philistines. Though he did not, ultimately, lead his people to victory, he demonstrated that it was possible to stand up and fight. He began to restore national pride to the people of Israel. It would take many more years, and many more battles, before King David would finally and decisively defeat the Philistines. But Samson had planted the seeds – just like my grandfather.

# 17

| | | | |
|---|---|---|---|
| 1 | There was a man in the hill country of Ephraim whose name was Micah. | *vai-hee EESH may-har ef-RA-yim ush-MO mee-KHAI-hu* | וַיְהִי־אִישׁ מֵהַר־אֶפְרָיִם וּשְׁמוֹ מִיכָיְהוּ: <br> א |
| 2 | He said to his mother, "The eleven hundred shekels of silver that were taken from you, so that you uttered an imprecation that you repeated in my hearing—I have that silver; I took it." "Blessed of GOD be my son," said his mother. | *va-YO-mer l'-i-MO E-lef u-may-AH ha-KE-sef a-SHER lu-kakh LAKH v'-AT a-LEET v'-GAM a-MART b'-oz-NAI hi-nay ha-KE-sef i-TEE a-NEE l'-kakh-TEEV va-TO-mer i-MO ba-RUKH b'-NEE la-do-NAI* | וַיֹּאמֶר לְאִמּוֹ אֶלֶף וּמֵאָה הַכֶּסֶף אֲשֶׁר לֻקַּח־לָךְ (ואתי) [וְאַתְּ] אָלִית וְגַם אָמַרְתְּ בְּאָזְנַי הִנֵּה־הַכֶּסֶף אִתִּי אֲנִי לְקַחְתִּיו וַתֹּאמֶר אִמּוֹ בָּרוּךְ בְּנִי לַיהֹוָה: <br> ב |
| 3 | He returned the eleven hundred shekels of silver to his mother; but his mother said, "I herewith consecrate the silver to GOD, transferring it to my son to make a sculptured image and a molten image. I now return it to you." | *va-YA-shev et e-lef u-may-AH ha-KE-sef l-i-MO va-TO-mer i-MO hak-DAYSH hik-DASH-tee et ha-KE-sef la-do-NAI mi-ya-DEE liv-NEE la-a-SOT PE-sel u-ma-say-KHAH v'-a-TAH a-shee-VE-nu LAKH* | וַיָּשֶׁב אֶת־אֶלֶף־וּמֵאָה הַכֶּסֶף לְאִמּוֹ וַתֹּאמֶר אִמּוֹ הַקְדֵּשׁ הִקְדַּשְׁתִּי אֶת־הַכֶּסֶף לַיהֹוָה מִיָּדִי לִבְנִי לַעֲשׂוֹת פֶּסֶל וּמַסֵּכָה וְעַתָּה אֲשִׁיבֶנּוּ לָךְ: <br> ג |

4 | So when he gave the silver back to his mother, his mother took two hundred shekels of silver and gave it to a smith. He made of it a sculptured image and a molten image, which were kept in the house of Micah.

*va-YA-shev et ha-KE-sef l-i-MO va-ti-KAKH i-MO ma-TA-yim KE-sef va-ti-t'-NAY-hu la-tzo-RAYF va-ya-a-SAY-hu PE-sel u-ma-say-KHAH vai-HEE b'-VAYT mee-KHAI-hu*

וַיָּשֶׁב אֶת־הַכֶּסֶף לְאִמּוֹ וַתִּקַּח אִמּוֹ מָאתַיִם כֶּסֶף וַתִּתְּנֵהוּ לַצּוֹרֵף וַיַּעֲשֵׂהוּ פֶּסֶל וּמַסֵּכָה וַיְהִי בְּבֵית מִיכָיְהוּ: ד

5 | Now this man Micah had a house of God; he had made an ephod and oracle idols and he had inducted one of his sons to be his priest.

*v'-ha-EESH mee-KHAH LO BAYT e-lo-HEEM va-YA-as ay-FOD ut-ra-FEEM vai-ma-LAY et YAD a-KHAD mi-ba-NAV vai-hee LO l'-kho-HAYN*

וְהָאִישׁ מִיכָה לוֹ בֵּית אֱלֹהִים וַיַּעַשׂ אֵפוֹד וּתְרָפִים וַיְמַלֵּא אֶת־יַד אַחַד מִבָּנָיו וַיְהִי־לוֹ לְכֹהֵן: ה

6 | In those days there was no king in Israel; everyone did as they pleased.

*ba-ya-MEEM ha-HAYM AYN ME-lekh b'-yis-ra-AYL EESH ha-ya-SHAR b'-ay-NAV ya-a-SEH*

בַּיָּמִים הָהֵם אֵין מֶלֶךְ בְּיִשְׂרָאֵל אִישׁ הַיָּשָׁר בְּעֵינָיו יַעֲשֶׂה: ו

7 | There was a young man from Bethlehem of Judah, from the clan seat of Judah; he was a Levite and had resided there as a sojourner.

*vai-hee NA-ar mi-BAYT LE-khem y'-hu-DAH mi-mish-PA-khat y'-hu-DAH v'-HU lay-VEE v'-HU gar SHAM*

וַיְהִי־נַעַר מִבֵּית לֶחֶם יְהוּדָה מִמִּשְׁפַּחַת יְהוּדָה וְהוּא לֵוִי וְהוּא גָר־שָׁם: ז

8 | This man had left the town of Bethlehem of Judah to take up residence wherever he could find a place. On his way, he came to the house of Micah in the hill country of Ephraim.

*va-YAY-lekh ha-EESH may-ha-EER mi-BAYT LE-khem y'-hu-DAH la-GUR ba-a-SHER yim-TZA va-ya-VO har ef-RA-yim ad BAYT mee-KHAH la-a-SOT dar-KO*

וַיֵּלֶךְ הָאִישׁ מֵהָעִיר מִבֵּית לֶחֶם יְהוּדָה לָגוּר בַּאֲשֶׁר יִמְצָא וַיָּבֹא הַר־אֶפְרַיִם עַד בֵּית מִיכָה לַעֲשׂוֹת דַּרְכּוֹ: ח

| | | | |
|---|---|---|---|
| 9 | "Where do you come from?" Micah asked him. He replied, "I am a Levite from Bethlehem of Judah, and I am traveling to take up residence wherever I can find a place." | *va-yo-mer LO mee-KHAH may-A-yin ta-VO va-YO-mer ay-LAV lay-VEE a-NO-khee mi-BAYT LE-khem y'-yu-DAH v'-a-no-KHEE ho-LAYKH la-GUR ba-a-SHER em-TZA* | וַיֹּאמֶר־לוֹ מִיכָה מֵאַיִן תָּבוֹא וַיֹּאמֶר אֵלָיו לֵוִי אָנֹכִי מִבֵּית לֶחֶם יְהוּדָה וְאָנֹכִי הֹלֵךְ לָגוּר בַּאֲשֶׁר אֶמְצָא: ט |
| 10 | "Stay with me," Micah said to him, "and be a father and a priest to me, and I will pay you ten shekels of silver a year, an allowance of clothing, and your food." The Levite went. | *va-YO-mer LO mee-KHAH sh'-VAH i-ma-DEE veh-yay LEE l'-AV ul-kho-HAYN v'-a-no-KHEE e-ten l'-KHA a-SE-ret KE-sef la-ya-MEEM v'-AY-rekh b'-ga-DEEM u-mikh-ya-TE-kha va-YAY-lekh ha-lay-VEE* | וַיֹּאמֶר לוֹ מִיכָה שְׁבָה עִמָּדִי וֶהְיֵה־לִי לְאָב וּלְכֹהֵן וְאָנֹכִי אֶתֶּן־לְךָ עֲשֶׂרֶת כֶּסֶף לַיָּמִים וְעֵרֶךְ בְּגָדִים וּמִחְיָתֶךָ וַיֵּלֶךְ הַלֵּוִי: י |
| 11 | The Levite agreed to stay with the man, and the youth became like one of his own sons. | *va-YO-el ha-lay-VEE la-SHE-vet et ha-EESH vai-HEE ha-NA-ar LO k'-a-KHAD mi-ba-NAV* | וַיּוֹאֶל הַלֵּוִי לָשֶׁבֶת אֶת־הָאִישׁ וַיְהִי הַנַּעַר לוֹ כְּאַחַד מִבָּנָיו: יא |
| 12 | Micah inducted the Levite, and the young man became his priest and remained in Micah's shrine. | *vai-ma-LAY mee-KHAH et YAD ha-lay-VEE vai-hee LO ha-NA-ar l'-kho-HAYN vai-HEE b'-VAYT mee-KHAH* | וַיְמַלֵּא מִיכָה אֶת־יַד הַלֵּוִי וַיְהִי־לוֹ הַנַּעַר לְכֹהֵן וַיְהִי בְּבֵית מִיכָה: יב |
| 13 | "Now I know," Micah told himself, "that GOD will make me prosper, since the Levite has become my priest." | *va-YO-mer mee-KHAH a-TAH ya-DA-tee kee yay-TEEV a-do-NAI LEE KEE ha-yah LEE ha-lay-VEE l'-kho-HAYN* | וַיֹּאמֶר מִיכָה עַתָּה יָדַעְתִּי כִּי־יֵיטִיב יְהוָה לִי כִּי הָיָה־לִי הַלֵּוִי לְכֹהֵן: יג |

# A Book That Never Grows Stale

Saul Bellow won more honors and recognition than any other writer of his era. Everywhere he went he was revered as a "wise man," and his award-winning books were read by untold thousands. By the time he died in 2005, he was considered one of the great writers of his generation.

But less than twenty years after his death, Bellow's writing no longer speaks to most people. Contemplating the dramatic fall in popularity of Bellow's books, the critic James Atlas writes: "Was it possible that even Saul Bellow's work would fade from the collective memory, that his books would one day molder on the shelf... their spines creased, the yellow pages crumbling? Then recede even further back in time... available only from Abe Books? Then become footnotes in some grad student's dissertation on twentieth-century American literature; and finally be forgotten altogether?"

Here today, gone tomorrow; there is no guarantee that even the very best books will remain relevant from generation to generation. But there is one exception: the Bible. Every verse in the Bible is Divinely inspired. Every verse, word and letter is eternally relevant!

A powerful example of this truth can be found towards the end of the Book of Judges, in the obscure story of Micah's idol.

The story begins with some good old-fashioned intra-family theft:

"There was a man in the hill country of Ephraim whose name was Micah. He said to his mother, 'The 1,100 shekalim of silver that were taken from you, so that you uttered a curse which you repeated in my hearing – I have that silver; I took it.' 'Blessed of GOD be my son,' said his mother." (Judges 17:1-2)

Overcome by temptation, Micah stole 1,100 pieces of silver from his mother. Though he ultimately returned the money, he did not do so because he felt guilty about taking advantage of his mother, but because he heard his mother utter a curse against the person who stole the silver from her, and he feared the consequences of that curse.

From the first two verses of this story, we learn that Micah is a strange sort of man – a man of contradictions. On the one hand, he stole from his own mother, a blatant violation of God's word, but at the very same time, he feared that God would strike him down because his mother had uttered a curse!

Micah's contradictory impulses continue to emerge as the story unfolds:

"He returned the 1,100 shekels of silver to his mother; but his mother said, 'I herewith consecrate the silver to God, transferring it to my son to make a sculptured image and a molten image. I now return it to you.' So when he gave the silver back to his mother, his mother took two hundred shekels of silver and gave it to a smith. He made of it a sculptured image and a molten image, which were kept in the house of Mica. Now the man Mica had a house of God; he made a breastplate and small idols and he inducted one of his sons to be his priest." (Judges 17:3-5)

Micah and his mother could have used the 1,100 pieces of silver for many purposes, but they admirably chose to dedicate it to God. There was only one problem: instead of donating the money to the Tabernacle, God's chosen dwelling place, they used the money to create an idol!

It appears that Micah believed in God, but felt he needed an alternative to the Tabernacle so he could better worship God according to his own preferences. As the next verse states: "In those days there was no king in Israel; every man did as he pleased" (Judges 17:6).

The story of Micah and his idol occurred over three thousand years ago – and yet it is more relevant in our time than ever before. Personally, I cannot think of a story that better illustrates one of the great religious challenges of our time. We live in an era of radical autonomy, when people believe they have the right to "pick and choose" from the Bible and practice only those teachings that personally speak to them. Like Micah, millions of people in our generation yearn for meaning in their lives – but they want it strictly on their own terms.

In 1985, the American sociologist Robert Bellah wrote about Sheila Larson, a nurse who "has actually named her religion (she calls it her 'faith') after herself." She said, "I believe in God. I'm not a religious fanatic. I can't remember the last time I went to church. My faith has carried me a long way. It's Sheilaism. Just my own little voice." She defined the principles of "Sheilaism" as "It's just try to love yourself and be gentle with yourself. You know, I guess, take care of each other. I think He would want us to take care of each other" (Habits of the Heart: Individualism and Commitment in American Life).

"Only that shall happen which has already happened, only that shall occur which has already occurred; there is nothing new beneath the sun!" (Ecclesiastes 1:9).

Sheilaism, at its core, is "Micah-ism." Both, of course, share the same fatal flaw. As human beings, we are here in this world to serve God – and we must do so the way that God wants us to. Otherwise, religion will devolve into a self-serving exercise that makes us feel good about ourselves, rather than authentic service of God. And such a service will inevitably fail.

Micah's idol, Sheilaism, Saul Bellows' books – all of these works of man are destined, ultimately, to wind up in the dustbin of history. Only the Bible, God's eternal word, continues to speak powerfully to our generation – and every generation!

# The Welcoming Idolater

Reading the story of Micah and his idol, I am bowled over by this man's sheer audacity. According to Jewish tradition, Micah established a house of idolatry a mere three miles from the Tabernacle in Shiloh. Micah's house of idolatry was so close to God's holy Tabernacle, "the smoke of the two altars mingled on account of their proximity" (Talmud Sanhedrin 103b).

Given Micah's arrogance and the severity of the sin of idolatry, one would surely expect God to bring His wrath down upon Micah, in both this world and the next. Surprisingly, however, the sages do not include Micah on their list of evil people who do not have a portion in the world to come. Though Micah was clearly a sinner who caused thousands of others to sin, he does not qualify for "God's most wanted list"!

Why is Micah spared from eternal punishment?

The answer can be found in a short conversation between Micah and a poor Levite from Bethlehem who was looking for a new beginning.

"'Stay with me,' Micah said to him, 'and be a father and a priest to me, and I will pay you ten shekels of silver a year, an allowance of clothing, and your food.' The Levite went. The Levite agreed to stay with the man, and the youth became like one of his own sons" (Judges 17:10-11).

Yes, Micah was an idolater who led the masses of Israel astray. But he was also, it seems, a very warm and welcoming guy.

The sages powerfully capture Micah's complexity: "The angels wished to throw down [Micah's] idol; but God said to them, 'Leave it alone; for Micah offers bread to travelers'" (Talmud Sanhedrin 103b). In other words, despite Micah's terrible sin of idolatry, God was willing to bear Micah's failings because he excelled at hospitality!

Micah's hospitality stood in sharp contrast to the way people were treated at the Tabernacle, only three miles away. There, the sons of the high priest, Hofni and Phineas, treated the Israelite pilgrims who traveled great distances to the Tabernacle with disdain:

"Now Eli [the high priest's] sons were scoundrels; they paid no heed to God. This is how the priests used to deal with the people: When anyone brought a sacrifice, the priest's boy would come along with a three-pronged fork while the meat was boiling, and he would thrust it into the cauldron, or the kettle, or the great pot, or the small cooking-pot; and whatever the fork brought up, the priest would take away on it. This was the practice at Shiloh with all the Israelites who came there" (I Samuel 2:12-14).

The contrast between the corrupt and inhospitable priests in the holy Tabernacle and the idolatrous but welcoming Micah – only three miles apart! – could not have been starker. And whereas Micah was spared God's wrath, the evil priests of the Tabernacle would soon meet their end in a disastrous battle against the Philistines.

What are we to make of this strange situation? I believe the Bible is teaching us critically important lessons for life.

By tolerating Micah and punishing Hofni and Phineas, God demonstrated that He cares more for the well-being of His children on earth than He cares for His own glory. As the sages so powerfully stated: "Hospitality to wayfarers is greater than welcoming the presence of God Himself" (Talmud Shabbat 127a). It is worth reflecting on God's awesome humility, for we too should care more about the well-being of God's children than we do for our own honor and reputation.

At the same time, we learn that devotion to God is meaningless if our devotion does not transform the way we interact with others. Yes, we must study the Bible, pray with great fervor and attend services regularly. But if our religious devotion does not make us kinder and more loving to our fellow man, we are missing the point.

Maimonides, the great Jewish thinker, emphasizes this point: "When a person eats and drinks [in celebration of a religious holiday], he is obligated to feed converts, orphans, widows, and others who are destitute and poor. In contrast, a person who locks the gates of his courtyard and eats and drinks with his children and his wife, without feeding the poor and the embittered, is [not indulging in] rejoicing associated with a mitzvah, but rather the rejoicing of his gut" (Laws of Festivals, 6:18).

"Love your fellow as yourself: I am Hashem." (Leviticus 19:18).

# 18

יח

| | | |
|---|---|---|

In those days there was no king in Israel, and in those days the tribe of Dan was seeking a territory in which to settle; for to that day no territory had fallen to their lot among the tribes of Israel.

*ba-ya-MEEM ha-HAYM AYN ME-lekh b'-yis-ra-AYL u-va-ya-MEEM ha-HAYM SHAY-vet ha-da-NEE m'-va-kesh LO na-kha-LAH la-SHE-vet KEE lo na-f'-LAH LO ad ha-YOM ha-HU b'-tokh shiv-TAY yis-ra-AYL b'-na-kha-LAH*

בַּיָּמִים הָהֵם אֵין מֶלֶךְ בְּיִשְׂרָאֵל וּבַיָּמִים הָהֵם שֵׁבֶט הַדָּנִי מְבַקֶּשׁ־ לוֹ נַחֲלָה לָשֶׁבֶת כִּי לֹא־נָפְלָה לּוֹ עַד־הַיּוֹם הַהוּא בְּתוֹךְ־שִׁבְטֵי יִשְׂרָאֵל בְּנַחֲלָה: א

The Danites sent out five of their number, from their clan seat at Zorah and Eshtaol—valiant men—to spy out the land and explore it. "Go," they told them, "and explore the land." When they had advanced into the hill country of Ephraim as far as the house of Micah, they stopped there for the night.

*va-yish-l'-KHU v'-nay DAN mi-mish-pakh-TAM kha-mi-SHAH a-na-SHEEM mik-tzo-TAM a-na-SHEEM b'-nay KHA-yil mi-tzor-AH u-may-esh-ta-OL l'-ra-GAYL et ha-A-retz ul-khok-RAH va-yo-m'-RU a-lay-HEM l'-KHU khik-RU et ha-A-retz va-ya-VO-u har ef-RA-yim ad BAYT mee-KHAH va-ya-LEE-nu SHAM*

וַיִּשְׁלְחוּ בְנֵי־דָן מִמִּשְׁפַּחְתָּם חֲמִשָּׁה אֲנָשִׁים מִקְצוֹתָם אֲנָשִׁים בְּנֵי־חַיִל מִצָּרְעָה וּמֵאֶשְׁתָּאֹל לְרַגֵּל אֶת־הָאָרֶץ וּלְחָקְרָהּ וַיֹּאמְרוּ אֲלֵהֶם לְכוּ חִקְרוּ אֶת־הָאָרֶץ וַיָּבֹאוּ הַר־ אֶפְרַיִם עַד־בֵּית מִיכָה וַיָּלִינוּ שָׁם: ב

3

While in the vicinity of Micah's house, they recognized the speech of the young Levite, so they went over and asked him, "Who brought you to these parts? What are you doing in this place? What is your business here?"

*HAY-mah im BAYT mee-KHAH v'-HAY-mah hi-KEE-ru et KOL ha-NA-ar ha-lay-VEE va-ya-SU-ru SHAM va-YO-m'-ru LO mee he-vee-a-KHA ha-LOM u-mah a-TAH o-SEH ba-ZEH u-mah l'-KHA FOH*

הֵמָּה עִם־בֵּית מִיכָה וְהֵמָּה הִכִּירוּ אֶת־קוֹל הַנַּעַר הַלֵּוִי וַיָּסוּרוּ שָׁם וַיֹּאמְרוּ לוֹ מִי־הֱבִיאֲךָ הֲלֹם וּמָה־אַתָּה עֹשֶׂה בָּזֶה וּמַה־לְּךָ פֹה: ג

4

He replied, "Thus and thus Micah did for me—he hired me and I became his priest."

*va-YO-mer a-lay-HEM ka-ZOH v'-kha-ZEH A-sah LEE mee-KHAH va-yis-k'-RAY-nee va-e-hee LO l'-kho-HAYN*

וַיֹּאמֶר אֲלֵהֶם כָּזֹה וְכָזֶה עָשָׂה לִי מִיכָה וַיִּשְׂכְּרֵנִי וָאֱהִי־לוֹ לְכֹהֵן: ד

5

They said to him, "Please, inquire of God; we would like to know if the mission on which we are going will be successful."

*va-YO-m'-ru LO sh'-al NA vay-lo-HEEM v'-nay-d'-AH ha-tatz-LI-akh dar-KAY-nu a-SHER a-NAKH-nu ho-l'-KHEEM a-LE-ha*

וַיֹּאמְרוּ לוֹ שְׁאַל־ נָא בֵאלֹהִים וְנֵדְעָה הֲתַצְלִיחַ דַּרְכֵּנוּ אֲשֶׁר אֲנַחְנוּ הֹלְכִים עָלֶיהָ: ה

6

"Go in peace," the priest said to them, "GOD views with favor the mission you are going on."

*va-YO-mer la-HEM ha-ko-HAYN l'-KHU l'-sha-LOM NO-khakh a-do-NAI dar-k'-KHEM a-SHER tay-l'-khu VAH*

וַיֹּאמֶר לָהֶם הַכֹּהֵן לְכוּ לְשָׁלוֹם נֹכַח יְהוָה דַּרְכְּכֶם אֲשֶׁר תֵּלְכוּ־ בָהּ: ו

7

The five men went on and came to Laish. They observed the people in it dwelling carefree, after the manner of the Sidonians, a tranquil and unsuspecting people, with no one in the land to molest them and with no hereditary ruler. Moreover, they were distant from the Sidonians and had no dealings with anybody.

*va-yay-l'-KHU kha-MAY-shet ha-a-na-SHEEM va-ya-VO-u LAI-shah va-yir-U et ha-AM a-sher b'-kir-BAH yo-SHE-vet la-VE-takh k'-mish-PAT tzi-do-NEEM sho-KAYT u-vo-TAY-akh v'-ayn makh-LEEM da-VAR ba-A-retz yo-RAYSH E-tzer ur-kho-KEEM HAY-mah mi-tzee-do-NEEM v'-da-VAR ayn la-HEM im a-DAM*

וַיֵּלְכוּ חֲמֵשֶׁת הָאֲנָשִׁים וַיָּבֹאוּ לָיְשָׁה וַיִּרְאוּ אֶת־הָעָם אֲשֶׁר־בְּקִרְבָּהּ יוֹשֶׁבֶת־לָבֶטַח כְּמִשְׁפַּט צִדֹנִים שֹׁקֵט וּבֹטֵחַ וְאֵין־מַכְלִים דָּבָר בָּאָרֶץ יוֹרֵשׁ עֶצֶר וּרְחֹקִים הֵמָּה מִצִּידֹנִים וְדָבָר אֵין־לָהֶם עִם־אָדָם: ז

8

When [the spies] came back to their clans at Zorah and Eshtaol, their fellows asked them, "How did you fare?"

*va-ya-VO-u el a-khay-HEM tzor-AH v'-esh-ta-OL va-yo-m'-RU la-HEM a-khay-HEM MAH a-TEM*

וַיָּבֹאוּ אֶל־אֲחֵיהֶם צָרְעָה וְאֶשְׁתָּאֹל וַיֹּאמְרוּ לָהֶם אֲחֵיהֶם מָה אַתֶּם: ח

9

They replied, "Let us go at once and attack them! For we found that the land was very good, and you are sitting idle! Don't delay; go and invade the land and take possession of it,

*va-yo-m'-RU KU-mah v'-na-a-LEH a-lay-HEM KEE ra-EE-nu et ha-A-retz v'-hi-NAY to-VAH m'-OD v'-a-TEM makh-SHEEM al tay-a-tz'-LU la-LE-khet la-VO la-RE-shet et ha-A-retz*

וַיֹּאמְרוּ קוּמָה וְנַעֲלֶה עֲלֵיהֶם כִּי רָאִינוּ אֶת־הָאָרֶץ וְהִנֵּה טוֹבָה מְאֹד וְאַתֶּם מַחְשִׁים אַל־תֵּעָצְלוּ לָלֶכֶת לָבֹא לָרֶשֶׁת אֶת־הָאָרֶץ: ט

10

for God has delivered it into your hand. When you come, you will come to an unsuspecting people; and the land is spacious and nothing on earth is lacking there."

*k'-vo-a-KHEM ta-VO-u el AM bo-TAY-akh v'-ha-A-retz ra-kha-VAT ya-DA-yim kee n'-ta-NAH e-lo-HEEM b'-yed-KHEM ma-KOM a-SHER ayn SHAM makh-SOR kol da-VAR a-SHER ba-A-retz*

כְּבֹאֲכֶם תָּבֹאוּ אֶל־עַם בֹּטֵחַ וְהָאָרֶץ רַחֲבַת יָדַיִם כִּי־נְתָנָהּ אֱלֹהִים בְּיֶדְכֶם מָקוֹם אֲשֶׁר אֵין־שָׁם מַחְסוֹר כָּל־דָּבָר אֲשֶׁר בָּאָרֶץ:

י

11

They departed from there, from the clan seat of the Danites, from Zorah and Eshtaol, six hundred strong, girt with weapons of war.

*va-yis-U mi-SHAM mi-mish-PA-khat ha-da-NEE mi-tzor-AH u-may-esh-ta-OL shaysh may-OT EESH kha-GUR k'-LAY mil-kha-MAH*

וַיִּסְעוּ מִשָּׁם מִמִּשְׁפַּחַת הַדָּנִי מִצׇּרְעָה וּמֵאֶשְׁתָּאֹל שֵׁשׁ־מֵאוֹת אִישׁ חָגוּר כְּלֵי מִלְחָמָה:

יא

12

They went up and encamped at Kiriath-jearim in Judah. That is why that place is called "the Camp of Dan" to this day; it lies west of Kiriath-jearim.

*va-ya-a-LU va-ya-kha-NU b'-kir-YAT y'-a-REEM bee-hu-DAH al KAYN ka-r'-U la-ma-KOM ha-HU ma-kha-nay DAN AD ha-YOM ha-ZEH hi-NAY a-kha-RAY kir-YAT y'-a-REEM*

וַיַּעֲלוּ וַיַּחֲנוּ בְּקִרְיַת יְעָרִים בִּיהוּדָה עַל־כֵּן קָרְאוּ לַמָּקוֹם הַהוּא מַחֲנֵה־דָן עַד הַיּוֹם הַזֶּה הִנֵּה אַחֲרֵי קִרְיַת יְעָרִים:

יב

13

From there they passed on to the hill country of Ephraim and arrived at the house of Micah.

*va-ya-av-RU mi-SHAM har ef-RA-yim va-ya-VO-u ad BAYT mee-KHAH*

וַיַּעַבְרוּ מִשָּׁם הַר־אֶפְרָיִם וַיָּבֹאוּ עַד־בֵּית מִיכָה:

יג

14 Here the five men who had gone to spy out the Laish region remarked to their clans, "Do you know, there is an ephod in these houses, and oracle idols, and a sculptured image and a molten image? Now you know what you have to do."

*va-ya-a-NU kha-MAY-shet ha-a-na-SHEEM ha-ho-l'-KHEEM l'-ra-GAYL et ha-A-retz LA-yish va-yo-m'-RU el a-khay-HEM hai-da-TEM KEE YAYSH ba-ba-TEEM ha-AY-leh ay-FOD ut-ra-FEEM u-FE-sel u-ma-say-KHAH v'-a-TAH d'-U mah ta-a-SU*

יד וַיַּעֲנוּ חֲמֵשֶׁת הָאֲנָשִׁים הַהֹלְכִים לְרַגֵּל אֶת־הָאָרֶץ לַיִשׁ וַיֹּאמְרוּ אֶל־אֲחֵיהֶם הַיְדַעְתֶּם כִּי יֵשׁ בַּבָּתִּים הָאֵלֶּה אֵפוֹד וּתְרָפִים וּפֶסֶל וּמַסֵּכָה וְעַתָּה דְּעוּ מַה־תַּעֲשׂוּ׃

15 So they turned off there and entered the home of the young Levite at Micah's house and greeted him.

*va-ya-SU-ru SHA-mah va-ya-VO-u el bayt ha-NA-ar ha-lay-VEE BAYT mee-KHAH va-yish-a-lu LO l'-sha-LOM*

טו וַיָּסוּרוּ שָׁמָּה וַיָּבֹאוּ אֶל־בֵּית־הַנַּעַר הַלֵּוִי בֵּית מִיכָה וַיִּשְׁאֲלוּ־לוֹ לְשָׁלוֹם׃

16 The six hundred Danites, girt with their weapons of war, stood at the entrance of the gate,

*v'-shaysh may-OT EESH kha-gu-REEM k'-LAY mil-kham-TAM ni-tza-VEEM PE-takh ha-SHA-ar a-SHER mi-b'-nay DAN*

טז וְשֵׁשׁ־מֵאוֹת אִישׁ חֲגוּרִים כְּלֵי מִלְחַמְתָּם נִצָּבִים פֶּתַח הַשָּׁעַר אֲשֶׁר מִבְּנֵי־דָן׃

17 while the five who had gone to spy out the land went inside and took the sculptured image, the ephod, the oracle idols, and the molten image. The priest was standing at the entrance of the gate, and the six hundred men girt with their weapons of war,

*va-ya-a-LU kha-MAY-shet ha-a-na-SHEEM ha-ho-l'-KHEEM l'-ra-GAYL et ha-A-retz BA-u SHA-mah la-k'-KHU et ha-PE-sel v'-et ha-ay-FOD v'-et ha-t'-ra-FEEM v'-et ha-ma-say-KHAH v'-ha-ko-HAYN ni-TZAV PE-takh ha-SHA-ar v'-shaysh may-OT ha-EESH he-kha-GUR k'-LAY ha-mil-kha-MAH*

יז וַיַּעֲלוּ חֲמֵשֶׁת הָאֲנָשִׁים הַהֹלְכִים לְרַגֵּל אֶת־הָאָרֶץ בָּאוּ שָׁמָּה לָקְחוּ אֶת־הַפֶּסֶל וְאֶת־הָאֵפוֹד וְאֶת־הַתְּרָפִים וְאֶת־הַמַּסֵּכָה וְהַכֹּהֵן נִצָּב פֶּתַח הַשַּׁעַר וְשֵׁשׁ־מֵאוֹת הָאִישׁ הֶחָגוּר כְּלֵי הַמִּלְחָמָה׃

18

while the others
entered Micah's
house and took the
sculptured image,
the molten image,
the ephod, and
the oracle idols.
The priest said to
them, "What are you
doing?"

*v'-AY-leh BA-u BAYT
mee-KHAH va-yik-KHU
et PE-sel ha-ay-FOD
v'-et ha-t'-ra-FEEM v'-et
ha-ma-say-KHAH va-
YO-mer a-lay-HEM ha-
ko-HAYN MAH a-TEM
o-SEEM*

וְאֵ֙לֶּה֙ בָּ֣אוּ בֵּ֣ית מִיכָ֔ה
וַיִּקְח֗וּ אֶת־פֶּ֤סֶל
הָֽאֵפוֹד֙ וְאֶת־הַתְּרָפִ֔ים
וְאֶת־הַמַּסֵּכָ֑ה וַיֹּ֣אמֶר
אֲלֵיהֶ֗ם הַכֹּהֵ֔ן מָ֥ה
אַתֶּ֖ם עֹשִֽׂים: יח

19

But they said to him,
"Be quiet; put your
hand on your mouth!
Come with us and be
our father and priest.
Would you rather be
priest to one man's
household, or be
priest to a tribe and
clan in Israel?"

*va-YO-m'-ru LO ha-
kha-RAYSH SEEM
ya-d'-KHA al PEE-kha
v'-LAYKH i-MA-nu veh-
yay LA-nu l'-AV ul-kho-
HAYN ha-TOV he-yo-t'-
KHA kho-HAYN l'-VAYT
EESH e-KHAD O
he-yo-t'-KHA kho-HAYN
l'-SHAY-vet ul-mish-pa-
KHAH b'-yis-ra-AYL*

וַיֹּאמְרוּ ל֩וֹ הַחֲרֵ֨שׁ
שִֽׂים־יָדְךָ֤ עַל־פִּ֙יךָ֙ וְלֵ֣ךְ
עִמָּ֔נוּ וֶהְיֵה־לָ֖נוּ לְאָ֣ב
וּלְכֹהֵ֑ן הֲט֣וֹב ׀ הֱיוֹתְךָ֣
כֹהֵ֗ן לְבֵית֙ אִ֣ישׁ אֶחָ֔ד
א֚וֹ הֱיוֹתְךָ֣ כֹהֵ֔ן לְשֵׁ֖בֶט
וּלְמִשְׁפָּחָ֥ה בְּיִשְׂרָאֵֽל: יט

20

The priest was
delighted. He took
the ephod, the
oracle idols, and the
sculptured image,
and he joined the
people.

*va-yeey-TAV LAYV ha-
ko-HAYN va-yi-KAKH et
ha-ay-FOD v'-et ha-t'-
ra-FEEM v'-et ha-PA-
sel va-ya-VO b'-KE-rev
ha-AM*

וַיִּיטַב֙ לֵ֣ב הַכֹּהֵ֔ן וַיִּקַּח֙
אֶת־הָ֣אֵפ֔וֹד וְאֶת־
הַתְּרָפִ֖ים וְאֶת־הַפָּ֑סֶל
וַיָּבֹ֖א בְּקֶ֥רֶב הָעָֽם: כ

21

They set out again,
placing the children,
the cattle, and their
household goods in
front.

*va-yif-NU va-yay-LAY-
khu va-ya-SEE-mu et
ha-TAF v'-et ha-mik-
NEH v'-et ha-k'-vu-DAH
lif-nay-HEM*

וַיִּפְנ֖וּ וַיֵּלֵ֑כוּ וַיָּשִׂ֨ימוּ
אֶת־הַטַּ֧ף וְאֶת־הַמִּקְנֶ֛ה
וְאֶת־הַכְּבוּדָּ֖ה לִפְנֵיהֶֽם: כא

| | | | |
|---|---|---|---|
| 22 | They had already gone some distance from Micah's house, when Micah's neighbors mustered and caught up with the Danites. | *HAY-mah hir-KHEE-ku mi-BAYT mee-KHAH v'-ha-a-na-SHEEM a-SHER ba-ba-TEEM a-SHER im BAYT mee-KHAH niz-a-KU va-yad-BEE-ku et b'-nay DAN* | הֵמָּה הִרְחִיקוּ מִבֵּית מִיכָה וְהָאֲנָשִׁים אֲשֶׁר בַּבָּתִּים אֲשֶׁר עִם־בֵּית מִיכָה נִזְעֲקוּ וַיַּדְבִּיקוּ אֶת־בְּנֵי־דָן: כב |
| 23 | They called out to the Danites, who turned around and said to Micah, "What's the matter? Why have you mustered?" | *va-yik-r'-U el b'-nay DAN va-ya-SAY-bu p'-nay-HEM va-yo-m'-RU l'-mee-KHAH mah LAKH KEE niz-AK-ta* | וַיִּקְרְאוּ אֶל־בְּנֵי־דָן וַיַּסֵּבּוּ פְּנֵיהֶם וַיֹּאמְרוּ לְמִיכָה מַה־לְּךָ כִּי נִזְעָקְתָּ: כג |
| 24 | He said, "You have taken my priest and the gods that I made, and walked off! What do I have left? How can you ask, 'What's the matter'?" | *va-YO-mer et e-lo-HAI a-sher a-SEE-tee l'-kakh-TEM v'-et ha-ko-HAYN va-tay-l'-KHU u-mah LEE OD u-mah ZEH to-m'-RU ay-LAI mah LAKH* | וַיֹּאמֶר אֶת־אֱלֹהַי אֲשֶׁר־עָשִׂיתִי לְקַחְתֶּם וְאֶת־הַכֹּהֵן וַתֵּלְכוּ וּמַה־לִּי עוֹד וּמַה־זֶּה תֹּאמְרוּ אֵלַי מַה־לָּךְ: כד |
| 25 | But the Danites replied, "Don't do any shouting at us, or some desperate party might attack you, and you and your family would lose your lives." | *va-yo-m'-RU ay-LAV b'-nay DAN al tish-MA ko-l'-KHA i-MA-nu pen yif-g'-U va-KHEM a-na-SHEEM ma-RAY NE-fesh v'-a-saf-TAH naf-sh'-KHA v'-NE-fesh bay-TE-kha* | וַיֹּאמְרוּ אֵלָיו בְּנֵי־דָן אַל־תַּשְׁמַע קוֹלְךָ עִמָּנוּ פֶּן־יִפְגְּעוּ בָכֶם אֲנָשִׁים מָרֵי נֶפֶשׁ וְאָסַפְתָּה נַפְשְׁךָ וְנֶפֶשׁ בֵּיתֶךָ: כה |
| 26 | So Micah, realizing that they were stronger than he, turned back and went home; and the Danites went on their way, | *va-yay-l'-KHU v'-nay DAN l'-dar-KAM va-YAR mee-KHAH kee kha-za-KEEM HAY-mah mi-ME-nu va-YI-fen va-YA-shov el bay-TO* | וַיֵּלְכוּ בְנֵי־דָן לְדַרְכָּם וַיַּרְא מִיכָה כִּי־חֲזָקִים הֵמָּה מִמֶּנּוּ וַיִּפֶן וַיָּשָׁב אֶל־בֵּיתוֹ: כו |

27 taking the things Micah had made and the priest he had acquired. They proceeded to Laish, a people tranquil and unsuspecting, and they put them to the sword and burned down the town.

*v'-HAY-mah la-k'-KHU AYT a-sher a-SAH mee-KHAH v'-et ha-ko-HAYN a-SHER ha-yah LO va-ya-VO-u al LA-yish al AM sho-KAYT u-vo-TAY-akh va-ya-KU o-TAM l'-fee KHA-rev v'-et ha-EER sa-r'-FU va-AYSH*

וְהֵמָּה לָקְחוּ אֵת אֲשֶׁר־עָשָׂה מִיכָה וְאֶת־הַכֹּהֵן אֲשֶׁר הָיָה־לוֹ וַיָּבֹאוּ עַל־לַיִשׁ עַל־עַם שֹׁקֵט וּבֹטֵחַ וַיַּכּוּ אוֹתָם לְפִי־חָרֶב וְאֶת־הָעִיר שָׂרְפוּ בָאֵשׁ: כז

28 There was none to come to the rescue, for it was distant from Sidon and they had no dealings with anyone; it lay in the valley of Beth-rehob. They rebuilt the town and settled there,

*v'-AYN ma-TZEEL KEE r'-kho-kah HEE mi-tzee-DON v'-da-VAR ayn la-HEM im a-DAM v'-HEE ba-AY-mek a-SHER l'-vayt r'-KHOV va-yiv-NU et ha-EER va-YAY-sh'-vu VAH*

וְאֵין מַצִּיל כִּי רְחוֹקָה־הִיא מִצִּידוֹן וְדָבָר אֵין לָהֶם עִם־אָדָם וְהִיא בָּעֵמֶק אֲשֶׁר לְבֵית־רְחוֹב וַיִּבְנוּ אֶת־הָעִיר וַיֵּשְׁבוּ בָהּ: כח

29 and they named the town Dan, after their ancestor Dan who was Israel's son. Originally, however, the name of the town was Laish.

*va-yik-r'-U shaym ha-EER DAN b'-SHAYM DAN a-vee-HEM a-SHER yu-LAD l'-yis-ra-AYL v'-u-LAM LA-yish shaym ha-EER la-ri-sho-NAH*

וַיִּקְרְאוּ שֵׁם־הָעִיר דָּן בְּשֵׁם דָּן אֲבִיהֶם אֲשֶׁר יוּלַּד לְיִשְׂרָאֵל וְאוּלָם לַיִשׁ שֵׁם־הָעִיר לָרִאשֹׁנָה: כט

30 The Danites set up the sculptured image for themselves; and Jonathan son of Gershom son of Manasseh, and his descendants, served as priests to the Danite tribe until the land went into exile.

*va-ya-KEE-mu la-HEM b'-nay DAN et ha-PA-sel vee-ho-na-TAN ben gay-r'-SHOM ben m'-na-SHEH HU u-va-NAV ha-YU kho-ha-NEEM l'-SHAY-vet ha-da-NEE ad YOM g'-LOT ha-A-retz*

וַיָּקִימוּ לָהֶם בְּנֵי־דָן אֶת־הַפָּסֶל וִיהוֹנָתָן בֶּן־גֵּרְשֹׁם בֶּן־מְנַשֶּׁה הוּא וּבָנָיו הָיוּ כֹהֲנִים לְשֵׁבֶט הַדָּנִי עַד־יוֹם גְּלוֹת הָאָרֶץ: ל

31

They maintained the sculptured image that Micah had made throughout the time that the House of God stood at Shiloh.

*va-ya-SEE-mu la-HEM et PE-sel mee-KHAH a-SHER a-SAH kol y'-MAY he-YOT bayt ha-e-lo-HEEM b'-shi-LOH*

לא

וַיָּשִׂימוּ לָהֶם אֶת־פֶּסֶל מִיכָה אֲשֶׁר עָשָׂה כָּל־יְמֵי הֱיוֹת בֵּית־הָאֱלֹהִים בְּשִׁלֹה:

# 19

יט

| | | |
|---|---|---|
| In those days, when there was no king in Israel, a certain Levite residing at the other end of the hill country of Ephraim took to himself a concubine from Bethlehem in Judah. | *vai-HEE ba-ya-MEEM ha-HAYM u-ME-lekh AYN b'-yis-ra-AYL vai-HEE EESH lay-VEE GAR b'-yark'-TAY har ef-RA-yim va-yi-KAKH LO i-SHAH fee-LE-gesh mi-BAYT LE-khem y'-hu-DAH* | וַיְהִי בַּיָּמִים הָהֵם וּמֶלֶךְ אֵין בְּיִשְׂרָאֵל וַיְהִי אִישׁ לֵוִי גָּר בְּיַרְכְּתֵי הַר־אֶפְרַיִם וַיִּקַּח־לוֹ אִשָּׁה פִילֶגֶשׁ מִבֵּית לֶחֶם יְהוּדָה: |

1 (In those days...)  א

| | | |
|---|---|---|
| Once his concubine deserted him, leaving him for her father's house in Bethlehem in Judah; and she stayed there a full four months. | *va-tiz-NEH a-LAV pee-lag-SHO va-TAY-lekh may-i-TO el BAYT a-VEE-ha el BAYT LE-khem y'-hu-DAH va-t'-hee SHAM ya-MEEM ar-ba-AH kho-da-SHEEM* | וַתִּזְנֶה עָלָיו פִּילַגְשׁוֹ וַתֵּלֶךְ מֵאִתּוֹ אֶל־בֵּית אָבִיהָ אֶל־בֵּית לֶחֶם יְהוּדָה וַתְּהִי־שָׁם יָמִים אַרְבָּעָה חֳדָשִׁים: |

2  ב

| | | |
|---|---|---|
| Then her husband set out, with an attendant and a pair of donkeys, and went after her to woo her and to win her back. She admitted him into her father's house; and when the young woman's father saw him, he received him warmly. | *va-YA-kom ee-SHAH va-YAY-lekh a-kha-RE-ha l'-da-BAYR al li-BAH la-ha-shee-VAH v'-na-a-RO i-MO v'-TZE-med kha-mo-REEM va-t'-vee-AY-hu BAYT a-VEE-ha va-yir-AY-hu a-VEE ha-na-a-RAH va-yis-MAKH lik-ra-TO* | וַיָּקָם אִישָׁהּ וַיֵּלֶךְ אַחֲרֶיהָ לְדַבֵּר עַל־לִבָּהּ (להשיבו) [לַהֲשִׁיבָהּ] וְנַעֲרוֹ עִמּוֹ וְצֶמֶד חֲמֹרִים וַתְּבִיאֵהוּ בֵּית אָבִיהָ וַיִּרְאֵהוּ אֲבִי הַנַּעֲרָה וַיִּשְׂמַח לִקְרָאתוֹ: |

3  ג

4

His father-in-law, the young woman's father, pressed him, and he stayed with him three days; they ate and drank and lodged there.

*va-ya-kha-zek BO kho-t'-NO a-VEE ha-na-a-RAH va-YAY-shev i-TO sh'-LO-shet ya-MEEM va-yo-kh'-LU va-yish-TU va-ya-LEE-nu SHAM*

וַיַּחֲזֶק־בּוֹ אָבִי הַנַּעֲרָה וַיֵּשֶׁב אִתּוֹ שְׁלֹשֶׁת יָמִים וַיֹּאכְלוּ וַיִּשְׁתּוּ וַיָּלִינוּ שָׁם:

ד

5

Early in the morning of the fourth day, he started to leave; but the young woman's father said to his son-in-law, "Eat something to give you strength, then you can leave."

*vai-HEE ba-YOM ha-r'-vee-EE va-yash-KEE-mu va-BO-ker va-YA-kom la-LE-khet va-YO-mer a-VEE ha-na-a-RAH el kha-ta-NO s'-AD li-b'-KHA pat LE-khem v'-a-KHAR tay-LAY-khu*

וַיְהִי בַּיּוֹם הָרְבִיעִי וַיַּשְׁכִּימוּ בַבֹּקֶר וַיָּקָם לָלֶכֶת וַיֹּאמֶר אֲבִי הַנַּעֲרָה אֶל־חֲתָנוֹ סְעָד לִבְּךָ פַּת־לֶחֶם וְאַחַר תֵּלֵכוּ:

ה

6

So the two of them sat down and they feasted together. Then the young woman's father said to the man, "Won't you stay overnight and enjoy yourself?"

*va-yay-sh'-VU va-yo-kh'-LU sh'-nay-HEM yakh-DAV va-yish-TU va-YO-mer a-VEE ha-na-a-RAH el ha-EESH ho-el NA v'-LEEN v'-yeey-TAV li-BE-kha*

וַיֵּשְׁבוּ וַיֹּאכְלוּ שְׁנֵיהֶם יַחְדָּו וַיִּשְׁתּוּ וַיֹּאמֶר אֲבִי הַנַּעֲרָה אֶל־הָאִישׁ הוֹאֶל־נָא וְלִין וְיִיטַב לְבֶךָ:

ו

7

The man started to leave, but his father-in-law kept urging him until he turned back and spent the night there.

*va-YA-kom ha-EESH la-LE-khet va-yif-tzar BO kho-t'-NO va-YA-shov va-YA-len SHAM*

וַיָּקָם הָאִישׁ לָלֶכֶת וַיִּפְצַר־בּוֹ חֹתְנוֹ וַיָּשָׁב וַיָּלֶן שָׁם:

ז

8 Early in the morning of the fifth day, he was about to leave, when the young woman's father said, "Come, have a bite." The two of them ate, dawdling until past noon.

*va-yash-KAYM ba-BO-ker ba-YOM ha-kha-mee-SHEE la-LE-khet va-YO-mer a-VEE ha-na-a-RAH s'-ad NA l'-va-v'-KHA v'-hit-mah-m'-HU ad n'-TOT ha-YOM va-yo-kh'-LU sh'-nay-HEM*

וַיַּשְׁכֵּם בַּבֹּקֶר בַּיּוֹם הַחֲמִישִׁי לָלֶכֶת וַיֹּאמֶר אֲבִי הַנַּעֲרָה סְעָד־נָא לְבָבְךָ וְהִתְמַהְמְהוּ עַד־נְטוֹת הַיּוֹם וַיֹּאכְלוּ שְׁנֵיהֶם: ח

9 Then the man, his concubine, and his attendant started to leave. His father-in-law, the young woman's father, said to him, "Look, the day is waning toward evening; do stop for the night. See, the day is declining; spend the night here and enjoy yourself. You can start early tomorrow on your journey and head for home."

*va-YA-kom ha-EESH la-LE-khet HU u-fee-lag-SHO v'-na-a-RO va-YO-mer LO kho-t'-NO a-VEE ha-na-a-RAH hi-NAY NA ra-FAH ha-YOM la-a-ROV lee-nu NA hi-NAY kha-NOT ha-YOM LEEN POH v'-yee-TAV l'-va-VE-kha v'-hish-kam-TEM ma-KHAR l'-dar-k'-KHEM v'-ha-lakh-TA l'-o-ha-LE-kha*

וַיָּקָם הָאִישׁ לָלֶכֶת הוּא וּפִילַגְשׁוֹ וְנַעֲרוֹ וַיֹּאמֶר לוֹ חֹתְנוֹ אֲבִי הַנַּעֲרָה הִנֵּה נָא רָפָה הַיּוֹם לַעֲרוֹב לִינוּ־נָא הִנֵּה חֲנוֹת הַיּוֹם לִין פֹּה וְיִיטַב לְבָבֶךָ וְהִשְׁכַּמְתֶּם מָחָר לְדַרְכְּכֶם וְהָלַכְתָּ לְאֹהָלֶךָ: ט

10 But the man refused to stay for the night. He set out and traveled as far as the vicinity of Jebus—that is, Jerusalem; he had with him a pair of laden donkeys, and his concubine was with him.

*v'-lo a-VAH ha-EESH la-LUN va-YA-kom va-YAY-lekh va-ya-VO ad NO-khakh y'-VUS HEE y'-ru-sha-LA-yim v'-i-MO TZE-med kha-mo-REEM kha-vu-SHEEM u-fee-lag-SHO i-MO*

וְלֹא־אָבָה הָאִישׁ לָלוּן וַיָּקָם וַיֵּלֶךְ וַיָּבֹא עַד־נֹכַח יְבוּס הִיא יְרוּשָׁלַ͏ִם וְעִמּוֹ צֶמֶד חֲמוֹרִים חֲבוּשִׁים וּפִילַגְשׁוֹ עִמּוֹ: י

|  |  |  | |
|---|---|---|---|
| 11 | Since they were close to Jebus, and the day was very far spent, the attendant said to his master, "Let us turn aside to this town of the Jebusites and spend the night in it." | *HAYM im y'-VUS v'-ha-YOM RAD m'-OD va-YO-mer ha-NA-ar el a-do-NAV l'-khah NA v'-na-SU-rah el eer hai-vu-SEE ha-ZOT v'-na-LEEN BAH* | הֵם עִם־יְבוּס וְהַיּוֹם רַד מְאֹד וַיֹּאמֶר הַנַּעַר אֶל־אֲדֹנָיו לְכָה־נָּא וְנָסוּרָה אֶל־עִיר־הַיְבוּסִי הַזֹּאת וְנָלִין בָּהּ: | יא |
| 12 | But his master said to him, "We will not turn aside to a town of aliens who are not of Israel, but will continue to Gibeah. | *va-YO-mer ay-LAV a-do-NAV LO na-SUR el EER nokh-REE a-SHER lo mi-b'-NAY yis-ra-AYL HAY-nah v'-a-VAR-nu ad giv-AH* | וַיֹּאמֶר אֵלָיו אֲדֹנָיו לֹא נָסוּר אֶל־עִיר נָכְרִי אֲשֶׁר לֹא־מִבְּנֵי יִשְׂרָאֵל הֵנָּה וְעָבַרְנוּ עַד־גִּבְעָה: | יב |
| 13 | Come," he said to his attendant, "let us approach one of those places and spend the night either in Gibeah or in Ramah." | *va-YO-mer l'-na-a-RO l'-KHA v'-nik-r'-VAH b'-a-KHAD ha-m'-ko-MOT v'-LA-nu va-giv-AH O va-ra-MAH* | וַיֹּאמֶר לְנַעֲרוֹ לְךְ וְנִקְרְבָה בְּאַחַד הַמְּקֹמוֹת וְלַנּוּ בַגִּבְעָה אוֹ בָרָמָה: | יג |
| 14 | So they traveled on, and the sun set when they were near Gibeah of Benjamin. | *va-ya-av-RU va-yay-LAY-khu va-ta-VO la-HEM ha-SHE-mesh AY-tzel ha-giv-AH a-SHER l'-vin-ya-MIN* | וַיַּעֲבֹרוּ וַיֵּלְכוּ וַתָּבֹא לָהֶם הַשֶּׁמֶשׁ אֵצֶל הַגִּבְעָה אֲשֶׁר לְבִנְיָמִן: | יד |
| 15 | They turned off there and went in to spend the night in Gibeah. He went and sat down in the town square, but nobody took them indoors to spend the night. | *va-ya-SU-ru SHAM la-VO la-LUN ba-giv-AH va-ya-VO va-YAY-shev bir-KHOV ha-EER v'-AYN EESH m'-a-sayf o-TAM ha-BAI-tah la-LUN* | וַיָּסֻרוּ שָׁם לָבוֹא לָלוּן בַּגִּבְעָה וַיָּבֹא וַיֵּשֶׁב בִּרְחוֹב הָעִיר וְאֵין אִישׁ מְאַסֵּף־אוֹתָם הַבַּיְתָה לָלוּן: | טו |

16 In the evening, an old man came along from his property outside the town. (This man hailed from the hill country of Ephraim and resided at Gibeah, where the locals were Benjaminites.)

*v'-hi-NAY EESH za-KAYN BA min ma-a-SAY-hu min ha-sa-DEH ba-E-rev v'-ha-EESH may-HAR ef-RA-yim v'-hu GAR ba-giv-AH v'-an-SHAY ha-ma-KOM b'-NAY y'-mee-NEE*

וְהִנֵּה אִישׁ זָקֵן בָּא מִֽמַּעֲשֵׂהוּ מִן־הַשָּׂדֶה בָּעֶרֶב וְהָאִישׁ מֵהַר אֶפְרַיִם וְהוּא־גָר בַּגִּבְעָה וְאַנְשֵׁי הַמָּקוֹם בְּנֵי יְמִינִי: טז

17 He happened to notice the wayfarer in the town square. "Where," the old man inquired, "are you going to, and where do you come from?"

*va-yi-SA ay-NAV va-YAR et ha-EESH ha-o-RAY-akh bir-KHOV ha-EER va-YO-mer ha-EESH ha-za-KAYN A-nah tay-LAYKH u-may-A-yin ta-VO*

וַיִּשָּׂא עֵינָיו וַיַּרְא אֶת־הָאִישׁ הָאֹרֵחַ בִּרְחֹב הָעִיר וַיֹּאמֶר הָאִישׁ הַזָּקֵן אָנָה תֵלֵךְ וּמֵאַיִן תָּבוֹא: יז

18 He replied, "We are traveling from Bethlehem in Judah to the other end of the hill country of Ephraim. That is where I live. I made a journey to Bethlehem of Judah, and now I am on my way to the House of GOD, and nobody has taken me indoors.

*va-YO-mer ay-LAV o-v'-REEM a-NAKH-nu mi-bayt LE-khem y'-hu-DAH ad yar-k'-TAY har ef-RA-yim mi-SHAM a-NO-khee va-ay-LAYKH ad BAYT LE-khem y'-hu-DAH v'-et BAYT a-do-NAI a-NEE ho-LAYKH v'-AYN EESH m'-a-SAYF o-TEE ha-BAI-tah*

וַיֹּאמֶר אֵלָיו עֹבְרִים אֲנַחְנוּ מִבֵּֽית־לֶחֶם יְהוּדָה עַד־יַרְכְּתֵי הַר־אֶפְרַיִם מִשָּׁם אָנֹכִי וָאֵלֵךְ עַד־בֵּית לֶחֶם יְהוּדָה וְאֶת־בֵּית יְהֹוָה אֲנִי הֹלֵךְ וְאֵין אִישׁ מְאַסֵּף אוֹתִי הַבָּֽיְתָה: יח

19

We have both bruised straw and feed for our donkeys, and bread and wine for me and your handmaid, and for the attendant with your servants. We lack nothing."

*v'-gam TE-ven gam mis-PO YAYSH la-kha-mo-RAY-nu v'-GAM LE-khem va-YA-yin yesh LEE v'-la-a-ma-TE-kha v'-la-NA-ar im a-va-DE-kha AYN makh-SOR kol da-VAR*

וְגַם־תֶּבֶן גַּם־מִסְפּוֹא יֵשׁ לַחֲמוֹרֵינוּ וְגַם לֶחֶם וָיַיִן יֶשׁ־לִי וְלַאֲמָתֶךָ וְלַנַּעַר עִם־עֲבָדֶיךָ אֵין מַחְסוֹר כָּל־דָּבָר: יט

20

"Rest easy," said the old man. "Let me take care of all your needs. Do not on any account spend the night in the square."

*va-YO-mer ha-EESH ha-za-KAYN sha-LOM LAKH RAK kol makh-so-r'-KHA a-LAI RAK ba-r'-KHOV al ta-LAN*

וַיֹּאמֶר הָאִישׁ הַזָּקֵן שָׁלוֹם לָךְ רַק כָּל־מַחְסוֹרְךָ עָלָי רַק בָּרְחוֹב אַל־תָּלַן: כ

21

And he took him into his house. He mixed fodder for the donkeys; then they bathed their feet and ate and drank.

*vai-vee-AY-hu l'-vay-TO va-YA-vol la-kha-mo-REEM va-yir-kha-TZU rag-lay-HEM va-yo-kh'-LU va-yish-TU*

וַיְבִיאֵהוּ לְבֵיתוֹ (ויבול) [וַיָּבָל] לַחֲמוֹרִים וַיִּרְחֲצוּ רַגְלֵיהֶם וַיֹּאכְלוּ וַיִּשְׁתּוּ: כא

22

While they were enjoying themselves, the townsmen, a depraved lot, had gathered about the house and were pounding on the door. They called to the aged owner of the house, "Bring out that man who's come into your house, so that we can be intimate with him."

*HAY-mah may-tee-VEEM et li-BAM v'-hi-NAY an-SHAY ha-EER an-SHAY v'-nay v'-li-YA-al na-SA-bu et ha-BA-yit mit-da-p'-KEEM al ha-DA-let va-yo-m'-RU el ha-EESH BA-al ha-BA-yit ha-za-KAYN lay-MOR ho-TZAY et ha-EESH a-sher BA el bay-t'-KHA v'-nay-da-E-nu*

הֵמָּה מֵיטִיבִים אֶת־לִבָּם וְהִנֵּה אַנְשֵׁי הָעִיר אַנְשֵׁי בְנֵי־בְלִיַּעַל נָסַבּוּ אֶת־הַבַּיִת מִתְדַּפְּקִים עַל־הַדָּלֶת וַיֹּאמְרוּ אֶל־הָאִישׁ בַּעַל הַבַּיִת הַזָּקֵן לֵאמֹר הוֹצֵא אֶת־הָאִישׁ אֲשֶׁר־בָּא אֶל־בֵּיתְךָ וְנֵדָעֶנּוּ: כב

192

23 The owner of the house went out and said to them, "Please, my friends, do not commit such a wrong. Since this fellow has entered my house, do not perpetrate this outrage.

*va-yay-TZAY a-lay-HEM ha-EESH BA-al ha-BA-yit va-YO-mer a-lay-HEM al a-KHAI al ta-RAY-u NA a-kha-RAY a-sher BA ha-EESH ha-ZEH el bay-TEE al ta-a-SU et ha-n'-va-LAH ha-ZOT*

וַיֵּצֵא אֲלֵיהֶם הָאִישׁ בַּעַל הַבַּיִת וַיֹּאמֶר אֲלֵהֶם אַל־אַחַי אַל־תָּרֵעוּ נָא אַחֲרֵי אֲשֶׁר־בָּא הָאִישׁ הַזֶּה אֶל־בֵּיתִי אַל־תַּעֲשׂוּ אֶת־הַנְּבָלָה הַזֹּאת: כג

24 Look, here is my virgin daughter, and his concubine. Let me bring them out to you. Use them, do what you like with them; but don't do that outrageous thing to this fellow."

*hi-NAY vi-TEE ha-b'-tu-LAH u-fee-lag-SHAY-hu o-tzee-ah NA o-TAM v'-a-NU o-TAM va-a-SU la-HEM ha-TOV b'-ay-nay-KHEM v'-la-EESH ha-ZEH LO ta-a-SU d'-VAR ha-n'-va-LAH ha-ZOT*

הִנֵּה בִתִּי הַבְּתוּלָה וּפִילַגְשֵׁהוּ אוֹצִיאָה־נָּא אוֹתָם וְעַנּוּ אוֹתָם וַעֲשׂוּ לָהֶם הַטּוֹב בְּעֵינֵיכֶם וְלָאִישׁ הַזֶּה לֹא תַעֲשׂוּ דְּבַר הַנְּבָלָה הַזֹּאת: כד

25 But the others would not listen to him. So the man seized his concubine and pushed her out to them. They raped her and abused her all night long until morning; and they let her go when dawn broke.

*v'-lo a-VU ha-a-na-SHEEM lish-MO-a LO va-ya-kha-ZAYK ha-EESH b'-FEE-lag-SHO va-yo-TZAY a-lay-HEM ha-KHUTZ va-yay-d'-U o-TAH va-yit-a-l'-lu VAH kol ha-LAI-lah ad ha-BO-ker vai-shal-KHU-ha ka-a-LOT ha-SHA-khar*

וְלֹא־אָבוּ הָאֲנָשִׁים לִשְׁמֹעַ לוֹ וַיַּחֲזֵק הָאִישׁ בְּפִילַגְשׁוֹ וַיֹּצֵא אֲלֵיהֶם הַחוּץ וַיֵּדְעוּ אוֹתָהּ וַיִּתְעַלְּלוּ־בָהּ כָּל־הַלַּיְלָה עַד־הַבֹּקֶר וַיְשַׁלְּחוּהָ (בעלות) [כַּעֲלוֹת] הַשָּׁחַר: כה

26 Toward morning the woman came back; and as it was growing light, she collapsed at the entrance of the very house where her husband was.

*va-ta-VO ha-i-SHAH lif-NOT ha-BO-ker va-ti-POL PE-takh bayt ha-EESH a-sher a-do-NE-ha SHAM ad ha-OR*

וַתָּבֹא הָאִשָּׁה לִפְנוֹת הַבֹּקֶר וַתִּפֹּל פֶּתַח בֵּית־הָאִישׁ אֲשֶׁר־אֲדוֹנֶיהָ שָּׁם עַד־הָאוֹר: כו

27

When her husband arose in the morning, he opened the doors of the house and went out to continue his journey; and there was the woman, his concubine, lying at the entrance of the house, with her hands on the threshold.

*va-YA-kom a-do-NE-ha ba-BO-ker va-yif-TAKH dal-TOT ha-BA-yit va-yay-TZAY la-LE-khet l'-dar-KO v'-hi-NAY ha-i-SHAH fee-lag-SHO no-FE-let PE-takh ha-BA-yit v'-ya-DE-ha al ha-SAF*

וַיָּקָם אֲדֹנֶיהָ בַּבֹּקֶר וַיִּפְתַּח דַּלְתוֹת הַבַּיִת וַיֵּצֵא לָלֶכֶת לְדַרְכּוֹ וְהִנֵּה הָאִשָּׁה פִילַגְשׁוֹ נֹפֶלֶת פֶּתַח הַבַּיִת וְיָדֶיהָ עַל־הַסַּף: כז

28

"Get up," he said to her, "let us go." But there was no reply. So the man placed her on the donkey and set out for home.

*va-YO-mer ay-LE-ha KU-mee v'-nay-LAY-kha v'-AYN o-NEH va-yi-ka-KHE-ha al ha-kha-MOR va-ya-KOM ha-EESH va-YAY-lekh lim-ko-MO*

וַיֹּאמֶר אֵלֶיהָ קוּמִי וְנֵלֵכָה וְאֵין עֹנֶה וַיִּקָּחֶהָ עַל־הַחֲמוֹר וַיָּקָם הָאִישׁ וַיֵּלֶךְ לִמְקֹמוֹ: כח

29

When he came home, he picked up a knife, and took hold of his concubine and cut her up limb by limb into twelve parts. He sent them throughout the territory of Israel.

*va-ya-VO el bay-TO va-yi-KAKH et ha-ma-a-KHE-let va-ya-kha-ZAYK b'-fee-lag-SHO vai-na-t'-KHE-ha la-a-tza-ME-ha lish-NAYM a-SAR n'-ta-KHEEM vai-sha-l'-KHE-ha b'-KHOL g'-VUL yis-ra-AYL*

וַיָּבֹא אֶל־בֵּיתוֹ וַיִּקַּח אֶת־הַמַּאֲכֶלֶת וַיַּחֲזֵק בְּפִילַגְשׁוֹ וַיְנַתְּחֶהָ לַעֲצָמֶיהָ לִשְׁנֵים עָשָׂר נְתָחִים וַיְשַׁלְּחֶהָ בְּכֹל גְּבוּל יִשְׂרָאֵל: כט

30

And everyone who saw it cried out, "Never has such a thing happened or been seen from the day the Israelites came out of the land of Egypt to this day! Put your mind to this; take counsel and decide."

*v'-ha-YAH khol ha-ro-EH v'-a-MAR lo nih-y'-TAH v'-lo nir-a-TAH ka-ZOT l'-mi-YOM a-LOT b'-NAY yis-ra-AYL may-E-retz mitz-RA-yim AD ha-YOM ha-ZEH see-mu la-KHEM a-LE-ha U-tzu v'-da-BAY-ru*

וְהָיָה כָל־הָרֹאֶה וְאָמַר לֹא־נִהְיְתָה וְלֹא־נִרְאֲתָה כָּזֹאת לְמִיּוֹם עֲלוֹת בְּנֵי־יִשְׂרָאֵל מֵאֶרֶץ מִצְרַיִם עַד הַיּוֹם הַזֶּה שִׂימוּ־לָכֶם עָלֶיהָ עֻצוּ וְדַבֵּרוּ: ל

# 20

ב

| | | |
|---|---|---|
| 1 | Thereupon all the Israelites—from Dan to Beer-sheba and [from] the land of Gilead—marched forth, and the community assembled as one, before GOD at Mizpah. | *va-yay-tz'-U kol b'-NAY yis-ra-AYL va-ti-ka-HAYL ha-ay-DAH k'-EESH e-KHAD l'-mi-DAN v'-ad b'-AYR SHE-va v'-E-retz ha-gil-AD el a-do-NAI ha-mitz-PAH* |

וַיֵּצְאוּ כָּל־בְּנֵי יִשְׂרָאֵל וַתִּקָּהֵל הָעֵדָה כְּאִישׁ אֶחָד לְמִדָּן וְעַד־בְּאֵר שֶׁבַע וְאֶרֶץ הַגִּלְעָד אֶל־יְהֹוָה הַמִּצְפָּה: א

All the leaders of the people [and] all the tribes of Israel presented themselves in the assembly of God's people, 400,000 fighters on foot.—

*va-yit-ya-tz'-VU pi-NOT kol ha-AM KOL shiv-TAY yis-ra-AYL bik-HAL AM ha-e-lo-HEEM ar-BA may-OT E-lef EESH rag-LEE sho-LAYF KHA-rev*

וַיִּתְיַצְּבוּ פִּנּוֹת כָּל־הָעָם כֹּל שִׁבְטֵי יִשְׂרָאֵל בִּקְהַל עַם הָאֱלֹהִים אַרְבַּע מֵאוֹת אֶלֶף אִישׁ רַגְלִי שֹׁלֵף חָרֶב: ב

The Benjaminites heard that the Israelites had come up to Mizpah. —The Israelites said, "Tell us, how did this evil thing happen?"

*va-yish-m'-U b'-NAY vin-ya-MIN kee a-LU v'-NAY yis-ra-AYL ha-mitz-PAH va-yo-m'-RU b'-NAY yis-ra-AYL da-b'-RU ay-KHAH nih-y'-TAH ha-ra-AH ha-ZOT*

וַיִּשְׁמְעוּ בְּנֵי בִנְיָמִן כִּי־עָלוּ בְנֵי־יִשְׂרָאֵל הַמִּצְפָּה וַיֹּאמְרוּ בְּנֵי יִשְׂרָאֵל דַּבְּרוּ אֵיכָה נִהְיְתָה הָרָעָה הַזֹּאת: ג

And that Levite, the husband of the murdered woman, replied, "My concubine and I came to Gibeah of Benjamin to spend the night.

*va-YA-an ha-EESH ha-lay-VEE EESH ha-i-SHAH ha-nir-tz'-KHAH va-yo-MAR ha-giv-A-tah a-SHER l'-vin-ya-MIN BA-tee a-NEE u-fee-lag-SHEE la-LUN*

וַיַּעַן הָאִישׁ הַלֵּוִי אִישׁ הָאִשָּׁה הַנִּרְצָחָה וַיֹּאמַר הַגִּבְעָתָה אֲשֶׁר לְבִנְיָמִן בָּאתִי אֲנִי וּפִילַגְשִׁי לָלוּן: ד

<table>
<tr><td>5</td><td>The citizens of Gibeah set out to harm me. They gathered against me around the house in the night; they meant to kill me, and they abused my concubine until she died.</td><td>*va-ya-KU-mu a-LAI ba-a-LAY ha-giv-AH va-ya-SO-bu a-LAI et ha-BA-yit LAI-lah o-TEE di-MU la-ha-ROG v'-et pee-lag-SHEE i-NU va-ta-MOT*</td><td>וַיָּקֻמוּ עָלַי בַּעֲלֵי הַגִּבְעָה וַיָּסֹבּוּ עָלַי אֶת־הַבַּיִת לָיְלָה אוֹתִי דִּמּוּ לַהֲרֹג וְאֶת־פִּילַגְשִׁי עִנּוּ וַתָּמֹת:<br>ה</td></tr>
<tr><td>6</td><td>So I took hold of my concubine and I cut her in pieces and sent them through every part of Israel's territory. For an outrageous act of depravity had been committed in Israel.</td><td>*va-o-KHAYZ b'-fee-lag-SHEE va-a-na-t'-KHE-ha va-a-sha-l'-KHE-ha b-khol s'-DAY na-kha-LAT yis-ra-AYL KEE a-SU zi-MAH un-va-LAH b'-yis-ra-AYL*</td><td>וָאֹחֵז בְּפִילַגְשִׁי וָאֲנַתְּחֶהָ וָאֲשַׁלְּחֶהָ בְּכָל־שְׂדֵה נַחֲלַת יִשְׂרָאֵל כִּי עָשׂוּ זִמָּה וּנְבָלָה בְּיִשְׂרָאֵל:<br>ו</td></tr>
<tr><td>7</td><td>Now you are all Israelites; produce a plan of action here and now!"</td><td>*hi-NAY khu-l'-KHEM b'-NAY yis-ra-AYL ha-VU la-KHEM da-VAR v'-ay-TZAH ha-LOM*</td><td>הִנֵּה כֻלְּכֶם בְּנֵי יִשְׂרָאֵל הָבוּ לָכֶם דָּבָר וְעֵצָה הֲלֹם:<br>ז</td></tr>
<tr><td>8</td><td>Then all the people rose as one and declared, "We will not go back to our homes, we will not enter our houses!</td><td>*va-YA-kom kol ha-AM k'-EESH e-KHAD lay-MOR LO nay-LAYKH EESH l'-o-ha-LO v'-LO na-SUR EESH l'-vay-TO*</td><td>וַיָּקָם כָּל־הָעָם כְּאִישׁ אֶחָד לֵאמֹר לֹא נֵלֵךְ אִישׁ לְאָהֳלוֹ וְלֹא נָסוּר אִישׁ לְבֵיתוֹ:<br>ח</td></tr>
<tr><td>9</td><td>But this is what we will do to Gibeah: [we will wage war] against it according to lot.</td><td>*v'-a-TAH ZEH ha-da-VAR a-SHER na-a-SEH la-giv-AH a-LE-ha b'-go-RAL*</td><td>וְעַתָּה זֶה הַדָּבָר אֲשֶׁר נַעֲשֶׂה לַגִּבְעָה עָלֶיהָ בְּגוֹרָל:<br>ט</td></tr>
</table>

| | | | |
|---|---|---|---|
| 10 | We will take from all the tribes of Israel ten of every hundred, a hundred of every thousand, and a thousand of every ten thousand to supply provisions for the troops—to prepare for their going to Geba in Benjamin for all the outrage it has committed in Israel." | *v'-la-KAKH-nu a-sa-RAH a-na-SHEEM la-may-AH l'-KHOL shiv-TAY yis-ra-AYL u-may-AH la-E-lef v'-E-lef la-r'-va-VAH la-KA-khat tzay-DAH la-AM la-a-SOT l'-vo-AM l'-GE-va bin-ya-MIN k'-KHOL ha-n'-va-LAH a-SHER a-SAH b'-yis-ra-AYL* | וְלָקַחְנוּ עֲשָׂרָה אֲנָשִׁים לַמֵּאָה לְכֹל שִׁבְטֵי יִשְׂרָאֵל וּמֵאָה לָאֶלֶף וְאֶלֶף לָרְבָבָה לָקַחַת צֵדָה לָעָם לַעֲשׂוֹת לְבוֹאָם לְגֶבַע בִּנְיָמִן כְּכָל־הַנְּבָלָה אֲשֶׁר עָשָׂה בְּיִשְׂרָאֵל: |
| 11 | So Israel's forces, united as one, massed against the town. | *va-yay-a-SAYF kol EESH yis-ra-AYL el ha-EER k'-EESH e-KHAD kha-vay-REEM* | וַיֵּאָסֵף כָּל־אִישׁ יִשְׂרָאֵל אֶל־הָעִיר כְּאִישׁ אֶחָד חֲבֵרִים: יא |
| 12 | And the tribes of Israel sent agents through the whole tribe of Benjamin, saying, "What is this evil thing that has happened among you? | *va-yish-l'-KHU shiv-TAY yis-ra-AYL a-na-SHEEM b'-khol shiv-TAY vin-ya-MIN lay-MOR MAH ha-ra-AH ha-ZOT a-SHER nih-y'-TAH ba-KHEM* | וַיִּשְׁלְחוּ שִׁבְטֵי יִשְׂרָאֵל אֲנָשִׁים בְּכָל־שִׁבְטֵי בִנְיָמִן לֵאמֹר מָה הָרָעָה הַזֹּאת אֲשֶׁר נִהְיְתָה בָּכֶם: יב |
| 13 | Come, hand over those scoundrels in Gibeah so that we may put them to death and stamp out the evil from Israel." But the Benjaminites would not yield to the demand of their fellow Israelites. | *v'-a-TAH t'-NU et ha-a-na-SHEEM b'-NAY v'-li-YA-al a-SHER ba-giv-AH un-mee-TAYM un-va-a-RAH ra-AH mi-yis-ra-AYL v'-LO a-VU [b'-NAY] vin-ya-MIN lish-MO-a b'-KOL a-khay-HEM b'-nay yis-ra-AYL* | וְעַתָּה תְּנוּ אֶת־הָאֲנָשִׁים בְּנֵי־בְלִיַּעַל אֲשֶׁר בַּגִּבְעָה וּנְמִיתֵם וּנְבַעֲרָה רָעָה מִיִּשְׂרָאֵל וְלֹא אָבוּ [בְּנֵי] בִּנְיָמִן לִשְׁמֹעַ בְּקוֹל אֲחֵיהֶם בְּנֵי־יִשְׂרָאֵל: יג |

| | | |
|---|---|---|
| 14 | So the Benjaminites gathered from their towns to Gibeah in order to take the field against the Israelites. | *va-yay-a-s'-FU v'-nay vin-ya-MIN min he-a-REEM ha-giv-A-tah la-TZAYT la-mil-kha-MAH im b'-NAY yis-ra-AYL* | וַיֵּאָסְפוּ בְנֵי־בִנְיָמִן מִן־הֶעָרִים הַגִּבְעָתָה לָצֵאת לַמִּלְחָמָה עִם־ בְּנֵי יִשְׂרָאֵל: | יד |
| 15 | On that day the Benjaminites mustered from the towns 26,000 fighters, mustered apart from the inhabitants of Gibeah; 700 elite troops | *va-yit-pa-k'-DU v'-NAY vin-ya-MIN ba-YOM ha-HU may-he-a-REEM es-REEM v'-shi-SHAH E-lef EESH SHO-layf KHA-rev l'-VAD mi-yo-sh'-VAY ha-giv-AH hit-pa-k'-DU sh'-VA may-OT EESH ba-KHUR* | וַיִּתְפָּקְדוּ בְנֵי בִנְיָמִן בַּיּוֹם הַהוּא מֵהֶעָרִים עֶשְׂרִים וְשִׁשָּׁה אֶלֶף אִישׁ שֹׁלֵף חָרֶב לְבַד מִיֹּשְׁבֵי הַגִּבְעָה הִתְפָּקְדוּ שְׁבַע מֵאוֹת אִישׁ בָּחוּר: | טו |
| 16 | of these forces—700 of the best troops— were left-handed. Every one of them could sling a stone at a hair and not miss. | *mi-KOL ha-AM ha-ZEH sh'-VA may-OT EESH ba-KHUR i-TAYR yad y'-mee-NO kol ZEH ko-LAY-a ba-E-ven el ha-sa-a-RAH v'-LO ya-kha-TI* | מִכֹּל הָעָם הַזֶּה שְׁבַע מֵאוֹת אִישׁ בָּחוּר אִטֵּר יַד־יְמִינוֹ כָּל־זֶה קֹלֵעַ בָּאֶבֶן אֶל־הַשַּׂעֲרָה וְלֹא יַחֲטִא: | טז |
| 17 | Israel's side—other than Benjamin— mustered 400,000 fighters, every one of them a warrior. | *v'-EESH yis-ra-AYL hit-pa-k'-DU l'-VAD mi-bin-ya-MIN ar-BA may-OT E-lef EESH SHO-layf KHA-rev kol ZEH EESH mil-kha-MAH* | וְאִישׁ יִשְׂרָאֵל הִתְפָּקְדוּ לְבַד מִבִּנְיָמִן אַרְבַּע מֵאוֹת אֶלֶף אִישׁ שֹׁלֵף חָרֶב כָּל־זֶה אִישׁ מִלְחָמָה: | יז |
| 18 | They proceeded to Bethel and inquired of God; the Israelites asked, "Who of us shall advance first to fight the Benjaminites?" And GOD replied, "Judah first." | *va-ya-KU-mu va-ya-a-LU vayt AYL va-yish-a-LU vay-lo-HEEM va-yo-m'-RU b'-NAY yis-ra-AYL MEE ya-a-leh LA-nu va-t'-khi-LAH la-mil-kha-MAH im b'-NAY vin-ya-MIN va-YO-mer a-do-ANI y'-hu-DAH va-t'-khi-LAH* | וַיָּקֻמוּ וַיַּעֲלוּ בֵית־אֵל וַיִּשְׁאֲלוּ בֵאלֹהִים וַיֹּאמְרוּ בְּנֵי יִשְׂרָאֵל מִי יַעֲלֶה־לָּנוּ בַתְּחִלָּה לַמִּלְחָמָה עִם־בְּנֵי בִנְיָמִן וַיֹּאמֶר יְהוָה יְהוּדָה בַתְּחִלָּה: | יח |

| |  |  |  |
|---|---|---|---|
| 19 | So the Israelites arose in the morning and encamped against Gibeah. | *va-ya-KU-mu v'-nay yis-ra-AYL ba-BO-ker va-ya-kha-NU al ha-giv-AH* | וַיָּקוּמוּ בְנֵי־יִשְׂרָאֵל בַּבֹּקֶר וַיַּחֲנוּ עַל־הַגִּבְעָה: יט |
| 20 | Israel's side took the field against the Benjaminites; Israel's force drew up in battle order against them at Gibeah. | *va-yay-TZAY EESH yis-ra-AYL la-mil-kha-MAH im bin-ya-MIN va-ya-ar-KHU i-TAM eesh yis-ra-AYL mil-kha-MAH el ha-giv-AH* | וַיֵּצֵא אִישׁ יִשְׂרָאֵל לַמִּלְחָמָה עִם־בִּנְיָמִן וַיַּעַרְכוּ אִתָּם אִישׁ־יִשְׂרָאֵל מִלְחָמָה אֶל־הַגִּבְעָה: כ |
| 21 | But the Benjaminites issued from Gibeah, and that day they struck down 22,000 of the Israelites. | *va-yay-tz'-U v'-nay vin-ya-MIN min ha-giv-AH va-yash-KHEE-tu v'-yis-ra-AYL ba-YOM ha-HU sh'-NA-yim v'-es-REEM E-lef EESH ar-TZAH* | וַיֵּצְאוּ בְנֵי־בִנְיָמִן מִן־הַגִּבְעָה וַיַּשְׁחִיתוּ בְיִשְׂרָאֵל בַּיּוֹם הַהוּא שְׁנַיִם וְעֶשְׂרִים אֶלֶף אִישׁ אָרְצָה: כא |
| 22 | Now the army—Israel's force—rallied and again drew up in battle order at the same place as they had on the first day. | *va-yit-kha-ZAYK ha-AM EESH yis-ra-AYL va-yo-SI-fu la-a-ROKH mil-kha-MAH ba-ma-KOM a-sher A-r'-khu SHAM ba-YOM ha-ri-SHON* | וַיִּתְחַזֵּק הָעָם אִישׁ יִשְׂרָאֵל וַיֹּסִפוּ לַעֲרֹךְ מִלְחָמָה בַּמָּקוֹם אֲשֶׁר־עָרְכוּ שָׁם בַּיּוֹם הָרִאשׁוֹן: כב |
| 23 | For the Israelites had gone up and wept before GOD until evening. They had inquired of GOD, "Shall we again join battle with our kinsmen the Benjaminites?" And GOD had replied, "March against them." | *va-ya-a-LU v'-nay yis-ra-AYL va-yiv-KU lif-nay a-do-NAI ad ha-E-erv va-yish-a-LU va-do-NAI lay-MOR ha-o-SEEF la-GE-shet la-mil-kha-MAH im b'-NAY vin-ya-MIN a-KHEE va-YO-mer a-do-NAI a-LU ay-LAV* | וַיַּעֲלוּ בְנֵי־יִשְׂרָאֵל וַיִּבְכּוּ לִפְנֵי־יְהוָה עַד־הָעֶרֶב וַיִּשְׁאֲלוּ בַיהוָה לֵאמֹר הַאוֹסִיף לָגֶשֶׁת לַמִּלְחָמָה עִם־בְּנֵי בִנְיָמִן אָחִי וַיֹּאמֶר יְהוָה עֲלוּ אֵלָיו: כג |

| | | | |
|---|---|---|---|
| 24 | The Israelites advanced against the Benjaminites on the second day. | *va-yik-r'-VU v'-nay yis-ra-AYL el b'-NAY vin-ya-MIN ba-YOM ha-shay-NEE* | וַיִּקְרְבוּ בְנֵי־יִשְׂרָאֵל אֶל־בְּנֵי בִנְיָמִן בַּיּוֹם הַשֵּׁנִי: כד |
| 25 | But the Benjaminites came out from Gibeah against them on the second day and struck down 18,000 more of the Israelites, all of them fighters. | *va-yay-TZAY vin-ya-MIN lik-ra-TAM min ha-giv-AH ba-YOM ha-shay-NEE va-yash-KHEE-tu viv-NAY yis-ra-AYL OD sh'-mo-NAT a-SAR E-lef EESH AR-tzah kol AY-leh SHO-l'-fay KHA-rev* | וַיֵּצֵא בִנְיָמִן לִקְרָאתָם מִן־הַגִּבְעָה בַּיּוֹם הַשֵּׁנִי וַיַּשְׁחִיתוּ בִבְנֵי יִשְׂרָאֵל עוֹד שְׁמֹנַת עָשָׂר אֶלֶף אִישׁ אָרְצָה כָּל־אֵלֶּה שֹׁלְפֵי חָרֶב: כה |
| 26 | Then all the Israelites, all the army, went up and came to Bethel and they sat there, weeping before GOD. They fasted that day until evening, and presented burnt offerings and offerings of well-being to GOD. | *va-ya-a-LU kol b'-NAY yis-ra-AYL v'-khol ha-AM va-ya-VO-u vayt AYL va-yiv-KU va-YAY-sh'-vu SHAM lif-NAY a-do-NAI va-ya-TZU-mu va-yom ha-HU ad ha-A-rev va-ya-a-LU o-LOT ush-la-MEEM lif-NAY a-do-NAI* | וַיַּעֲלוּ כָל־בְּנֵי יִשְׂרָאֵל וְכָל־הָעָם וַיָּבֹאוּ בֵית־אֵל וַיִּבְכּוּ וַיֵּשְׁבוּ שָׁם לִפְנֵי יְהוָה וַיָּצוּמוּ בַיּוֹם־הַהוּא עַד־הָעָרֶב וַיַּעֲלוּ עֹלוֹת וּשְׁלָמִים לִפְנֵי יְהוָה: כו |
| 27 | The Israelites inquired of GOD (for the Ark of God's Covenant was there in those days, | *va-yish-a-LU v'-nay yis-ra-AYL ba-do-NAI v'-SHAM a-RON b'-REET ha-e-lo-HEEM ba-ya-MEEM ha-HAYM* | וַיִּשְׁאֲלוּ בְנֵי־יִשְׂרָאֵל בַּיהוָה וְשָׁם אֲרוֹן בְּרִית הָאֱלֹהִים בַּיָּמִים הָהֵם: כז |

28
and Phinehas son of Eleazar son of Aaron the priest ministered before [God] in those days), "Shall we again take the field against our kinsmen the Benjaminites, or shall we not?" GOD answered, "Go up, for tomorrow I will deliver them into your hands."

*u-feen-KHAS ben el-a-ZAR ben a-ha-RON o-MAYD l'-fa-NAV ba-ya-MEEM ha-HAYM lay-MOR ha-o-SEEF OD la-TZAYT la-mil-kha-MAH im b'-nay vin-ya-MIN a-KHEE im ekh-DAL va-YO-mer a-do-NAI a-LU KEE ma-KHAR e-t'-NE-nu v'-ya-DE-kha*

וּפִינְחָס בֶּן־אֶלְעָזָר בֶּן־אַהֲרֹן עֹמֵד לְפָנָיו בַּיָּמִים הָהֵם לֵאמֹר הַאוֹסִף עוֹד לָצֵאת לַמִּלְחָמָה עִם־בְּנֵי־ בִנְיָמִן אָחִי אִם־אֶחְדָּל וַיֹּאמֶר יְהוָה עֲלוּ כִּי מָחָר אֶתְּנֶנּוּ בְיָדֶךָ: כח

29
Israel put men in ambush against Gibeah on all sides.

*va-YA-sem yis-ra-AYL o-r'-VEEM el ha-giv-AH sa-VEEV*

וַיָּשֶׂם יִשְׂרָאֵל אֹרְבִים אֶל־הַגִּבְעָה סָבִיב: כט

30
And on the third day, the Israelites went up against the Benjaminites, as before, and engaged them in battle at Gibeah.

*va-ya-a-LU v'-nay yis-ra-AYL el b'-NAY vin-ya-MIN ba-YOM ha-sh'-lee-SHEE va-ya-ar-KHU el ha-giv-AH k'-FA-am b'-FA-am*

וַיַּעֲלוּ בְנֵי־יִשְׂרָאֵל אֶל־בְּנֵי בִנְיָמִן בַּיּוֹם הַשְּׁלִישִׁי וַיַּעַרְכוּ אֶל־ הַגִּבְעָה כְּפַעַם בְּפָעַם: ל

31
The Benjaminites dashed out to meet the army and were drawn away from the town onto the roads, of which one runs to Bethel and the other to Gibeah. As before, they started out by striking some of the men dead in the open field, about 30 of the Israelites.

*va-yay-tz'-U v'-nay vin-ya-MIN lik-RAT ha-AM hon-t'-KU min ha-EER va-ya-KHAY-lu l'-ha-KOT may-ha-AM kha-la-LEEM k'-FA-am b'-FA-am bam-si-LOT a-SHER a-KHAT o-LAH vayt AYL v'-a-KHAT giv-A-tah ba-sa-DEH kish-lo-SHEEM EESH b'-yis-ra-AYL*

וַיֵּצְאוּ בְנֵי־בִנְיָמִן לִקְרַאת הָעָם הָנְתְּקוּ מִן־הָעִיר וַיָּחֵלּוּ לְהַכּוֹת מֵהָעָם חֲלָלִים כְּפַעַם בְּפַעַם בַּמְסִלּוֹת אֲשֶׁר אַחַת עֹלָה בֵית־ אֵל וְאַחַת גִּבְעָתָה בַּשָּׂדֶה כִּשְׁלֹשִׁים אִישׁ בְּיִשְׂרָאֵל: לא

32

The Benjaminites thought, "They are being routed before us as previously." But the Israelites had planned: "We will take to flight and draw them away from the town to the roads."

*va-YO-m'-ru b'-NAY vin-ya-MIN ni-ga-FEEM HAYM l'-fa-NAY-nu k'-va-ri-sho-NAH uv-NAY yis-ra-AYL a-m'-RU na-NU-sah un-ta-k'-NU-hu min ha-EER el ham-si-LOT*

וַיֹּאמְרוּ בְּנֵי בִנְיָמִן נִגָּפִים הֵם לְפָנֵינוּ כְּבָרִאשֹׁנָה וּבְנֵי יִשְׂרָאֵל אָמְרוּ נָנוּסָה וּנְתַקְנוּהוּ מִן־הָעִיר אֶל־הַמְסִלּוֹת: לב

33

And while the main body of Israel's force had moved away from their positions and had drawn up in battle order at Baal-tamar, the Israelite ambush was rushing out from its position at Maareh-geba.

*v'-KHOL EESH yis-ra-AYL KA-mu mi-m'-ko-MO va-ya-ar-KHU b'-VA-al ta-MAR v'-o-RAYV yis-ra-AYL may-GEE-akh mi-m'-ko-MO mi-MA-a-ray GA-va*

וְכֹל אִישׁ יִשְׂרָאֵל קָמוּ מִמְּקוֹמוֹ וַיַּעַרְכוּ בְּבַעַל תָּמָר וְאֹרֵב יִשְׂרָאֵל מֵגִיחַ מִמְּקֹמוֹ מִמַּעֲרֵה גָבַע: לג

34

Thus 10,000 of the best troops from all Israel came to a point south of Gibeah, and the battle was furious. Before they realized that disaster was approaching,

*va-ya-VO-u mi-NE-ged la-giv-AH a-SE-ret a-la-FEEM EESH ba-KHUR mi-kol yis-ra-AYL v'-ha-mil-kha-MAH ka-VAY-dah v'-HAYM LO ya-d'-U kee no-GA-at a-lay-HEM ha-ra-AH*

וַיָּבֹאוּ מִנֶּגֶד לַגִּבְעָה עֲשֶׂרֶת אֲלָפִים אִישׁ בָּחוּר מִכָּל־יִשְׂרָאֵל וְהַמִּלְחָמָה כָּבֵדָה וְהֵם לֹא יָדְעוּ כִּי־נֹגַעַת עֲלֵיהֶם הָרָעָה: לד

35

GOD routed the Benjaminites before Israel. That day the Israelites slew 25,100 of the Benjaminites, all of them fighters.

*va-yi-GOF a-do-NAI et bin-ya-MIN lif-NAY yis-ra-AYL va-yash-KHEE-tu b'-NAY yis-ra-AYL b'-vin-ya-MIN ba-YOM ha-HU es-REEM va-kha-mi-SHAH E-lef u-may-AH EESH kol AY-leh SHO-layf KHA-rev*

וַיִּגֹּף יְהוָה אֶת־בִּנְיָמִן לִפְנֵי יִשְׂרָאֵל וַיַּשְׁחִיתוּ בְנֵי יִשְׂרָאֵל בְּבִנְיָמִן בַּיּוֹם הַהוּא עֶשְׂרִים וַחֲמִשָּׁה אֶלֶף וּמֵאָה אִישׁ כָּל־אֵלֶּה שֹׁלֵף חָרֶב: לה

**36**

Then the Benjaminites realized that they were routed. Now Israel's force had yielded ground to the Benjaminites, for they relied on the ambush that they had laid against Gibeah.

*va-yir-U v'-nay vin-ya-MIN KEE ni-GA-fu va-yi-t'-NU EESH yis-ra-AYL ma-KOM l'-vin-ya-MIN KEE va-t'-KHU el ha-o-RAYV a-SHER SA-mu el ha-giv-AH*

וַיִּרְאוּ בְנֵי־בִנְיָמִן כִּי נִגָּפוּ וַיִּתְּנוּ אִישׁ־ יִשְׂרָאֵל מָקוֹם לְבִנְיָמִן כִּי בָטְחוּ אֶל־הָאֹרֵב אֲשֶׁר שָׂמוּ אֶל־הַגִּבְעָה: לו

**37**

One ambush quickly deployed against Gibeah, and the other ambush advanced and put the whole town to the sword.

*v'-ha-o-RAYV hay-KHEE-shu va-yif-sh'-TU el ha-giv-AH va-yim-SHOKH ha-o-RAYV va-YAKH et kol ha-EER l'-fee KHA-rev*

וְהָאֹרֵב הֵחִישׁוּ וַיִּפְשְׁטוּ אֶל־הַגִּבְעָה וַיִּמְשֹׁךְ הָאֹרֵב וַיַּךְ אֶת־ כָּל־הָעִיר לְפִי־חָרֶב: לז

**38**

A time had been agreed upon by Israel's force with those in ambush: When a huge column of smoke was sent up from the town,

*v'-ha-mo-AYD ha-YAH l'-EESH yis-ra-AYL im ha-o-RAYV HE-rev l'-ha-a-lo-TAM mas-AT he-a-SHAN min ha-EER*

וְהַמּוֹעֵד הָיָה לְאִישׁ יִשְׂרָאֵל עִם־הָאֹרֵב הֶרֶב לְהַעֲלוֹתָם מַשְׂאַת הֶעָשָׁן מִן־הָעִיר: לח

**39**

Israel's force was to turn about in battle. Benjamin had begun by striking dead about 30 men from Israel's force, and they thought, "They are being routed before us as in the previous fighting."

*va-ya-ha-FOKH eesh yis-ra-AYL ba-mil-kha-MAH u-vin-ya-MIN hay-KHAYL l'-ha-KOT kha-la-LEEM b'-eesh yis-ra-AYL kish-lo-SHEEM EESH KEE a-m'-RU AKH ni-GOF ni-GAF HU l'-fa-NAY-nu ka-mil-kha-MAH ha-ri-sho-NAH*

וַיַּהֲפֹךְ אִישׁ־יִשְׂרָאֵל בַּמִּלְחָמָה וּבִנְיָמִן הֵחֵל לְהַכּוֹת חֲלָלִים בְּאִישׁ־ יִשְׂרָאֵל כִּשְׁלֹשִׁים אִישׁ כִּי אָמְרוּ אַךְ נִגּוֹף נִגָּף הוּא לְפָנֵינוּ כַּמִּלְחָמָה הָרִאשֹׁנָה: לט

| | | |
|---|---|---|
| 40 | But when the column, the pillar of smoke, began to rise from the city, the Benjaminites looked behind them, and there was the whole town going up in smoke to the sky! | *v'-ha-mas-AYT hay-KHAY-lah la-a-LOT min ha-EER a-MUD a-SHAN va-YI-fen bin-ya-MIN a-kha-RAV v'-hi-NAY a-LAH kh'-leel ha-EER ha-sha-MAI-mah* | וְהַמַּשְׂאֵת הֵחֵלָּה לַעֲלוֹת מִן־הָעִיר עַמּוּד עָשָׁן וַיִּפֶן בִּנְיָמִן אַחֲרָיו וְהִנֵּה עָלָה כְלִיל־הָעִיר הַשָּׁמָיְמָה: מ |
| 41 | And now Israel's force turned about, and Benjamin's force was thrown into panic, for they realized that disaster had overtaken them. | *v'-EESH yis-ra-AYL ha-FAKH va-yi-ba-HAYL EESH bin-ya-MIN KEE ra-AH kee na-g'-AH a-LAV ha-ra-AH* | וְאִישׁ יִשְׂרָאֵל הָפַךְ וַיִּבָּהֵל אִישׁ בִּנְיָמִן כִּי רָאָה כִּי־נָגְעָה עָלָיו הָרָעָה: מא |
| 42 | They retreated before Israel's force along the road to the wilderness, where the fighting caught up with them; meanwhile those from the towns were massacring them in it. | *va-yif-NU lif-NAY EESH yis-ra-AYL el DE-rekh ha-mid-BAR v'-ha-mil-kha-MAH hid-bee-KAT-hu va-a-SHER may-HE-a-REEM mash-khee-TEEM o-TO b'-to-KHO* | וַיִּפְנוּ לִפְנֵי אִישׁ יִשְׂרָאֵל אֶל־דֶּרֶךְ הַמִּדְבָּר וְהַמִּלְחָמָה הִדְבִּיקָתְהוּ וַאֲשֶׁר מֵהֶעָרִים מַשְׁחִיתִים אוֹתוֹ בְּתוֹכוֹ: מב |
| 43 | They encircled the Benjaminites, pursued them, and trod them down [from] Menuhah to a point opposite Gibeah on the east. | *ki-t'-RU et bin-ya-MIN hir-dee-FU-hu m'-nu-KHAH hid-ree-KHU-hu AD NO-khakh ha-giv-AH mi-miz-rakh SHA-mesh* | כִּתְּרוּ אֶת־בִּנְיָמִן הִרְדִיפֻהוּ מְנוּחָה הִדְרִיכֻהוּ עַד נֹכַח הַגִּבְעָה מִמִּזְרַח־שָׁמֶשׁ: מג |
| 44 | That day 18,000 of the Benjaminites fell, all of them brave men. | *va-yi-p'-LU mi-bin-ya-MIN sh'-mo-nah a-SAR E-lef EESH et kol AY-leh an-shay KHA-yil* | וַיִּפְּלוּ מִבִּנְיָמִן שְׁמֹנָה־עָשָׂר אֶלֶף אִישׁ אֶת־כָּל־אֵלֶּה אַנְשֵׁי־חָיִל: מד |

| | | | |
|---|---|---|---|
| 45 | They turned and fled to the wilderness, to the Rock of Rimmon; but [the Israelites] picked off another 5,000 on the roads and, continuing in hot pursuit of them up to Gidom, they slew 2,000 more. | *va-yif-NU va-ya-NU-su ha-mid-BA-rah el SE-la ha-ri-MON vai-o-l'-LU-hu bam-si-LOT kha-MAY-shet a-la-FEEM EESH va-yad-BEE-ku a-kha-RAV ad gid-OM va-ya-KU mi-ME-nu al-PA-yim EESH* | וַיִּפְנוּ וַיָּנֻסוּ הַמִּדְבָּרָה אֶל־סֶלַע הָרִמּוֹן וַיְעֹלְלֻהוּ בַּמְסִלּוֹת חֲמֵשֶׁת אֲלָפִים אִישׁ וַיַּדְבִּיקוּ אַחֲרָיו עַד־גִּדְעֹם וַיַּכּוּ מִמֶּנּוּ אַלְפַּיִם אִישׁ: מה |
| 46 | Thus the Benjaminite fighters who fell that day numbered 25,000, all of them brave men. | *vai-HEE khol ha-no-f'-LEEM mi-bin-ya-MIN es-REEM va-kha-mi-SHAH E-lef EESH sho-LAYF KHE-rev ba-YOM ha-HU et kol AY-leh an-shay KHA-yil* | וַיְהִי כָל־הַנֹּפְלִים מִבִּנְיָמִן עֶשְׂרִים וַחֲמִשָּׁה אֶלֶף אִישׁ שֹׁלֵף חֶרֶב בַּיּוֹם הַהוּא אֶת־כָּל־אֵלֶּה אַנְשֵׁי־חָיִל: מו |
| 47 | But 600 others turned and fled to the wilderness, to the Rock of Rimmon; they remained at the Rock of Rimmon four months. | *va-yif-NU va-ya-NU-su ha-mid-BA-rah el SE-la ha-ri-MON SHAYSH may-OT EESH va-yay-sh'-VU b'-SE-la ri-MON ar-ba-AH kho-da-SHEEM* | וַיִּפְנוּ וַיָּנֻסוּ הַמִּדְבָּרָה אֶל־סֶלַע הָרִמּוֹן שֵׁשׁ מֵאוֹת אִישׁ וַיֵּשְׁבוּ בְּסֶלַע רִמּוֹן אַרְבָּעָה חֳדָשִׁים: מז |
| 48 | Israel's force, meanwhile, turned back to the rest of the Benjaminites and put them to the sword—towns, people, cattle—everything that remained. Finally, they set fire to all the towns that were left. | *v'-EESH yis-ra-AYL SHA-vu el b'-NAY vin-ya-MIN va-ya-KUM l'-fee KHE-rev may-EER m'-TOM ad b'-hay-MAH AD kol ha-nim-TZA GAM kol he-a-REEM ha-nim-tza-OT shi-l'-KHU va-AYSH* | וְאִישׁ יִשְׂרָאֵל שָׁבוּ אֶל־בְּנֵי בִנְיָמִן וַיַּכּוּם לְפִי־חֶרֶב מֵעִיר מְתֹם עַד־בְּהֵמָה עַד כָּל־הַנִּמְצָא גַּם כָּל־הֶעָרִים הַנִּמְצָאוֹת שִׁלְּחוּ בָאֵשׁ: מח |

# 21

## כא

| |  |  |  |
|---|---|---|---|

1 — Now Israel's forces had taken an oath at Mizpah: "None of us must ever give his daughter in marriage to a Benjaminite."

*v'-EESH yis-ra-AYL nish-BA ba-mitz-PAH lay-MOR EESH mi-ME-nu lo yi-TAYN bi-TO l'-vin-ya-MIN l'-i-SHAH*

וְאִישׁ יִשְׂרָאֵל נִשְׁבַּע בַּמִּצְפָּה לֵאמֹר אִישׁ מִמֶּנּוּ לֹא־יִתֵּן בִּתּוֹ לְבִנְיָמִן לְאִשָּׁה: א

2 — The people came to Bethel and sat there before God until evening. They wailed and wept bitterly,

*va-ya-VO ha-AM bayt AYL va-YAY-sh'-vu SHAM ad ha-E-rev lif-NAY ha-e-lo-HEEM va-yis-U ko-LAM va-yiv-KU b'-KHEE ga-DOL*

וַיָּבֹא הָעָם בֵּית־אֵל וַיֵּשְׁבוּ שָׁם עַד־הָעֶרֶב לִפְנֵי הָאֱלֹהִים וַיִּשְׂאוּ קוֹלָם וַיִּבְכּוּ בְּכִי גָדוֹל: ב

3 — and they said, "O ETERNAL God of Israel, why has this happened in Israel, that one tribe must now be missing from Israel?"

*va-YO-m'-RU la-MAH a-do-NAI e-lo-HAY yis-ra-AYL HA-y'-tah ZOT b'-yis-ra-AYL l'-hi-pa-KAYD ha-YOM mi-yis-ra-AYL SHAY-vet e-KHAD*

וַיֹּאמְרוּ לָמָה יְהוָה אֱלֹהֵי יִשְׂרָאֵל הָיְתָה זֹּאת בְּיִשְׂרָאֵל לְהִפָּקֵד הַיּוֹם מִיִּשְׂרָאֵל שֵׁבֶט אֶחָד: ג

4 — Early the next day, the people built an altar there, and they brought burnt offerings and offerings of well-being.

*vai-HEE mi-ma-kho-RAT va-yash-KEE-mu ha-AM va-yiv-nu SHAM miz-BAY-akh va-ya-a-LU o-LOT ush-la-MEEM*

וַיְהִי מִמָּחֳרָת וַיַּשְׁכִּימוּ הָעָם וַיִּבְנוּ־שָׁם מִזְבֵּחַ וַיַּעֲלוּ עֹלוֹת וּשְׁלָמִים: ד

5 The Israelites asked, "Is there anyone from all the tribes of Israel who failed to come up to the assembly before GOD ?" For a solemn oath had been taken concerning anyone who did not go up to GOD at Mizpah: "He shall be put to death."

*va-yo-m'-RU b'-NAY yis-ra-AYL MEE a-SHER lo a-LAH va-ka-HAL mi-kol shiv-TAY yis-ra-AYL el a-do-NAI KEE ha-sh'-vu-AH ha-g'-do-LAH ha-y'-TAH la-a-SHER lo a-LAH el a-do-NAI ha-mitz-PAH lay-MOR MOT yu-MAT*

ה וַיֹּאמְרוּ בְּנֵי יִשְׂרָאֵל מִי אֲשֶׁר לֹא־עָלָה בַקָּהָל מִכָּל־שִׁבְטֵי יִשְׂרָאֵל אֶל־יְהֹוָה כִּי הַשְּׁבוּעָה הַגְּדוֹלָה הָיְתָה לַאֲשֶׁר לֹא־עָלָה אֶל־יְהֹוָה הַמִּצְפָּה לֵאמֹר מוֹת יוּמָת:

6 The Israelites now relented toward their kin the Benjaminites, and they said, "This day one tribe has been cut off from Israel!

*va-yi-na-kha-MU b'-NAY yis-ra-AYL el bin-ya-MIN a-KHEEV va-yo-m'-RU nig-DA ha-YOM SHAY-vet e-KHAD mi-yis-ra-AYL*

ו וַיִּנָּחֲמוּ בְּנֵי יִשְׂרָאֵל אֶל־בִּנְיָמִן אָחִיו וַיֹּאמְרוּ נִגְדַּע הַיּוֹם שֵׁבֶט אֶחָד מִיִּשְׂרָאֵל:

7 What can we do to provide wives for those who are left, seeing that we have sworn by GOD not to give any of our daughters to them in marriage?"

*mah na-a-SEH la-HEM la-no-ta-REEM l'-na-SHEEM va-a-NAKH-nu nish-BA-nu va-do-NAI l'-vil-TEE tayt la-HEM mi-b'-no-TAY-nu l'-na-SHEEM*

ז מַה־נַּעֲשֶׂה לָהֶם לַנּוֹתָרִים לְנָשִׁים וַאֲנַחְנוּ נִשְׁבַּעְנוּ בַיהֹוָה לְבִלְתִּי תֵּת־לָהֶם מִבְּנוֹתֵינוּ לְנָשִׁים:

8 They inquired, "Is there anyone from the tribes of Israel who did not go up to GOD at Mizpah?" Now no one from Jabesh-gilead had come to the camp, to the assembly.

*va-yo-m'-RU MEE e-KHAD mi-shiv-TAY yis-ra-AYL a-SHER lo a-LAH el a-do-NAI ha-mitz-PAH v'-hi-NAY LO va EESH el ha-ma-kha-NEH mi-ya-VAYSH gil-AD el ha-ka-HAL*

ח וַיֹּאמְרוּ מִי אֶחָד מִשִּׁבְטֵי יִשְׂרָאֵל אֲשֶׁר לֹא־עָלָה אֶל־יְהֹוָה הַמִּצְפָּה וְהִנֵּה לֹא בָא־אִישׁ אֶל־הַמַּחֲנֶה מִיָּבֵישׁ גִּלְעָד אֶל־הַקָּהָל:

| 9 | For, when the roll of the troops was taken, not one of the inhabitants of Jabesh-gilead was present. | va-yit-pa-KAYD ha-AM v'-hi-NAY ayn SHAM EESH mi-yo-sh'-VAY ya-VAYSH gil-AD | וַיִּתְפָּקֵד הָעָם וְהִנֵּה אֵין־שָׁם אִישׁ מִיּוֹשְׁבֵי יָבֵשׁ גִּלְעָד: | ט |

| 10 | So the assemblage dispatched 12,000 of the warriors, instructing them as follows: "Go and put the inhabitants of Jabesh-gilead to the sword, women and children included. | va-yish-l'-khu SHAM ha-ay-DAH sh'-naym a-SAR E-lef EESH mi-b'-NAY he-KHA-yil vai-tza-VU o-TAM lay-MOR l'-KHU v'-hi-kee-TEM et yo-sh'-VAY ya-VAYSH gil-AD l'-fee KHE-rev v'-ha-na-SHEEM v'-ha-TAF | וַיִּשְׁלְחוּ־שָׁם הָעֵדָה שְׁנֵים־עָשָׂר אֶלֶף אִישׁ מִבְּנֵי הֶחָיִל וַיְצַוּוּ אוֹתָם לֵאמֹר לְכוּ וְהִכִּיתֶם אֶת־יוֹשְׁבֵי יָבֵשׁ גִּלְעָד לְפִי־חֶרֶב וְהַנָּשִׁים וְהַטָּף: | י |

| 11 | This is what you are to do: Proscribe every male, and every woman who has known a man carnally." | v'-ZEH ha-da-VAR a-SHER ta-a-SU kol za-KHAR v'-khol i-SHAH yo-DA-at misk-kav za-KHAR ta-kha-REE-mu | וְזֶה הַדָּבָר אֲשֶׁר תַּעֲשׂוּ כָּל־זָכָר וְכָל־אִשָּׁה יֹדַעַת מִשְׁכַּב־זָכָר תַּחֲרִימוּ: | יא |

| 12 | They found among the inhabitants of Jabesh-gilead 400 maidens who had not known a man carnally; and they brought them to the camp at Shiloh, which is in the land of Canaan. | va-yim-tz'-U mi-yo-sh'-VAY ya-VAYSH gil-AD ar-BA may-OT na-a-RAH v'-tu-LAH a-SHER lo ya-d'-AH EESH l'-mish-KAV za-KHAR va-ya-VI-u o-TAM el ha-ma-kha-NEH shi-LOH a-SHER b'-E-retz k'-NA-an | וַיִּמְצְאוּ מִיּוֹשְׁבֵי יָבֵישׁ גִּלְעָד אַרְבַּע מֵאוֹת נַעֲרָה בְתוּלָה אֲשֶׁר לֹא־יָדְעָה אִישׁ לְמִשְׁכַּב זָכָר וַיָּבִאוּ אוֹתָם אֶל־הַמַּחֲנֶה שִׁלֹה אֲשֶׁר בְּאֶרֶץ כְּנָעַן: | יב |

| 13 | Then the whole community sent word to the Benjaminites who were at the Rock of Rimmon, and offered them terms of peace. | va-yish-l'-KHU kol ha-ay-DAH vai-da-b'-RU el b'-NAY vin-ya-MIN a-SHER b'-SE-la ri-MON va-yik-r'-U la-HEM sha-LOM | וַיִּשְׁלְחוּ כָּל־הָעֵדָה וַיְדַבְּרוּ אֶל־בְּנֵי בִנְיָמִן אֲשֶׁר בְּסֶלַע רִמּוֹן וַיִּקְרְאוּ לָהֶם שָׁלוֹם: | יג |

| | | | |
|---|---|---|---|
| 14 | Thereupon the Benjaminites returned, and they gave them the maidens who had been spared from the women of Jabesh-gilead. But there were not enough of them. | *va-YA-shov bin-ya-MIN ba-AYT ha-HEE va-yi-t'-NU la-HEM ha-na-SHEEM a-SHER khi-YU mi-n'-SHAY ya-VAYSH gil-AD v'-lo ma-tz'-U la-HEM KAYN* | וַיָּשָׁב בִּנְיָמִן בָּעֵת הַהִיא וַיִּתְּנוּ לָהֶם הַנָּשִׁים אֲשֶׁר חִיּוּ מִנְּשֵׁי יָבֵשׁ גִּלְעָד וְלֹא־מָצְאוּ לָהֶם כֵּן: יד |
| 15 | Now the people had relented toward Benjamin, for GOD had made a breach in the tribes of Israel. | *v'-ha-AM ni-KHAM l'-vin-ya-MIN kee a-SAH a-do-NAI PE-retz b'-shiv-TAY yis-ra-AYL* | וְהָעָם נִחָם לְבִנְיָמִן כִּי־עָשָׂה יְהֹוָה פֶּרֶץ בְּשִׁבְטֵי יִשְׂרָאֵל: טו |
| 16 | So the elders of the community asked, "What can we do about wives for those who are left, since the women of Benjamin have been killed off?" | *va-yo-m'-RU zik-NAY ha-ay-DAH mah na-a-SEH la-no-ta-REEM l'-na-SHEEM kee nish-m'-DAH mi-bin-ya-MIN i-SHAH* | וַיֹּאמְרוּ זִקְנֵי הָעֵדָה מַה־נַּעֲשֶׂה לַנּוֹתָרִים לְנָשִׁים כִּי־נִשְׁמְדָה מִבִּנְיָמִן אִשָּׁה: טז |
| 17 | For they said, "There must be a saving remnant for Benjamin, that a tribe may not be blotted out of Israel; | *va-yo-m'-RU y'-ru-SHAT p'-lay-TAH l'-vin-ya-MIN v'-lo yi-ma-KHEH SHAY-vet mi-yis-ra-AYL* | וַיֹּאמְרוּ יְרֻשַּׁת פְּלֵיטָה לְבִנְיָמִן וְלֹא־יִמָּחֶה שֵׁבֶט מִיִּשְׂרָאֵל: יז |
| 18 | yet we cannot give them any of our daughters as wives," since the Israelites had taken an oath: "Cursed be anyone who gives a wife to Benjamin!" | *va-a-NAKH-nu LO nu-KHAL la-TAYT la-HEM na-SHEEM mi-b'-no-TAY-nu kee nish-b'-U v'-nay yis-ra-AYL lay-MOR a-RUR no-TAYN i-SHAH l'-vin-ya-MIN* | וַאֲנַחְנוּ לֹא נוּכַל לָתֶת־לָהֶם נָשִׁים מִבְּנוֹתֵינוּ כִּי־נִשְׁבְּעוּ בְנֵי־יִשְׂרָאֵל לֵאמֹר אָרוּר נֹתֵן אִשָּׁה לְבִנְיָמִן: יח |

**19**

They said, "The annual feast of GOD is now being held at Shiloh." (It lies north of Bethel, east of the highway that runs from Bethel to Shechem, and south of Lebonah.)

*va-yo-m'-RU hi-NAY khag a-do-NAI b'-shi-LO mi-ya-MEEM ya-MEE-mah a-SHER mi-tz'-FO-nah l'-vayt AYL miz-r'-KHAH ha-SHE-mesh lim-si-LAH ha-o-LAH mi-bayt AYL sh'-KHE-mah u-mi-NE-gev lil-vo-NAH*

וַיֹּאמְרוּ הִנֵּה חַג־יְהֹוָה בְּשִׁלוֹ מִיָּמִים יָמִימָה אֲשֶׁר מִצְּפוֹנָה לְבֵית־אֵל מִזְרְחָה הַשֶּׁמֶשׁ לִמְסִלָּה הָעֹלָה מִבֵּית־אֵל שְׁכֶמָה וּמִנֶּגֶב לִלְבוֹנָה: יט

**20**

So they instructed the Benjaminites as follows: "Go and lie in wait in the vineyards.

*vai-tza-VU et b'-NAY vin-ya-MIN lay-MOR l'-KHU va-a-rav-TEM ba-k'-ra-MEEM*

(ויצו) [וַיְצַוּוּ] אֶת־בְּנֵי בִנְיָמִן לֵאמֹר לְכוּ וַאֲרַבְתֶּם בַּכְּרָמִים: כ

**21**

As soon as you see the daughters of Shiloh coming out to join in the dances, come out from the vineyards; let each of you seize a wife from among the daughters of Shiloh, and be off for the land of Benjamin.

*ur-ee-TEM v'-hi-NAY im yay-tz'-U b'-not shi-LO la-KHUL ba-m'-kho-LOT vee-tza-TEM min ha-k'-ra-MEEM va-kha-taf-TEM la-KHEM EESH ish-TO mi-b'-NOT shee-LO va-ha-lakh-TEM E-retz bin-ya-MIN*

וּרְאִיתֶם וְהִנֵּה אִם־יֵצְאוּ בְנוֹת־שִׁילוֹ לָחוּל בַּמְּחֹלוֹת וִיצָאתֶם מִן־הַכְּרָמִים וַחֲטַפְתֶּם לָכֶם אִישׁ אִשְׁתּוֹ מִבְּנוֹת שִׁילוֹ וַהֲלַכְתֶּם אֶרֶץ בִּנְיָמִן: כא

**22**

And if their fathers or brothers come to us to complain, we shall say to them, 'Be generous to them for our sake! We could not provide any of them with a wife on account of the war, and you would have incurred guilt if you yourselves had given them [wives].'"

*v'-ha-YAH kee ya-VO-u a-vo-TAM O a-khay-HEM la-REEV ay-LAY-nu v'-a-MAR-nu a-lay-HEM kha-NU-nu o-TAM KEE LO la-KAKH-nu EESH ish-TO ba-mil-kha-MAH KEE LO a-TEM n'-ta-TEM la-HEM ka-AYT te-SHA-mu*

וְהָיָה כִּי־יָבֹאוּ אֲבוֹתָם אוֹ אֲחֵיהֶם (לרוב) [לָרִיב] אֵלֵינוּ וְאָמַרְנוּ אֲלֵיהֶם חָנּוּנוּ אוֹתָם כִּי לֹא לָקַחְנוּ אִישׁ אִשְׁתּוֹ בַּמִּלְחָמָה כִּי לֹא אַתֶּם נְתַתֶּם לָהֶם כָּעֵת תֶּאְשָׁמוּ: כב

23 | The Benjaminites did so. They took to wife, from the dancers whom they carried off, as many as they themselves numbered. Then they went back to their own territory, and rebuilt their towns and settled in them. | *va-ya-a-su KHAYN b'-NAY vin-ya-MIN va-yis-U na-SHEEM l'-mis-pa-RAM min ha-m'-kho-l'-LOT a-SHER ga-ZA-lu va-yay-l'-KHU va-ya-SHU-vu el na-kha-la-TAM va-yiv-NU et he-a-REEM va-yay-sh'-VU ba-HEM* | וַיַּעֲשׂוּ־כֵן בְּנֵי בִנְיָמִן וַיִּשְׂאוּ נָשִׁים לְמִסְפָּרָם מִן־הַמְּחֹלְלוֹת אֲשֶׁר גָּזָלוּ וַיֵּלְכוּ וַיָּשׁוּבוּ אֶל־נַחֲלָתָם וַיִּבְנוּ אֶת־הֶעָרִים וַיֵּשְׁבוּ בָּהֶם: | כג

24 | Thereupon the Israelites dispersed to their own tribes and clans; everyone departed for their own territory. | *va-yit-ha-l'-KHU mi-SHAM b'-nay yis-ra-AYL ba-AYT ha-HEE EESH l'-shiv-TO ul-mish-pakh-TO va-yay-tz'-U mi-SHAM EESH l'-na-kha-la-TO* | וַיִּתְהַלְּכוּ מִשָּׁם בְּנֵי־יִשְׂרָאֵל בָּעֵת הַהִיא אִישׁ לְשִׁבְטוֹ וּלְמִשְׁפַּחְתּוֹ וַיֵּצְאוּ מִשָּׁם אִישׁ לְנַחֲלָתוֹ: | כד

25 | In those days there was no king in Israel; everyone did as they pleased. | *ba-ya-MEEM ha-HAYM AYN ME-lekh b'-yis-ra-AYL EESH ha-ya-SHAR b'-ay-NAV ya-a-SEH* | בַּיָּמִים הָהֵם אֵין מֶלֶךְ בְּיִשְׂרָאֵל אִישׁ הַיָּשָׁר בְּעֵינָיו יַעֲשֶׂה: | כה

# Take a Wife and Find Joy!

"Awake, awake, O Zion! Clothe yourself in splendor; put on your robes of majesty, Jerusalem, holy city! For the uncircumcised and the unclean shall never enter you again" (Isaiah 52:1).

In the Bible, horrific events are almost inevitably followed by opportunities for healing and redemption. Time and time again, the people of Israel fall into a deep slumber of sin and impurity. But the cry of the prophets to wake up inevitably pierces through the nation's sleepiness, and they awaken with a spiritual strength they had forgotten they possessed. After the fall, man is given the chance to begin again.

Of all the terrible moments described in the Bible, the story of the concubine of Gibeah is certainly one of the very worst. Moral degradation, civil war, and the slaughter of thousands – this story has it all! And yet, in the aftermath of the destruction, we find an extraordinary ray of light.

In their rage at the sinful tribe of Benjamin, the tribes of Israel swore that they would never again give their daughters to the men of Benjamin as wives. But in the aftermath of the war, only 400 Benjamite men were left alive. If they could not marry the daughters of the other eleven tribes, the tribe of Benjamin would die out and disappear!

To solve the problem and get around their oath, the people of Israel came up with an ingenious solution. Instead of "giving" their daughters to the men of Benjamin, the men of Benjamin would "take" their daughters as wives:

"'They said, "The annual feast of GOD is now being held at Shiloh.' ... So they instructed the Benjaminites as follows: 'Go and lie in wait in the vineyards. As soon as you see the girls of Shiloh coming out to join in the dances, come out from the vineyards; let each of you seize a wife from among the girls of Shiloh, and be off for the land of Benjamin...' The Benjaminites did so. They took as wives, from the dancers whom they carried off, as many as they themselves numbered. Then they went back to their own territory, and rebuilt their towns and settled in them." (Judges 21:18-23)

In Jewish thought, this moment of rapprochement and magnanimity is no mere detail in the larger story of the Book of Judges. According to the sages, this sweet story of the men of Israel allowing the men of Benjamin to "take" their daughters as wives was a foundational moment in Jewish history:

"Rabbi Simeon ben Gamaliel said: there never were in Israel greater days of joy than the fifteenth of Av and the day of atonement (Yom Kippur)... What happened on the 15th of Av? Rabbi Joseph said in the name of R. Nahman: It is the day on which the tribe of Benjamin was permitted to re-enter the congregation [of Israel]..." (Babylonian Talmud, Taanit 26b, 30b)

In Jewish tradition, the 15th day of the Hebrew month of Av – the day the tribe of Benjamin was allowed to marry into the other tribes of Israel – is one of the two happiest days of the year (along with Yom Kippur, the Day of Atonement). Incredibly, this joyful day occurs only six days after the saddest day of the Jewish calendar, the 9th of Av, when both the first and second Temples in Jerusalem were destroyed.

Why is this day so joyous? For it is a constant reminder to us all that even after great failure, tragedy and brokenness, it is possible to begin again and start anew. God does not give up on us, and so we must never give up on ourselves. The tribe of Benjamin sinned terribly and was almost completely destroyed – but God, and the other tribes, refused to let Benjamin disappear.

The Sages explain that the seeds of the redemption of Israel, which will come to full bloom in the Book of Samuel, were planted at this propitious moment at the end of the Book of Judges. According to tradition, a young man named Saul – destined to become the first King of Israel – was one of the 400 Benjamite men who took a wife and started a family on the 15th of Av. And so the Book of Judges, which contains so many painful and tragic moments, ends with a story of comfort, hope and redemption.

May we, too, soon find comfort and redemption!

# Is Civil War
# on the Horizon?

"It's time for Americans to wake up to a fundamental reality: the continued unity of the United States of America cannot be guaranteed. At this moment in history, there is not a single important cultural, religious, political, or social force that is pulling Americans together more than it is pushing us apart. We cannot assume that a continent-sized, multi-ethnic, multi-faith democracy can remain united forever, and it will not remain united if our political class cannot and will not adapt to an increasingly diverse and divided American public." (David French, Divided We Fall: America's Secession Threat and How to Restore Our Nation).

Each new day brings another story about America and Israel tearing themselves apart. Partisan hatred has been on the rise for years in the United States, while left-wing protests have become daily events throughout Israel. Unsurprisingly, the growing enmity has led to threats of political violence and even talk of secession.

How can we prevent our countries from self-imploding? The answer, as always, can be found in the Bible, and specifically in the sordid and tragic story of the concubine at Gibeah.

In a horrific, Sodom-like story, the people of Gibeah, a town of the tribe of Benjamin, abused and raped a woman traveling through their town until she died. Her husband cut up her body into pieces and sent them to the tribes of Israel, leading the other eleven tribes to ultimately declare war on the tribe of Benjamin. The war was disastrous for all sides; tens of thousands of soldiers were killed in battle, and almost the entire tribe of Benjamin was wiped out.

When the war ended with only a few hundred Benjamite men surviving, the eleven tribes came to a terrible realization:

"Now the men of Israel had taken an oath at Mizpah: 'None of us will give his daughter in marriage to a Benjaminite.' The people came to Bethel and sat there before God

214

until evening. They wailed and wept bitterly, and they said, 'O God of Israel, why has this happened in Israel, that one tribe must now be missing from Israel?'... For they said, "There must be a saving remnant for Benjamin, that a tribe may not be blotted out of Israel." (Judges 21:1-3,17).

The eleven tribes were so infuriated by the atrocities committed by the Benjamites that they charged into war, destroying entire Benjamite cities. Now, only a short time later, the eleven tribes cry bitterly over the destruction of Benjamin. What changed?

One of the great Biblical commentators of the 19th century, Rabbi Meir Leibush Wisser (1809 – 1879), explains the deeper significance of this moment: "Only now, after passions had cooled, did the people remember that they had sworn in anger not to give their daughters as wives to the men of Benjamin. Therefore, even though 600 men were left of the tribe of Benjamin, they could not find wives, for all the women of Benjamin had been killed. This would lead to the blotting out of the entire tribe of Benjamin, which would be a terrible wound to the people of Israel, for it is impossible for God's presence to rest upon the people of Israel without all twelve tribes. Therefore, if one tribe would be lost, the damage would be felt for all generations; it would be a brokenness that could not be fixed for all time."

Only after a terrible and avoidable tragedy did the people of Israel learn a critical lesson – that God's presence will only dwell among them if all twelve tribes of Israel unite! This is the most critical lesson of the Book of Judges – a lesson the nation had to learn before they could unite under kings Saul and David in the Book of Samuel and become a light unto the nations.

The lesson for both America and Israel is clear. Each nation will only be able to fulfill its Godly mission by first learning to appreciate the importance of each and every tribe – even those "tribes" that have sinned and turned away from God. Though we do not approve of their sinful ways, we must find a way to show them that we value them and need them. We must change the tone of our arguments; instead of threatening to "destroy" our opponents, we must treat them with respect – and patiently work to convince them of the truth!

Clearly, this won't be easy. But must we experience a civil war before learning this lesson? As David French writes, "Our nation's angriest culture warriors need to know the cost of their conflict. As they seek to crush their political and cultural enemies, they may destroy the nation they seek to rule." Let's do everything in our power to ensure that doesn't happen!

# Connect to Israel on a deeper level with
## *The Israel Bible*

The only Bible highlighting the special relationship between the Land and People of Israel. Through traditional and contemporary Jewish sources, *The Israel Bible* presents God's eternal and unchanging love for the Promised Land and His Chosen People from biblical times until today.

- 2,200 pages of side by side Hebrew and English
- Exclusive collection of maps, photos, charts and illustrations
- Hundreds of unique and inspiring study notes

Get your copy today at:
**www.israel365store.com**

For more inspiring
commentary, interactive maps,
educational videos, vivid
photographs and more, please
visit our website

**www.TheIsraelBible.com**

THE
**ISRAEL**
**BIBLE**